ANTHROPOLOGICAL PAPERS OF
THE UNIVERSITY OF ARIZONA
NUMBER 65

Tracking Prehistoric Migrations

Pueblo Settlers among the Tonto Basin Hohokam

Jeffery J. Clark

THE UNIVERSITY OF ARIZONA PRESS
TUCSON
2001

About the Author

JEFFERY J. CLARK is a senior project director at Desert Archaeology, Inc., a Cultural Resource Management firm in Tucson, Arizona. In addition to the Tonto Basin research reported in this monograph, he has worked extensively in central and southern Arizona and his current contract archaeology work involves public education projects in southeastern Arizona. He also has engaged in fieldwork in southwest Asia at Bronze and Iron Age sites in Israel, Syria, and Iraq. His research interests include architectural analysis, cultural affiliation, and migration. Dr. Clark received his B.A. degree from Cornell University in 1983 and earned his master's (1990) and doctoral (1997) degrees from the University of Arizona.

Cover: Migration routes in eastern Arizona during the late 13th and early 14th centuries A.D. (*see* Fig. 6.1).

THE UNIVERSITY OF ARIZONA PRESS

Copyright © 2001

The Arizona Board of Regents
All Rights Reserved

This book was set in 10.7/12 CG Times
∞ This book is printed on acid-free, archival-quality paper.
Manufactured in the United States of America.

2003 02 01   3 2 1

Library of Congress Cataloging-in-Publication Data

Clark, Jeffery J.
   Tracking prehistoric migrations : Pueblo settlers among the Tonto Basin Hohokam / Jeffery J. Clark.
      p. cm. -- (Anthropological papers of the University of Arizona; no. 65)
      Includes bibliographic references and index.
      ISBN 0-8165-2087-9 (pbk. : alk. paper)
      1. Hohokam culture. 2. Indians of North America--Arizona--Tonto Basin--Antiquities. 3. Salado culture. 4. Pueblo Indians--Arizona--Antiquities. 5. Tonto Basin (Ariz.)--Antiquities. 6. Arizona--Antiquities.
I. Title. II. Series.
   E99.H68 C53 2001
   979.1'55--dc21
                    00-012673

Contents

FIGURES

TABLES

Preface

Southwest archaeology's "Old Guard" recognized the importance of migration in the prehistory of the region, and population movement was accorded a central role in explanatory frameworks during the first half of the twentieth century. This distinguished group included Harold and Winifred Gladwin, Emil Haury, and Charles Di Peso, to name only a few of the principals. Many Native American groups inhabiting the contemporary Southwest have oral traditions in which migration plays a central role in how they define themselves, how they are related to each other, and how they came to live in the areas in which they currently reside.

Overall, the shift to processual archaeology during the 1960s can be considered a positive development in the discipline. Focus on the scientific method improved the standards by which archaeological data were evaluated. New analytical techniques were developed that drew from other sciences, including biology, botany, chemistry, geology, and climatology. Finally, emphasis on "archaeology as anthropology" directed research toward answering questions that have broad relevance to human behavior and social organization. However, the early proponents of this paradigm were perhaps a bit too zealous in their desire to change the discipline, and they discarded the good with the bad of the earlier paradigm in their "New Archaeology." Considering its previous importance, migration was one of the casualties and, with the exception of a few torch-bearing researchers, the topic has not been discussed seriously within the discipline until recently.

Few archaeological manifestations better reflect the ebb and flow of archaeological paradigms than the Salado horizon. The Salado has proven to be a remarkably malleable concept that has been hammered and molded to fit a variety of models, including those that are virtual antitheses of each other. Throughout the 1930s, 1940s, and 1950s when migration reigned supreme, the Salado was considered either an intrusive pueblo culture or a cultural blend of pueblo migrants and various local groups. During the 1960s, Salado research in southern and central Arizona was redirected away from the puebloan world toward internal development and continuity with earlier Hohokam-related groups inhabiting the same area. Although debated, the idea of an indigenous Salado prevailed in Hohokam archaeology throughout the 1970s and 1980s. By the mid-1990s, the importance of puebloan migration in the Salado horizon was again seriously considered and the issue of the ultimate cultural affiliation of the Salado became hotly contested. Debate continues to the present day and much of this monograph is devoted to this issue.

The recent interest in the Salado has been fueled by large Cultural Resource Management (CRM) projects in the Tonto Basin of east-central Arizona. Data collected by these projects have elevated the basin to one of the most thoroughly investigated areas in the entire Southwest. CRM projects funded by the Arizona Department of Transportation (ADOT) in advance of road realignments and the massive Roosevelt Lake project funded by the United States Bureau of Reclamation (BOR) have permitted intensive investigation of virtually every major zone in the lower elevations of the basin. The Tonto Basin has been called the Salado Heartland in the past and it played a key role in the initial conception of the Salado in the 1930s by the Gladwins working out of Gila Pueblo in Globe, Arizona.

This monograph developed out of my dissertation research, which was conducted as part of the BOR's Roosevelt Lake project, an undertaking that was accomplished in advance of raising Theodore Roosevelt Dam and the highwater mark of the lake. Approximately 150 sites, including seven platform mounds, were investigated during the course of the project and fieldwork was divided among three contractors: Arizona State University in Tempe and Desert Archaeology and Statistical Research, Inc., two contract firms in Tucson. Arizona State University had the largest portion of the contract and focused on the investigation of Classic period (A.D. 1200–1450) platform mound communities throughout the lower portion of the basin. Desert Archaeology's Roosevelt Community Development (RCD) project was an intensive study of the development of a single community in the eastern portion of the lower basin during an interval of more than 1200 years (A.D. 100–1325). To round out the research effort, Statistical

Research examined settlement in several areas in the lower basin that were less densely populated in prehistoric times.

The fieldwork phase of the Roosevelt Lake project took place in the early 1990s. Descriptive write-up and analysis continued through the middle of the decade. The first synthesis of this material was published in the mid-1990s and additional syntheses have followed to the present day. Considering the vast amount of data and the research potential of the basin, new synthetic treatments and reevaluation of existing works can be expected in the future, especially in light of ongoing CRM projects in the region.

My research focuses on assessing the scale and impact of puebloan migration into the eastern Tonto Basin during the early Classic period (A.D. 1200–1325). Primary emphasis is placed on Desert Archaeology's RCD study area north of the Salt River. Other work essential to understanding the archaeological record of the eastern basin was conducted by Arizona State University (ASU) in the Livingston Management area and on Schoolhouse Point Mesa to the south of the Salt River. Together these three project areas encompass the entire territory of a well-defined prehistoric irrigation community and to date this portion of the basin is by far the most intensively investigated area within the region.

After a general discussion of the current state of migration research in archaeology (Chapter 1), a considerable portion of this monograph is devoted to developing a reliable method of assessing the occurrence of migration. This method is tested using ethnoarchaeological case studies that are concerned with identifying different cultural groups living in close proximity as the result of population movement (Chapter 2). Following a brief summary of Salado and Tonto Basin research (Chapter 3), I use this approach to identify puebloan movements in the eastern basin and pinpoint the locations of migrant enclaves (Chapter 4). Specific data sets used in this assessment include the organization of domestic space and technological styles associated with architectural construction and utilitarian ceramic manufacture.

Two clarifications should be stated at the outset. The term "Salado polychrome," as used in this volume and by most archaeologists, does not refer to a specific ceramic type but to several related types that include Gila Black-on-red, Gila Polychrome, Pinto Black-on-red, Pinto Polychrome, and Tonto Polychrome. In a similar vein, the term "puebloan," as it is used in this monograph, is not restricted to a specific group (for example, Western Anasazi) or a particular region (such as Kayenta or Tusayan) in the northern and eastern Southwest. Rather, the term is used as a generic label for prehistoric groups living throughout this large region who constructed room blocks with coursed masonry walls and who made corrugated ceramic vessels using coil-and-scrape manufacturing techniques during the period of interest (A.D. 1200–1325). These *technological styles* can be readily contrasted with the styles associated with the indigenous groups occupying the Tonto Basin during the early Classic period. Although there are many attributes that can be used to define specific groups within the puebloan Southwest, such an exercise is beyond the scope of this monograph.

Following assessment of the scale of puebloan migration, possible origins of the migrants, their underlying motives for resettlement, and their impact on the local community are explored (Chapter 5). Although the scale of migration is limited, these movements significantly altered the trajectory of the community in the direction of increasing complexity and may have ultimately played an important role in its collapse shortly after the beginning of the fourteenth century A.D. Finally, the implications of the case study for the Salado horizon and migration studies in general are presented (Chapter 6). An important lesson to be drawn from this study is that migration often generates mixed cultural settings. Considering this outcome, research on postmigration contexts should be focused on the transformational character of *interaction* between socially distant groups living in close proximity rather than on the relative contributions of each group to the archaeological record.

Acknowledgments

This effort would have never left the ground without the unwavering support of Desert Archaeology and William Doelle. Other members of the RCD research team whose constant feedback stimulated thinking and sometimes elevated blood pressure include Douglas Craig, David Gregory, Miriam Stark, Mark Elson, Henry Wallace, James Heidke, and Deborah Swartz. I am also deeply indebted to the RCD and ASU staff and field crew for the high quality of archaeological data recorded from the Tonto Basin.

The community of archaeological scholars is fortunate to have well-working cooperative agreements with various federal and state government agencies. The results, sometimes surprising ones, of numerous massive joint research undertakings have revitalized our thinking about prehistory. Foremost here I thank the U.S. Bureau of Reclamation, especially Jon Czaplicki, for providing a subvention for publication of this volume. J. Scott Wood, Tonto National Forest archaeologist, deserves special mention in playing the role of devil's advocate with admirable vigor and tenacity. I would like to thank Glen Rice (Arizona State University) and Owen Lindauer (Arizona Department of Transportation) for their immense help in turning an unwieldy dissertation into a digestible monograph. The RCD peer review committee, which included Ben Nelson, Steve Lekson, Jeffrey Dean, David Wilcox, and Bureau of Reclamation archaeologist Thomas Lincoln, provided extensive and insightful comments that were carefully considered. I would also like to thank Paul Fish, Carol Kramer, David Killick (all at the University of Arizona), and Norman Yoffee (University of Michigan) for their feedback and encouragement. My parents, Jean and Jack Clark, deserve special appreciation for their unswerving support now and during my graduate student years.

Sarah Herr (Desert Archaeology) provided numerous suggestions and thoughtful criticisms that greatly improved the quality of this document. Discussions with my colleagues at Desert Archaeology, particularly James Vint, Patrick Lyons, Penny Dufoe Minturn, and Mike Lindeman, also generated considerable food for thought. Ron Beckwith drafted a number of the figures in this volume, including many in Chapter 4. Several figures were also drafted by Susan Hall (Desert Archaeology), including the cover illustration and the overall map of the Tonto Basin in Chapter 3. A number of other figures (as noted throughout the volume) were adapted from maps supplied by James Holmlund and Geo-Map, Inc. Nicves Zedeño (University of Arizona) furnished the Spanish Resumen. Carol Gifford, the series editor, expresses special recognition and appreciation to Dirk J. Harris, Support Systems Analyst, and his assistant Eric Hanson (all University of Arizona), for their computer assistance in scanning figures and for their patience and wisdom in serving as the interface between the editor and photoshop. I reserve a final thanks to Carol for her knack of turning archaeological jargon into standard English and her unique ability to trim away excess words, leaving only concise prose that cuts to the chase.

CHAPTER ONE

Revisiting Migration

Perhaps the most severe criticism that can be leveled at migration theory in anthropology is that, in the strictest sense, it does not exist. What we have been discussing are, properly speaking, not migration theories but distribution theories which presuppose migration. Yet anthropologists have shown little interest in addressing the movement of peoples as a subject for study in its own right. On the contrary, there has been an almost perverse refusal, alike on the part of archaeologists, linguists, and physical anthropologists, to consider the social, technological, and logistic mechanics of human movement.

(Adams and others 1978: 523)

Forty years of neglect have left migration studies behind the times in archaeology and anthropology. During this interval, methodological advances in the discipline have enhanced resolution of the archaeological record and added new multidisciplinary analyses such as paleobotany and petrography to the archaeologist's arsenal of analytical tools. In the American Southwest a vast amount of fieldwork during the past two decades, primarily as the result of Cultural Resource Management (CRM) efforts, has generated an impressive database that was unavailable to early investigators. Finally, significant theoretical advances in correlating artifact variability with specific forms of human behavior have taken place. In light of these developments, a fresh look at migration within the discipline is long overdue.

During the past fifteen years, prehistorians in various areas of the world have returned to studies of migration to help explain material culture patterns (Anthony 1990; Bogucki 1987; Lindsay 1987; Renfrew 1987; Rouse 1986). The Southwest is one region profoundly impacted by renewed interest in this dated concept. Although several researchers never abandoned migration during the 1970s and 1980s (Lindsay 1987; Reid 1989), the topic did not reenter the mainstream of the discipline until the mid-1990s. Since then migration has returned to Southwest archaeology with a vengeance (Adams 1996; Cameron 1995; Ciolek-Torrello 1997; Clark 1995, 1997; Clark and others 2000; Dean 1996;

Duff 1998; Mills 1998; Reid 1997; Rice 1998; Riggs 1998; Spielmann 1998; Ştark, Clark, and Elson 1995). This revival is ironically fitting, considering that the Southwest was a major wellspring of the processual archaeology that threw the 'migration' baby out with the bathwater in the first place (Anthony 1990).

In this monograph, I reconsider the role of migration in archaeological explanatory frameworks and develop a reliable method for evaluating the scale of population movement. This approach is used to assess the impact of puebloan migrations into an early Classic period (A.D. 1200–1325) irrigation community in the Tonto Basin of east-central Arizona. The interval of interest coincides with the earliest manifestation of the 'Salado' in the Tonto Basin, a phenomenon that has been variably defined in the past as a culture, problem, question, or ceramic horizon (Crown 1994: 11–16; Gladwin and Gladwin 1935; Nelson and LeBlanc 1986: 1–14). Southwestern archaeologists are still struggling to come to grips with the Salado, and the significance of migration in the formation of this horizon has been and continues to be the subject of considerable debate (Dean 2000).

DEFINING PREHISTORIC MIGRATION

To discuss prehistoric migration objectively, it is necessary to have a precise definition of the term that differentiates migration from the much larger category of human population movement. Because assessments of prehistoric migrations rely primarily on archaeological data, the definition should take into account the limitations of the archaeological record. Population movement was undoubtedly a frequent occurrence in prehistory, but many of these movements remain invisible to the archaeologist. Bearing these issues in mind, prehistoric migration can be defined as *a long-term residential relocation beyond community boundaries by one or more discrete social units as the result of a perceived decrease in the benefits of remaining residentially stable or a perceived increase in the benefits of relocating to prospective destinations.*

This definition has a number of advantages for the archaeologist. From a methodological perspective, it filters out a considerable amount of 'background noise', including movements by individuals such as marriage partners, traders, and itinerant craftsmen. Limiting migration to the movements of social units rather than individuals increases the likelihood that the migrant groups are of sufficient size to remain distinct from indigenous groups for an extended interval in their destination areas. Temporary visits, scheduled seasonal rounds, and localized movements (Cadwallader 1992; Preucel 1990) are also excluded in the definition, regardless of how many individuals were participating in these activities. This increases the probability that the migrants traversed a material culture boundary, enhancing their visibility in the archaeological record with respect to indigenous groups. Although many population movements that fit this definition will continue to go unnoticed, establishing numerical thresholds for migrant unit size and distance traveled introduces an unacceptable level of arbitrariness.

The impact of migration in destination areas can be expected to be proportional to the size and social distance of the migrant units with respect to the indigenous population. The definition thus focuses our attention on population movements that are more likely to have significant impact rather than on inconsequential movements.

The definition also emphasizes the discrete character of migrant units, both en route (Anthony 1990: 902) and in destination areas. This important aspect of the 'new migration' can be contrasted with older models based on waves of migrants advancing along continuous fronts. Although displacement of one cultural group by another is possible, migration often generates co-residence contexts in which socially distant groups suddenly find themselves living in close proximity (Clark and others 2000; Mills 1998; Riggs 1998). This outcome can only be recognized using a model that views migration as a series of discontinuous movements by discrete social units.

Finally, population movements meeting the conditions of this definition are less likely to appear to the archaeologist as random events and more likely to be considered processes. Migration processes are initiated by spatially uneven changes in social and economic conditions within the 'known world' of the prospective migrants. Although the size of individual migrant units can be as small as a single household, general patterns can be found in the movements associated with large migrations because of common 'pushes' out of homelands and 'pulls' into specific destination areas (Anthony 1990: 898–900).

INVESTIGATING MIGRATION

Research on prehistoric migration can be subdivided into four broad categories: (1) detection in the archaeological record, (2) motivation for movement, (3) organization and logistical requirements of the migrant unit on the move, and (4) socioeconomic impact of migrants in destination areas. Each is considered briefly in the following sections.

Detection

Although detecting the occurrence and scale of migration is largely a methodological issue, it must be accomplished before the other three topics can be addressed. Demonstrating migration in the archaeological record can be difficult in even the most obvious examples because alternative explanations often exist for observed patterns that require little or no population movement. Especially difficult is proving that limited migration has occurred in areas inhabited by substantial populations. Advances in material culture studies during the past forty years provide considerable refinement in isolating specific classes of artifacts and types of attributes that can be used to track migrations. Based on these advances, a basic strategy for assessing the occurrence and scale of migration is developed in Chapter 2. This approach is evaluated using ethnoarchaeological and ethnohistoric case studies drawn from various regions around the world.

Motivation

At a macroregional scale, large migrations should be viewed as directed processes regardless of the size of each migrant unit. A basic assumption underlying a processual approach to migration is that independently acting households behave predictably when confronted with spatially uneven changes in social and economic conditions within their known world. These changes can be broken down into pushes from premigration settlements and pulls into destination areas (Anthony 1990: 899). Migrations, especially those covering long distances, involve considerable risk for the social units involved. Perceived benefits in emigrating from a particular region must outweigh both the risks inherent to moving and the benefits of staying put, or else migration will not occur.

Economic and environmental pushes such as drought, disease, resource over-exploitation, and demographic pushes such as population pressure are potentially identifiable if such data can be resolved at a fine-grained scale. Although more difficult to demonstrate from archaeological data, social and political factors, including factional disputes, may also play an important role in decisions to move (Herr and Clark 1997; Stanislawski 1973; Whiteley 1988).

Similar to pushes, there are also economic, environmental, demographic, and social pulls into prospective destinations. In the Southwest, obvious environmental pulls include perennial water and arable land. In times of environmental fluctuation and drought, movement from upland areas more dependent on precipitation to perennial rivers and springs would be expected (Adams 1996: 54; Dean 1996: 39; Fish and Fish 1993: 101; Varien and others 1996: 104–106). However, these areas were not devoid of settlement prior to migration and previous contacts with groups in prospective destinations probably weighed heavily in choosing final resettlement areas (Anthony 1990). Previous kin links and exchange relations may have provided the social contacts that facilitated the acceptance of new immigrants into existing communities. If communities practicing irrigation agriculture or other intensive subsistence strategies had labor requirements that were not always met by local populations, they might have welcomed immigrants as additions to the local labor pool (Fish and Fish 1993).

At a regional scale and beyond, commonalities in pushes and pulls can generate patterning in movement despite the fact that the migrant units themselves are acting independently. Stepping back from community to region, the seemingly chaotic moves of individual migrant units merge to form comprehensible lines and arrows. Migration processes once initiated can be self-propagating, because population movement itself may exert strong pushes and pulls. In terms of pushes, migrants entering a region can cause local socioeconomic conditions to deteriorate, triggering further movements by these groups, the local inhabitants, or a combination of both. Serial displacements may take place repeatedly along the migration route. With respect to pulls, once migrants have established a foothold within a destination, the initial enclaves may attract other groups from the same source area (Alvarez 1987: 133–138; Anthony 1990: 904; Lefferts 1977: 39; Stone 1996: 150, 151). Both pushes and pulls intrinsic to migration give this process an internal dynamic.

Organization and Logistics

Migrant groups do not travel randomly across the landscape and seldom enter unknown territory. Instead, they travel along established lines of communication or trade (Anthony 1990: 902; Cameron 1995; Herr and Clark 1997). Movements by discrete migrant units can be more accurately modeled as channelized "jumps" between optimal zones rather than radiating waves, with the success of previous moves determining future ones (Anthony 1990: 902–903). One would expect intervening areas between destinations to exhibit little material trace of the migrant population.

Several organizational and logistical variables constrain the size of migrant groups during movement. Important considerations include social organization in the homeland, physical distance traveled, terrain traversed, season of movement, and resources and other groups along the migration route. These variables affect the scale and structure of the migration and, hence, the impact of such movements en route and in destination areas.

The organization of migrant units and logistics of movement is perhaps the most difficult of the four subtopics to address with archaeological data. To date, archaeologists have turned to urban geography and modern sociology in modeling prehistoric migrations (Anthony 1990; Gmelch 1980). Although models borrowed from these disciplines have proven useful, the organization and logistical requirements of prehistoric migrations in traditional agricultural societies may differ substantially from those occurring in complex societies with high population densities, market economies, and advanced transportation technology. More promising sources of analogies are ethnographic, ethnohistoric, and ethnoarchaeological studies of societies with organizations and technologies more comparable to prehistoric groups. Unfortunately, few such studies focus on the movement of migrants (Herr and Clark 1997) and this is a research topic in which considerable work remains to be done.

Impact

Although displacement of one group by another is a possible outcome, more often migration results in the co-residence of different migrant groups and local groups within communities, settlements, and even households (Adams 1996; Clark 1997; Haury 1958; Lindsay 1987; Mills 1998; Reid 1989; Riggs 1998). In large migration processes, population movement, co-residence, and subsequent movement of one or more groups can rapidly generate a complicated sociocultural map. The impact of these movements varies substantially along migration routes and must be assessed one community at a time, which requires a shift in scale from regional process to local event. At this reduced scale, migration should be broken down into a series of related but discontinuous movements of discrete social units. Prehistoric migration can then be viewed as it was by indigenous populations, as abrupt influxes of foreign groups. At the very least, these influxes have an economic impact as population growth is increased at a level beyond the natural birth rate. More importantly, these movements place socially distant groups in close residential proximity. Although these groups may have had limited contact prior to immigration, such as long distance trade, they now are forced to share resources within a local setting, necessitating more intense and direct interaction.

Careful study of interaction between indigenous and different immigrant groups sheds light on the relationship between migration and the development of social complexity and inequality. The interval immediately following the first arrival of migrant groups is perhaps the most critical. During this period, a fluid context is generated in which new social networks rapidly emerge and crystallize that determine the course of subsequent interaction. This interaction may be cooperative, competitive, or oscillate between the two.

Heightened awareness of differences between groups may lead to expressions of ethnicity (De Vos and Romanucci-Ross 1975: 3, 9; Hodder 1979) and conflict along ethnic lines. Conflict has the potential of being particularly destructive as every community along the migration route is subjected to internal strife. In cases where the entry of new social groups dramatically impacts the trajectory of local communities, conflict between migrant and indigenous groups may result in the eventual displacement of one group or the other (Lindsay 1987; Wilcox and Haas 1994) or forced partitioning of local resources in favor of the dominant group (Barth 1969; Maquet 1970). Thus, conflict in the wake of migration is likely to lead to an appreciable increase in inequality.

Cooperative sharing of local resources between groups is also possible. In these instances, new integrative institutions may be required in the absence of kin ties to form stable communities (Crown 1994). These institutions must be of sufficient scale to bridge the social distances between the disparate groups. Kinship ties between migrant and indigenous groups may also develop rapidly through marriage alliances (Friedman and Rowlands 1977: 206–215) and the creation of fictive lineages (Henige 1974: 38–64).

Cooperation between groups does not necessarily mean the two groups are equal partners. Migrations of limited scale that do not disrupt extant communities or appreciably change land tenure systems place the newcomers at a distinct disadvantage in terms of access to land and resources. Numerical inferiority, unfamiliarity with the local environment, and the lack of better options may force immigrant groups into economic arrangements that are more beneficial to the indigenous population. These asymmetries can eventually destabilize and ultimately lead to the collapse of postmigration communities, especially if migrants continue to arrive and augment their relative power by weight of numbers. In these cases, if fine-grained resolution can be achieved, short intervals of co-residence may be discerned in outcomes in which one group ultimately displaces another.

These four subtopics of migration are discussed in greater detail in the following chapters. Detecting migration (Chapters 2 and 4) and assessing its impact (Chapter 5) are emphasized because they are amenable to standard forms of archaeological inquiry, including analyses of settlement pattern and of artifact and botanical assemblages. Although motivation for migration and the organizational and logistical requirements during movement are more difficult to reconstruct from archaeological data, particularly from a focused study in a destination area, the evidence that is available is also presented for the case study.

The American Southwest is a valuable source of examples of prehistoric migration because of the fine-tuned chronology and the vast amount of fieldwork accomplished in that region. Few areas in the Southwest rival the Tonto Basin with respect to the level of investigation using modern excavation and analytical techniques, much of it the result of cultural resource management work during the past twenty years. A 3-km by 6-km portion of the eastern basin was subjected to particularly intensive scrutiny. The development and collapse of the Meddler Point community is traced in this area over the course of 575 years. This example provides an ideal vantage point from which to study migration and assess the consequences of co-residence.

Detecting Prehistoric Migrations

Assessment of the occurrence and scale of prehistoric population movement is the crucial first step in any migration study. If this assessment cannot be accomplished with reasonable confidence, then subsequent models of migration are exercises in speculation. In the most compelling examples, migration is indicated by the depopulation of entire regions (Cameron 1991; Cameron and Tomka 1993; Dean 1996; Dean and others 1994; Varien and others 1996) or, in sparsely settled frontiers, by a dramatic increase in settlement (Longacre 1970; Martin 1973; Newcomb 1997; Reid and others 1996).

Demonstrating migration into regions already occupied by substantial populations is considerably more difficult, especially if population movement is on a limited scale and does not result in the displacement of local groups. To be detectable in the archaeological record, the migrants must have artifact assemblages that are discernibly different from those of the local groups. However, the appearance of new forms of material culture within a region can be explained by factors other than migration, such as exchange and emulation. Hence, a methodology is required that links changes in artifact assemblages specifically to population movement.

In his seminal treatment of the subject, Rouse (1958: 64; see also Reid 1997: 631) proposed five basic criteria for demonstrating migration:

1. Identify the migrating people as an intrusive unit in the region they have penetrated.
2. Trace this unit back to its homeland.
3. Determine that all occurrences of the unit are contemporaneous.
4. Establish the existence of favorable conditions for migration.
5. Demonstrate that some other hypothesis, such as independent invention or diffusion of traits, does not better fit the facts of the situation.

Although these criteria remain valid, they represent only general guidelines rather than a rigorous methodology. In particular, Criterion 5 does not specify the types of artifacts that should be used to demonstrate migration over competing explanations. All artifacts are not created equal in this regard, and advances in material culture studies over the past forty years have considerably refined the kinds of intrusive artifacts and attributes that indicate population movement.

Here I use literature pertaining to stylistic theory to isolate material indicators of migration. These indicators are comprised of artifact attributes that are *not* intentionally produced to convey messages. Variations in these attributes reflect unique cultural styles that can be used to track population movements of specific groups and to differentiate between groups with diverse origins when on-site production of the associated artifacts is demonstrated. Domestic spatial organization, preferences in foods and food preparation (foodways), and technological styles embedded in utilitarian items often meet these criteria and represent ideal data sets from which to assess migration.

Following the theoretical discussion, relevant material culture data sets are evaluated using ethnoarchaeological and ethnohistoric case studies drawn from a variety of contexts around the world. These studies are concerned either with tracking migrants on the move or differentiating among cultural groups living in close proximity as the result of migration.

THE FOUR "E-WORDS"

As can be inferred from Rouse's first two criteria, any assessment of archaeological migration is dependent on the appearance of new artifact forms within the region that have precedents outside that region. Demonstrating that a particular type of artifact is intrusive is a necessary condition of migration, but by itself is not sufficient proof. To generate a list of artifact types and attributes that are reliable indicators of migration, some discussion of human behavior is required (for detailed treatment, see Clark 1997: 45–76). Of particular interest are behaviors that produce artifact patterns that can be used to track migration and those that produce patterns that can be mistaken for migration. Behavior that produces artifact patterns that are often confused with migration can be divided into two broad categories: *exchange* and *emulation*. Because there is considerable overlap between patterns produced by these two behaviors and population movement, subsequent interpretations suffer from equifinality or the existence of alternative explanations for the same pattern that are equally probable. Behavior that is useful in assessing migration can also be placed into two broad categories: *ethnicity* and *enculturation*. Considering the instability of ethnic groups and the inconsistent manner in which these groups define themselves, the use of enculturation is considered a more promising approach.

Exchange

Exchange is a behavior that is particularly amenable to archaeological study because of its focus on the circulation of material goods. The most visible forms of exchange are those that circulate items that are conspicuous either because they are elaborately decorated or made from exotic raw materials. In the prehistoric American Southwest, long-distance exchange networks circulated conspicuous items such as decorated ceramics (Adams and others 1993; Blinman and Wilson 1993), marine shell (Bradley 1993; McGuire and Howard 1987), turquoise (Weigand and Harbottle 1993), copper bells (Vargas 1995), and macaws (Ruble 1996). The exchange of decorated pottery has been emphasized by Southwestern archaeologists in defining social and political boundaries (Graves 1982, 1994; Lekson 1996: 174; Plog 1980, 1990; Upham and others 1981).

Southwestern archaeologists have also used potential exchange goods, particularly decorated ceramics, to infer migration (Cordell 1995; Crown 1994; Dutton 1963; Gladwin and Gladwin 1935). Newly arrived migrants may have greater access to these goods than the indigenous inhabitants of a region if the items are produced near premigration settlement areas (Adams and others 1993; Montgomery and Reid 1990). In addition, producers of exchange goods may themselves immigrate and continue to manufacture these items in their new settlements (Crown 1994; Lindsay 1987; Triadan 1997). In either case, immigration would result in a dramatic increase of these goods within a particular region. In such examples, the appearance of decorated pots can be equated with the arrival of new peoples.

Despite several clear cases, a long list of cautionary tales warns against the use of exchange goods (especial-ly decorated ceramics) to track the movements of groups (Collett 1987; DeCorse 1989; Hodder 1979; Kramer 1977; Plog 1990; Pollock 1983). Exchange, as action at a distance (Renfrew 1975), can be conducted 'down-the-line' or by itinerant traders and requires little or no population movement. In cases where independent means of verification are lacking (like historical documents), determining whether the appearance of exchangeable goods is the result of migration or merely new trade contacts is often difficult. Because of the high potential for equifinality, items that circulate by exchange are unreliable indicators of migration unless local production can be demonstrated.

Emulation

Emulation of one group by another can produce artifact patterns that are more difficult to discern from migration than those generated by exchange because the new artifact forms are locally produced. There are many reasons why one group emulates the material culture of another, but for the purposes of this discussion, emulation is broken down into two basic categories: technological emulation and ideological emulation.

Technological Emulation

In the "Culture Area" paradigm of the early twentieth century, technological innovations were labeled "inventions." Inventions spread directly through migration or indirectly by diffusion (Adams and others 1978: 483–486; Anthony 1990: 896–897; Graebner 1911; Kossinna 1911), generating a distribution that radiated out from the source. Although overly simplistic, this dated concept remains valid at a general level for certain kinds of material culture. As discussed at length in selectionist and "culture as adaptation" models that borrow heavily from biological evolution, innovations that provide obvious adaptive or functional advantages over existing technologies are likely candidates for emulation by other groups (Braun 1995; Dunnell 1978; Leonard and Jones 1987). Thus, an argument may be offered that the appearance of these technologies and associated material culture within a region is the result of local imitation rather than migration. Examples of this process abound in the archaeological literature and only an illustrative case is provided here.

The role of migration in the spread of agriculture from southwest Asia to Europe, about 4500 to 3000 B.C., has been the subject of much discussion among Old World archaeologists. Many researchers tie the arrival of agriculture to the movements of Proto-Indo-Europeans (Anthony 1990: 905–908; Bogucki 1987; Renfrew 1987). These groups followed the fertile loess belt through central Europe, practicing a mixed strategy of cultivation and cattle herding. When they entered the northern European Plain, they came into contact with indigenous Mesolithic foragers. Although subsistence strategy and its associated toolkit may at first glance be an obvious candidate for differentiating between the two groups, the indigenous groups soon adopted the superior subsistence strategy of the migrants (Bogucki 1987; Sherratt 1990). To differentiate one group from another, archaeologists had to turn to other forms of material culture, such as funnel beakers, megalithic tombs, and Linear Pottery.

This example underscores a basic problem in relying on technological differences between groups to assess migration if such differences are of sufficient magnitude or character that one group possesses a distinct adaptive advantage over the other. In these cases, the archaeologist must resort to other forms of material culture to demonstrate that one group did not simply adopt the new technology because of its perceived benefits.

Ideological Emulation

The appearance of artifacts and architecture associated with religion and other high-level ideologies has also been used by archaeologists to demonstrate migration. In terms of religious architecture, the construction of Uruk-style temples in Syria at Habuba Kabira and Jebel Aruda in the fourth millennium B.C. is central to the argument for the presence of colonists from southern Mesopotamia along the middle and upper Euphrates (Algaze 1989). Similarly, the penetration of Arab and northern African groups into western Africa has been traced by the distribution of early mosques (McIntosh and McIntosh 1984: 91–92).

Mortuary practices have also been commonly used to trace population movements and to define boundaries between cultural groups (for example, DeCorse 1992: 183–185; Dolukhanov 1989: 275; Haury 1945: 43; Kus and Raharijaona 1990: 26–30; Santley and others 1987: 96). However, mortuary behavior is complex and may reflect multiple social dimensions (Binford 1971; Carr 1995c; Tainter 1978; Whittlesey 1978). One-to-one correlations between mortuary behavior and cultural groups are rare and more common are cases that produce inconclusive results (Crawford 1997; Larsson 1989).

Analogous to technological innovation, high-level ideologies as reflected in religion, mortuary practices, and other ritual behavior are also subject to emulation. In many cases, small-scale societies selectively borrow the ideologies and associated material culture of their more complex neighbors to serve local integrative needs (Craig and others 1998; Doelle and others 1995: 439) and to enhance their sociopolitical status (Rathje 1971). Under the label 'symbolic entrainment', this type of emulation is central to "Peer Polity Interaction" (Renfrew and Cherry 1986), which has been used as an alternative to migration in explaining the widespread distribution of ceremonial architecture, ritual paraphernalia, mortuary assemblages, and other ideological artifacts. In the Southwest, Peer Polity Interaction has been used to explain the spread of Mesoamerican ballcourts into southern and central Arizona (Wilcox 1991), the construction of great kivas and other Chacoan-style communal architecture in areas outside the San Juan Basin (Kintigh 1994), and platform mound building in areas outside the Phoenix Basin (Rice 1990a).

In general, linking high-level ideologies and religions with specific social groups is problematic. Although ideological and social boundaries can coincide, such ideologies often define interaction at the broadest of scales and include multiple societies (Crown 1994). Indeed, the interaction sphere concept, as developed by Caldwell (1965) to explain the Hopewell phenomenon, refers explicitly to a common ideology, as reflected in mortuary practices and ritual paraphernalia, shared by groups that possessed otherwise distinctive cultures and artifact assemblages. Artifacts associated with such ideologies are obviously not useful in discerning the movements of small social groups.

In evaluating population movement, the emulation of material culture with high ideological or technological value poses a problem analogous to that of items with high economic value circulating through exchange. Both emulation and exchange introduce certain forms of material culture into a region without significant population movement. Although migration can also introduce these goods, arguments based on these items are often equivocal because alternative explanations cannot be easily dismissed.

Ethnicity and Enculturation

Behaviors that are useful in assessing the occurrence and scale of migration include ethnicity and enculturation. Both define groups by shared identity, affiliation, and often settlement history. The primary difference between the two behaviors is that ethnicity is a conscious and active display of group identity based on common heritage (real or perceived) and enculturation is the process by which groups transmit culture knowledge between generations, both consciously and unconsciously. As such, ethnic and enculturative markers in artifact assemblages may be useful in tracking migrating groups. The presence of multiple ethnic or cultural groups within a region can often be attributed to recent migration, especially if only one group was present during earlier intervals in the sequence. The following sections explore the utility of both behaviors in migration research.

Ethnicity

Ethnic behavior is expressed as group solidarity, usually in opposition to similarly defined groups or larger polities in which these groups are embedded. This solidarity is based on any number of shared affiliations and identities, but often includes a common cultural heritage. On a general level, an ethnic group can be defined as a "self-perceived group of people who hold in common a set of traditions not shared by others with whom they are in contact. Such traditions typically include folk religious beliefs and practices, language, a sense of historical continuity, and common ancestry or place of origin" (De Vos 1975: 9). Kamp and Yoffee (1980: 87–89) and Shennan (1989: 14) define ethnicity as self-conscious identification with a particular social group based on real or fictitious common ancestries and origins.

At first glance, using ethnicity to trace migrations is an attractive option. Migration reshuffles the social map at both regional and local scales, placing previously unrelated social groups in close proximity (Reid 1997). Subsequent competition for local resources may heighten social tension (Hodder 1979) and stimulate the formation of ethnic groups whose membership is based on premigration origins. The presence of multiple ethnic groups in a region following an interval of ethnic homogeneity may constitute a compelling case for migration.

To identify ethnic groups in the archaeological record, symbols of these groups must be interpreted and isolated from the multitude of other messages that are conveyed in material culture, a task that requires a precise definition of ethnicity and an unambiguous list of ethnic markers. Unfortunately, such a definition and common criteria for membership have eluded anthropologists thus far (Alonso 1994). De Vos and Romanucci-Ross (1975: 3) list racial, territorial, economic, religious, cultural, aesthetic, and linguistic variables as potential criteria for ethnic group membership, noting

that ethnicity, "like any other form of social identity, is essentially subjective; a sense of social belonging and ultimate loyalty." In the absence of universal and objective criteria, ethnic groups may be difficult to reconstruct from archaeological data.

To complicate matters further for the archaeologist, historical evidence suggests that ethnicity is also highly situational and ethnic groups are unstable through time (Geary 1983; Kamp and Yoffee 1980). Contemporary ethnic boundaries rapidly develop and dissolve in response to external political threats or to economic pressures (David and others 1991; Hill 1989; Wolf 1984: 393–396). Ethnic group membership can be displayed when socially advantageous and hidden or suppressed when disadvantageous (Hodder 1979; Williams 1992). When and where ethnic identity is displayed often depends upon power relations among ethnic groups and between these groups and larger sociopolitical systems (Wallerstein 1973). Whether ethnicity, as it is defined for complex societies, existed prior to the industrial revolution and modern states (Bentley 1987; Gellner 1983) or the formation of early state societies (Emberling 1997; Smith 1986) has been the subject of considerable debate. Considering the instablity of ethnic groups and the coarse chronological resolution of many prehistoric sequences, finding such groups in the archaeological record is a formidable task without recourse to other sources of data such as written documents (for similar views, see Arutiunov and Khazanov 1981; Barth 1969; Shennan 1989: 14). This problem of detection limits our ability to track migrations through ethnic behavior. However, it may be possible to reconstruct ethnic behavior once migrant groups have been identified by other means.

Enculturation

In addition to displayed identities, social groups can be defined merely by the fact that they share a settlement history and have been in close contact throughout an extended interval. In small-scale agricultural societies, households are typically the basic social and corporate units (Hammel 1980: 251; Wilk 1991) and constitute "the next biggest thing on the social map after the individual" (Hammel 1984: 40). Basic enculturation (cultural training) and social reproduction are included in the range of functions preformed by households (Wilk and Netting 1984: 5–19). During the routine and rhythm of domestic life, specific ecological "where-to-do's," utilitarian "how-to-do's," and social "what-to-do's" are passed from old to young through active instruction and passive imitation (Netting 1993: 59, 63, 70–72).

Households in traditional agricultural societies that have formed stable settlements, communities, and larger social groups often develop common frameworks for transmitting cultural knowledge. This body of knowledge represents a shared tradition that can potentially be used to track the movements of associated households whether or not this collective consciously displays its identity. Unconscious and deeply embedded aspects of enculturation are often more stable through time than displayed identities such as ethnicity and more resistant to assimilation in mixed cultural settings generated by migration. Continuity in these embedded aspects within a region can be used as a proxy measure for settlement continuity. Conversely, their abrupt appearance in another region would indicate immigration of the associated group. Thus, the material correlates of deeply embedded aspects of enculturative background can be used to track the movements of the associated groups and identify their settlements when they enter regions occupied by groups with different backgrounds. To evaluate migration, we are concerned only with comparing similarities and differences within this set of correlates regardless of their meaning within the traditions that produced them.

FINDING ENCULTURATION IN ARTIFACT ASSEMBLAGES

To isolate artifact forms and attributes that reflect embedded aspects of enculturation, a brief digression into the history of interpreting stylistic variability in artifacts is required. During the first half of the twentieth century, Kossinna's (1911) *Siedlungarchäologie* and the concept of *Kulturkreise* or Culture Area (Graebner 1911) had a profound influence on both Old and New World archaeology (Childe 1950, 1956; Kluckhohn 1936).

The methodology for defining culture areas was relatively simple and could be applied directly to archaeological data. Once contemporaneous settlements and assemblages were defined by stratigraphic association or seriation, cultures were reconstructed by isolating "a plurality of well-defined diagnostic types that were repeatedly and exclusively associated with one another and, when plotted on a map, exhibited a recognizable distribution pattern" (Childe 1956: 123). Archaeological assemblages were equated with ethnographic societies and there was little consideration of the different types of human behavior that are reflected in the manufacture and use of various types of artifacts (Veit 1989: 39–42). In the American Southwest, adoption of the culture area approach led to the definition of the Hohokam, Mogollon, Anasazi, and Salado traditions (Gladwin and Gladwin 1930a, 1934, 1935; Haury 1936; 1945; Johnson 1965; Reed 1942; Wheat 1955).

Lewis Binford: Cultural Style and Drift

Processual archaeology represented the first systematic attempt to break down artifact variability and correlate it with specific behaviors. Influenced by the work of Julian Steward (1955), Lewis Binford (1965: 206–209) proposed an alternative to the culture area paradigm that partitioned sociocultural behavior with respect to three broad categories: cultural traditions, adaptive areas, and intersocietal interaction spheres, the last borrowed from Caldwell (1965). Artifact variability was attributed either to its primary or secondary function. Primary function was associated with an artifact's use as an adaptive tool and secondary function was related to style and cultural tradition. Processual archaeology focused almost exclusively on the former at the expense of the latter. Hence culture was largely viewed as an adaptation to the environment and the traditional and ideological aspects of culture were virtually ignored.

Binford (1963) also borrowed the concept of "cultural drift" from social anthropology and applied it to archaeological assemblages. This term was used to describe subtle variation in material culture that inevitably developed between groups who were not in frequent contact. Binford used the concept to explain variability in Late Archaic lithic assemblages associated with red ocher caches in Michigan.

Cultural drift was a direct analog of genetic drift in biological evolution and was attributed to random variation that did not significantly change the performance of the associated tool. Binford's cultural drift represented an attempt to isolate artifact variability that arose simply because of differences in settlement history and contact. This is the type of variability we can use to track the movements of specific groups. In fact, Binford (1963: 94) remarked that variability "observed in attribute classes suspected as amenable to the operation of the process of cultural drift should be investigated as hints to population expansions and migrations." Unfortunately, cultural drift was not explored further by Binford and the concept lay dormant within the processual paradigm.

Wobst, Wiessner, and Sackett: Style With and Without a Message

With the onset of postprocessual archaeology during the late 1970s and 1980s, topics largely ignored in processualist approaches such as ideology and symbolism reemerged in explanatory frameworks (for example, Hodder 1982). In the postprocessualist paradigm, cultures were no longer viewed as environmental adaptations but as texts subject to interpretation. Artifacts were not merely the tools of subsistence, but the words and sentences the archaeologist must read to interpret this text. Concomitant with this paradigm shift, there was a resurgence of interest in artifact style and intracultural meaning.

In his seminal article on stylistic behavior, Martin Wobst (1977) argued for a functional approach to style in line with the philosophy of processual archaeology. To Wobst (1977: 330, 335), style was consciously produced on visible media as a means of nonverbal communication within the associated culture. Information exchanged in this manner included important social messages regarding group and individual identity. Polly Wiessner (1983, 1984) took this approach a step further in explaining variability in artifact assemblages associated with Kalahari San groups of southern Africa. Wiessner subdivided "style with a message" into two dimensions based on the type of information conveyed. *Emblemic* style conveyed intentional messages about group affiliation and *assertive* style carried information concerning individual identity (Wiessner 1983: 257–258).

James Sackett approached style from a different perspective that ultimately led to a definition that was more abstract than that proposed by Wobst and Wiessner. Sackett's conception of style emerged from the famous Binford-Bordes debate on the meaning of artifact variability in lithic assemblages from the French Middle Paleolithic (Binford 1973; Bordes and de Sonneville-Bordes 1970; Sackett 1973). Binford attributed this variability to different tool types manufactured by a single cultural tradition and Bordes argued that this same variability reflected stylistic differences that could be attributed to more than one cultural tradition. In an attempt to find common ground between these two interpretations, Sackett placed style and function in a continuum in which one was the perfect complement of the other and both considered together accounted for all possible artifact variability (Sackett 1977: 370). For better or worse, Sackett introduced the concept of *isochrestic* variation as a means of articulating his abstract concept of style with tangible cultural behavior (Sackett 1982). The term means literally "equivalent in use" (Sackett 1985: 156) and refers to the fact that there is often more than one feasible method to accomplish the same function or, simply stated, "more than one way to skin a cat" (Sackett 1990: 33). Choices made from the range of options can also be considered stylistic behavior.

Differences in their approaches to style led to a debate in the 1980s between Sackett and Wiessner that rivaled the Binford-Bordes debate of the 1970s (Sackett 1985, 1986, 1990; Wiessner 1984, 1985, 1990). The discussion focused on Wiessner's ethnoarchaeological study of style in material culture produced by several Kalahari San groups (Wiessner 1983: 253–254). In a memorable experiment conducted by Wiessner (1983: 269), two infrequently interacting San groups were presented with projectile points produced by each other. This display generated considerable anxiety and discussion within each group as previously unrecognized differences in point manufacture were abruptly raised to a conscious level. In essence, Wiessner's experiment transformed enculturative differences in artifact manufacture to ethnic symbols. When asked to elaborate on the cause of these differences, Wiessner (1984: 195) elicited frustrated replies from members who stated they "made things in a certain way because everything must be made some way and that was the way their parents did it." Based on these comments Wiessner (1983: 273) cast the results of the experiment in a negative light and concluded that this type of variability was a source of distraction that interfered with interpreting stylistic messages. However, the San could not have presented a better response in support of Sackett's concept of *isochrestic* variation or Binford's "cultural drift." Because differences in point manufacture arose unconsciously through lack of contact, this variability cannot be easily explained and ultimately could only be attributed to enculturative background.

From the vantage point of hindsight, it is obvious that an unconscious and passive dimension of style lay outside the boundaries of Wobst's and Wiessner's "style with a message." However, Sackett's more generalized model could accommodate both types of style. Instead of reaching this conclusion, the debate merely polarized the two positions with little recognition of common ground. Much of this failure may be attributed to confusion over the meaning and usage of the term "isochrestic." By the early 1990s, there was considerable doubt whether a unified approach to style was possible in archaeology (Hegmon 1992; Wiessner 1990).

Christopher Carr: Physical and Contextual Visibility

Despite the skepticism generated by the Sackett-Wiessner debate, several researchers have subsequently attempted synthetic treatments of style (for example, Braun 1995; Carr 1995a, 1995b). Christopher Carr's "unified middle range theory of artifact design" is of particular interest because it provides a strategy to isolate specific artifact attributes that reflect enculturative background or "style without a message." Borrowing from Sackett, Wobst, and Wiessner, the goal of Carr's model is not to develop new conceptual tools for examining stylistic behavior, but to integrate the various theoretical stances that have emerged regarding stylistic behavior. As noted by Carr (1995a: 156), "the question is not which theory of style is 'right', but, rather, which kinds of formal attributes can reflect which kinds of processes—enculturation, communication...." Carr (1995a: 157) adopts a broad-based approach to style similar to Sackett's isochrestic model that extends the range of stylistic attributes beyond those that convey messages (Carr 1995b: 252).

In Carr's model (1995b: 173), artifact attributes are arranged hierarchically based on three criteria: (1) attribute and artifact visibility; (2) relative order of the attribute in the artifact design sequence; and (3) relative order of the attributes in the artifact production sequence. Following Wobst (1977: 330), Carr considered attribute and artifact visibility the most important of the three criteria in determining the potential for conveying messages. The degree of visibility indicates the size and character of the target audience.

Physical visibility is influenced by size of the attribute and associated artifact, frequency of attribute occurrence on the artifact, degree of contrast with other attributes, attribute complexity, and the relative order in which the attribute is manufactured within the production sequence. Although Carr (1995b: 185) gives priority to physical characteristics in determining an attribute's communication potential, the context of use must also be considered. The latter includes artifact ubiquity, average viewing time and distance, viewer attentiveness, openness of setting, number of viewers, and lighting conditions (Carr 1995b, Table 7.5).

As a rule, the higher the physical and contextual visibility of the attribute and associated artifact, the greater its message potential. Although high visibility is essential to communication, not all highly visible attributes convey social messages. In other words, high visibility is necessary but by itself is not a sufficient condition for communication, and other analyses must be conducted to determine whether or not messages are actually being conveyed. High visibility attributes are also more likely to be emulated or imitated by other groups and can be distributed widely without migration. Thus, they often are not reliable indicators of population movement.

Conversely, attributes with low physical and contextual visibility can be assumed to have little message potential. Low visibility attributes are inherently more stable through time than their visible counterparts because they are less subject to careful scrutiny and self-reflection. They are also less likely to be imitated or emulated. Stylistic similarities in low visibility attributes merely reflect shared settlement history and a common enculturative background (Carr 1995b: 195–198, 213). Differences in these attributes are the result of stylistic or cultural drift between noninteracting groups (Binford 1963; Braun 1995).

Domestic Spatial Organization, Foodways, and Embedded Technological Styles

This brief review of style and artifact variability has brought us close to our goal of isolating specific artifact types and attributes that reflect enculturative background and that can be used to evaluate migration. Archaeological theory has come a long way in assessing artifact variability since the early "Culture Area" paradigm. New Archaeology linked artifact function to adaptation and artifact style with cultural tradition, although its practitioners largely disregarded the latter. Renewed interest in ideology and cultural meaning in the late 1970s and 1980s resulted in the division of style into that which conveys messages and that which simply arises from settlement history. In the former, artifact style was shown to have function and, in the latter, artifact function was shown to have style. By assessing physical and contextual visibility, artifact attributes can be correlated with either type of style. This progression of knowledge seems straightforward, but it has taken forty years to achieve.

Carr (1995b: 246–250) provides only a basic framework for assessing visibility and assigning specific artifact attributes to either type of style. In terms of tracking migration, we need to look for attributes with low contextual visibility, wherein the number of viewers, openness of viewing setting, viewer attentiveness, and average viewing time are minimized (Carr 1995b, Table 7.5). Artifacts and architecture used in public contexts should be avoided because they are likely to be viewed for extended intervals by large audiences. Artifacts and architecture associated with ceremonies and rituals should also be avoided because these conspicuous events are likely to increase viewer attentiveness. Instead, everyday domestic contexts should be emphasized. The limited scale of domestic architecture places restrictions on the number of viewers and openness of setting. Although certain domestic activities may be rich in symbolism and meaning (Sterner 1989), many are conducted as part of a daily routine with little attentiveness or self-evaluation. A focus on domestic context places our search firmly in the domain of the household, which is the primary unit of enculturation in small-scale agricultural societies (Netting 1993: 59, 63, 70–72). The tools, installations, architecture, utilitarian vessels, and waste associated with domestic life are potentially rich in attributes that can be used to assess migration. As a rule, the more fundamental and mundane the artifact, the more likely it is to passively reflect enculturative background.

Material culture attributes associated with domestic contexts can be further culled by considering physical visibility (Carr 1995b, Table 7.5). Strategies for minimizing physical visibility include the selection of large attributes that cannot be viewed in their entirety or those so complex that they are not readily comprehensible. Domestic spatial organization is one such attribute that fits both criteria. Patterns of domestic spatial organization are often difficult to comprehend without a schematic representation such as a map, especially in settlements comprised of multiroomed buildings.

The organization of domestic space reflects the composition of households, the nature of activities undertaken in these basic units, and the degree to which households are integrated into larger social groups (Ferguson 1996; Flannery 1972; Fritz 1987; Hillier and Hanson 1984; Kent 1990; Lawrence and Low 1990; McGuire and Schiffer 1983). As such, domestic spatial organization can vary considerably between groups with different cultural backgrounds (Hillier and Hanson 1984: 27; Kent 1990; Rapaport 1969, 1990). Although aspects of domestic space can be highly symbolic (Kus and Raharijaona 1990: 23–29), the target audience is often small and limited to household members. Many patterns observed in the layout of domestic architecture have little message content and are merely the by-products of multiple construction episodes that reflect the changing needs of the resident household (Agorsah 1986; Goody 1971). The pattern of domestic spatial organization can be identified in archaeological sites from wall foundations, floors, and floor features. Build-

ing events can be reconstructed from wall bond-abut patterns, providing the excavator with a temporally compressed sequence that was unavailable to the original inhabitants (Haury 1985: 36). Finally, "local production" of domestic architecture is assured. Hence, domestic spatial organization represents an ideal data set for assessing migration.

At the other end of the size scale, attributes that are so small that they cannot be viewed without a visual aid are also ideal data sets for our purposes. Included in this set are tool use-wear patterns, microattributes of tools, and organic refuse. Organic remains are particularly useful because they contain valuable information as to the food preferences of the settlement inhabitants. Although plant staples and exploited animal species may not vary appreciably among different cultural groups inhabiting the same area, there are likely to be subtle differences in flavorings, meat cuts, and preparation techniques (Baker 1980; Cheek and Friedlander 1990; Evans 1980; DeFrance 1996). Such nuances have little message content and represent a potential source of variation that can be used to track the movements of specific groups.

A final strategy to minimize physical visibility focuses on the relative order an attribute is made within the production sequence of an artifact. All manufactured artifacts reflect the outcome of a series of technical options that compose a production sequence, or *chaîne d'operatoire* (Lemonnier 1986; Leroi-Gourhan 1964). As discussed by Binford (1963) in his model of cultural drift, nuances in the design and manufacture of tools with comparable functions can be expected among noninteracting groups simply because of the randomizing effect of independent choices made from a range of technical options. Such nuances constitute technological styles that are shared by artisans with a common enculturative background (Lechtman 1977; Sackett 1985: 158, 1990: 33; Stark and others 1998) or technological tradition (Childs 1991).

The earlier an attribute is produced within the production sequence, the more likely it is to be obscured by subsequent production steps of additive manufacturing processes (for example, ceramic manufacture, textile weaving, and wall construction) or removed by subsequent stages of reductive processes (ground stone and flaked stone manufacture). Early and intermediate manufacturing stages include raw material selection and basic forming techniques. Surface treatments and decoration are usually the final steps of the production process. In additive manufacturing processes, evidence of early stages of production often survive in the final product. The technical styles in these embedded attributes have little or no message content and represent another class of data from which migration can be assessed with reasonable confidence.

TESTING THE APPROACH

The above theoretical discussion has focused our search for reliable indicators of migration on low visibility attributes of artifacts and architecture associated with domestic contexts. Moving from theory to practice, the strategy presented is evaluated in this section using ethnoarchaeological and ethnohistoric case studies from Africa, North and South America, Asia, and Europe that focus on identifying cultural groups from material remains. In many of the examples, two or more different groups are residing in close proximity as the result of recent or past migration. Although the following literature survey is by no means exhaustive, it provides a representative cross section of examples that can be verified independently from sources other than archaeological data (for a more detailed presentation that includes archaeological cases studies, see Clark 1997: 105–144).

Material Culture Categories

To evaluate the strategy outlined in this chapter, various material markers evaluated in each case study are grouped into general categories with respect to physical and contextual visibility (Table 2.1). Attributes produced in early and intermediate stages of manufacturing processes and associated tools and installations are assigned to the "M–" categories in Table 2.1. This designation links nondecorative manufacturing steps (and associated technological styles) regardless of material type and differentiates them from the final, highly visible steps such as decoration (DE). Subcategories within the manufacturing process category (M–) represent specific materials and technologies, including ceramics (M–C), flaked stone (M–L), ground stone (M–G), textiles (M–T), metal (M–M), walls (M–W), and domestic installations (M–I).

The organization of architectural space represents another general category (A–) that should be considered separately from wall construction (M–W) and other manufacturing processes. Spatial organization is divided into that associated with domestic architecture (A–D) and that associated with public or ceremonial architecture (A–P). Considering the potential of foodways in assessing migration, preferences in food types and prep-

aration technqiues are assigned a separate category (FP). Subsistence strategy (SS), or the dominant mode of obtaining food resources, is treated separately from foodways. Finally, artifact forms that are used in special contexts or highly displayed are also grouped together regardless of material type and other considerations. These include projectile points (PP), personal ornamentation (PO), recreational and gaming paraphernalia (RG), and burial practices (BP).

Physical, contextual, and overall visibility was assessed for each category in Table 2.1. Physical visibility was evaluated in terms of attribute size, complexity, and degree of "embeddedness" in the final product, as discussed above. For example, many nondecorative manufacturing processes (raw materials selection, basic forming techniques, functional surface treatments) were assigned low-to-moderate physical visibility and differentiated from decorative steps (DE) with high visibility. Spatial organization in domestic architecture (A–D) was assigned a low rating in physical visibility based on the argument presented above, and public or ceremonial architecture (A–P) was assigned a high value because of large size, planned construction, and open layout to accommodate large social groups. Food preference (FP) was assigned a low-moderate value because of the range of size in this category, from large cuts of meat to small plants and from simple dishes to multi-ingredient stews and soups.

The high level of subjectivity in evaluating contextual visibility is reflected in the range of values assigned in Table 2.1. In assessing overall visibility, physical factors are given more weight than context. If an attribute is physically difficult to see, then it is likely to have low visibility regardless of where it is used. However, in categories assigned a moderate or high physical visibility, contextual factors then determined overall visibility. The Burial Practice category is perhaps the most difficult in which to assign an overall visibility, with extreme variability in physical visibility among potential mortuary offerings and in contextual visibility dependent on viewing customs.

The Sample

The examples used in this study are drawn from around the world and are organized by continent in Table 2.3 at the end of this chapter. The specific geographic and temporal settings and the relevant cultural groups are listed for each example. Each case study is evaluated in terms of the relative success of the studied material culture category in identifying specific cultural

Table 2.1. Material Culture Categories and Assessments of Physical, Contextual, and Overall Visibility

Attribute Code	Description	Physical Visibility	Contextual Visibility	Overall Visibility	Comments
A–D	Domestic architecture layout and spatial organization	Low	Low-moderate	Low	Internal organization and placement with regard to other such units
A–P	Public architecture layout and spatial organization	High	Moderate-high	High	Monumental and ceremonial architecture with an integrative function
BP	Burial practices	Moderate-high	Low-high	Low-high	Body treatment, funerary facilities, and mortuary offerings (overrides other classifications)
DE	Decorative techniques and designs	High	High	High	Nonutilitarian surface treatments on any media, including painted, sculpted, and molded designs
FP	Foodway preferences	Low-moderate	Low-moderate	Low-moderate	Food types and preparation techniques
M–C	Ceramic manufacture (nondecorative)	Low-high	Low-high	Low-high	Includes associated manufacturing tools and installations (see DE for decorative steps)
M–G	Ground stone tool manufacture	Low-moderate	Low-moderate	Low-moderate	Includes associated manufacturing tools, restricted to food processing tools
M–L	Flaked stone tool manufacture	Low-moderate	Low-moderate	Low-moderate	Includes associated manufacturing tools, projectile point morphology is considered separately (see PP)
M–I	Construction of domestic installations	Moderate-high	Low-moderate	Low-moderate	Includes hearths, storage facilities, and other installations associated with domestic architecture
M–M	Traditional metallurgy	Low-high	Low-high	Low-high	Emphasis on utilitarian metals, traditional technologies, and associated tools and installations
M–T	Textile manufacture (nondecorative)	Low	Low-moderate	Low	Emphasis on basic weaving techniques and cordage patterns rather than on decorative elements (see DE for the latter)
M–W	Wall and roof construction techniques	Low-high	Low-high	Low-high	Emphasis on domestic architecture
PO	Personal ornamentation	Moderate-high	High	High	Includes jewelry, designs on clothing, tattooing, cosmetic body modifications, and hairstyle (overrides other classifications)
PP	Projectile point morphology	High	Moderate-high	High	Emphasis on final morphology rather than on manufacture (see M–L for the latter)
RG	Recreational and gaming paraphernalia	Moderate-high	Low-high	Low-high	Includes items associated with the use of narcotic substances (overrides other classifications)
SS	Subsistence strategy	High	High	High	Emphasis on mode of subsistence and tools rather than on nuances in food choices and preparation (see FP)

A– Architectural spatial organization

M– Nondecorative steps in manufacturing processes, including raw materials selection, forming techniques, and nondecorative surface treatments

groups. One of three outcomes was possible: (1) the case study supported the use of the indicated category in differentiating groups (SP); (2) the case was a cautionary tale against using the indicated category in distinguishing between groups (CT); or (3) the case yielded inconclusive or mixed results (IN). Material data evaluated in each study were categorized using the designations in Table 2.1. In examples that utilized multiple categories, each was assessed separately.

Africa

The majority of contemporary ethnoarchaeological case studies used in the survey come from Africa. Examples cover the entire continent, including the Sahara, Sahel, and eastern and southern Africa. Notable ethnoarchaeological examples include studies of iron metallurgy as a technological tradition (Childs 1991; David and others 1991), DeCorse's (1989, 1992) research in West Africa, and Wiessner's (1983, 1984) seminal fieldwork with the Kalahari San that was the focus of the debate with Sackett. Sterner's work (1989) with the Sirak Bulahay in Cameroon provides an important cautionary tale against using decorated ceramics as ethnic markers. Collett's (1987) study of Ngoni and Kololo migrations from South Africa into Bantu-speaking areas argues against the use of ceramics altogether in tracing migrations in favor of domestic spatial organization. Hodder's (1979) ethnoarchaeological work in the Baringo district of Kenya suggests that the expression of ethnic differences is highly situational and dependent on the level of competition between groups for resources.

Americas

Many examples used in this study are derived from the Americas, where there has been considerable interest in the identification of minorities in the Colonial and post-Colonial archaeological record, particularly Afro-American and Chinese-American groups. In many of these examples, archaeological explanations are supported by historical documents. Plans of "shotgun" houses, manufacturing techniques reflected in Colono-Indian or "Yabba" utilitarian wares, and food preferences reflected in meat cuts that hearken back to West African traditions are generally considered the most reliable indicators of Afro-American households (Armstrong 1990; Baker 1980; Cheek and Friedlander 1990; Ferguson 1992). However, separating economic factors related to slavery from indicators of Afro-American culture is not always straightforward (Armstrong 1990).

For example, meat portions reflected in the faunal assemblages of Afro-American households may be more the result of poverty than voluntary food preferences (Otto 1980).

Early American Chinese households can be discerned by food preferences, including meat types and cuts, flavorings, and flavoring containers (Diehl and others 1998; Langenwalter 1980; McGuire 1982). Recreational pursuits also reflect cultural preferences, as reflected in gaming pieces and opium-smoking paraphernalia associated with Chinese households (Evans 1980). Food preferences evident in the faunal records from early Colonial sites in southern Peru can also be used to differentiate between Spanish and indigenous Incan groups (DeFrance 1996).

Northern European immigrants and their descendants can be identified in the backwoods frontiers of colonial North America from residential floorplans and log-cutting techniques that reflect Scandinavian origins (Jordan and Kaups 1989). In the early historic American Southwest, spatial layout and nonlocal construction techniques and materials associated with Tapicito Ruin identify the occupants as refugees of the Great Pueblo Revolt who lived amidst Navajo groups (Towner and Dean 1992).

Evaluations of cordage and weaving styles are largely derived from American examples, including one from Brazil (Newton 1974) and another from the American Southwest (Underhill 1944). These cases support the use of cordage patterns, especially spin direction, in identifying the enculturative background of the weaver.

Asia and Europe

Examples from Europe and Asia are derived from a variety of studies with different research goals. Barth's (1969) seminal work in Swat, Pakistan, provides one of the most insightful ethnographic case studies concerning ethnicity and an important cautionary tale against using subsistence strategy as an ethnic marker. Archaeological examples from the historic Near East are primarily concerned with ceramic distributions and include both supportive case studies (Dothan 1982; Emberling 1997; Esse 1992) and cautionary tales (Kramer 1977; Pollock 1983). Several examples use sources of data unavailable to prehistorians to reconstruct ethnic groups such as scripts, languages, and proper names (Kamp and Yoffee 1980; Larsen 1976). Finally, European examples are derived from the eastern portion of the continent, where ethnicity has reemerged as an important political issue following the collapse of the Soviet Union (Kobylínski 1989; Pálóczi-Horváth 1989).

Table 2.2. Relative Success of Material Catogories as Cultural Markers

Attribute Code	Description	Supportive Case Studies	Inconclusive Case Studies	Cautionary Tales
A–D	*Domestic architecture layout and spatial organization*	11	2	1
A–P	Public architecture layout and spatial organization	1	0	0
BP	Burial practices	4	3	3
DE	Decorative techniques and designs	9	2	7
FP	*Foodway preferences*	11	3	0
M–C	*Ceramic manufacture (nondecorative steps)*	10	2	1
M–G	*Ground stone tool manufacture*	1	0	0
M–L	*Flaked stone tool manufacture*	2	0	0
M–I	*Construction of domestic installations*	4	0	1
M–M	*Traditional metallurgy*	2	0	0
M–T	*Textile manufacture (nondecorative steps)*	3	0	0
M–W	*Wall and roof construction techniques*	4	0	1
PO	Personal ornamentation	5	2	4
PP	Projectile point morphology	2	0	2
RG	*Recreational and gaming paraphernalia*	2	0	0
SS	Subsistence strategy	1	0	1

NOTE: *Boldface denotes category potentially useful in assessing migration.*
A– Architectural spatial organization.
M– Nondecorative steps in manufacturing processes, including raw materials selection, forming techniques, and nondecorative surface treatments.

Survey Results

The above summary highlights research trends in identifying cultural groups through material remains from a wide variety of geographic and temporal settings. The relative success of each category listed in Table 2.1 in differentiating cultural groups living in close proximity is tallied in Table 2.2. Counts are provided of supportive cases, cautionary tales, and examples that yielded inconclusive results. Not surprisingly, many cases focus on ceramics (M–C and many of the DE case studies), including forming techniques, surface treatment, and decoration. Domestic architecture layout (A–D), food preferences (FP), burial practices (BP), and personal ornamentation (PO) have also been studied extensively as cultural markers, but few cases were found that used public architecture (A–P), projectile point morphology (PP), lithic manufacture (M–L), metallurgy (M–M), wall construction (M–W), subsistence strategy (SS), ground stone manufacture (M–G), and recreational and gaming practices (RG).

Figure 2.1 presents the results of the survey using the categories listed in Table 2.1. Categories with fewer than three examples (A–P, M–G, M–L, M–M, RG, SS) in Table 2.2 are not shown because of small sample size. The categories are ordered with respect to increas-

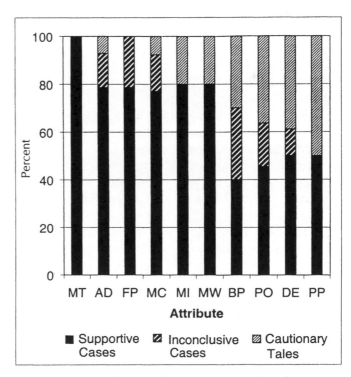

Figure 2.1. Case studies using material markers to identify cultural groups in diverse settings.

ing overall visibility. In general, an inverse relationship between attribute visibility and the reliability of a particular category as a cultural marker is indicated.

Both low visibility categories, domestic spatial organization and weaving-cordage style, received high scores. In the low-to-moderate visibility range, food preferences and, to a lesser extent, domestic installations also appear to be reliable indicators. The low-to-high category, as expected, produced variable results. However, if studies focusing on decoration are excluded, ceramic technological style yielded a relatively high score. Wall construction also represented a fairly reliable indicator of cultural background. Burial practices produced inconclusive results, although burial posture and body treatment may be more reliable indicators than associated mortuary offerings. Recreational and gaming practices and technological styles reflected in traditional metallurgy and in ground and flaked stone tool manufacture are promising avenues of research, but suffer from small sample sizes.

As predicted by Carr's model, high visibility categories yielded mixed results. Decorative elements (primarily on ceramics), personal ornamentation, projectile point styles, and subsistence strategy identify different groups in several examples, but the overall success rate in each of these categories is 50 percent or less. Variable results in these categories can be attributed to the different types of information that is conveyed on highly visible media. Selecting correctly from the multitude of potential messages would be an extremely difficult task for the prehistorian.

Overall, the literature survey lends substantial support to the strategy of using attributes with low physical and contextual visibility to identify groups with different enculturative backgrounds and settlement histories. This strategy maximizes the level of confidence in assessing migration by selecting attributes and associated artifacts that are not usually exchanged or emulated and thus do not circulate without the groups that produce them. It also selects for attributes that are likely to survive for extended intervals in the co-residence contexts often generated by migration. Of course, the more attributes within this set one can bring to bear on the evaluation, the stronger the argument for migration. This approach represents a substantial refinement of Rouse's general criteria for demonstrating migration that were presented at the beginning of the chapter.

Specific data sets that proved to be especially useful in tracking the movement of different groups include domestic spatial organization, foodways, and embedded technological styles reflected in the nondecorative production steps of ceramic vessels, textiles, walls, domestic installations, and other utilitarian items. These data sets must be tailored to fit the specific requirements of each case study. In selecting specific attributes, the strengths and weaknesses of the recovered artifact sample, the difficulty in determining production area, and the sensitivity of each attribute in differentiating between various migrant and local groups require careful consideration.

Evaluating the scale of migration is a necessary first step that must be accomplished with reasonable confidence or subsequent discussions of consequences are on tenuous ground. Once migration has been evaluated and the settlements of various migrants and local groups have been identified at maximum resolution, then decorative elements, public architecture, and other data sets with high message potential can be studied to assess the impact of migration. Using a paint-by-numbers analogy, the first step of any reliable assessment of migration is to reconstruct a background pattern of enculturative history. This pattern can be subsequently colored by data gleaned from more conspicuous forms of material culture.

With a strategy for detecting migrations developed, we turn to the Salado and the Tonto Basin. The intensive level of fieldwork in this region during the past twenty years has generated an impressive database that encompasses large samples of multiple artifacts and attributes that we can use to evaluate migration, including domestic spatial organization, wall construction, and utilitarian ceramic manufacture. These fortunate circumstances have provided abundant data with which to explore the consequences of migration, both in the interval immediately following the arrival of the first migrants and in succeeding generations.

Table 2.3 on the following pages provides case studies from around the world that were used to evaluate the effectiveness of using certain artifacts and attributes as markers of migration in the archaeological record (additional details are in Clark 1997).

A–D	Domestic architecture layout and spatial organization
A–P	Public architecture layout and spatial organization
BP	Burial practices
DE	Decorative techniques and designs
FP	Foodway preferences
M–C	Ceramic manufacture (nondecorative)
M–G	Ground stone tool manufacture
M–L	Flaked stone tool manufacture
M–I	Construction of domestic installations
M–M	Traditional metallurgy
M–T	Textile manufacture (nondecorative)
M–W	Wall and roof construction techniques
PO	Personal ornamentation
PP	Projectile point morphology
RG	Recreational and gaming paraphernalia
SS	Subsistence strategy

Table 2.3. Ethnoarchaeological, Ethnohistoric, and Experimental Case Studies that Assess the Use of Material Culture as Ethnic and Enculturative Markers

Source	Context	Cultural Groups	Material Markers	Results*
Africa				
Agorsah 1986	Contemporary and historic Waie villages in the Northern Volta Basin, Ghana	Guang-speaking Nchumuru	A–D	SP
Childs 1991	Contemporary sub-Saharan Africa; particularly Zimbabwe	Bantu-speaking groups; Ma Shona culture	M–M	SP
Collett 1987	Historic and contemporary southern Africa	Migration of Ngoni and Kololo groups from Swazi to Bantu-speaking areas	A–D, DE	SP for A–D; CT for DE
David and others 1991	Contemporary North Cameroon	Maha and Wandala groups in dispersed communities	A–D, A–I, BP, M–M	SP for all
DeCorse 1989	Contemporary Sierra Leone	Limba, Yalunka, and Kuranko groups	DE	CT
DeCorse 1992	Historic Gold Coast; Elmina settlement	Asante and Fante Akan-speaking groups; Europeans	A–D, M–C, FP, BP, M–W	SP for BP, A–D, FP, M–C; CT for M–W
Hodder 1979	Contemporary western Kenya; Baringo District	Cattle herding ethnic-tribal groups with limited agriculture	A–D, PO, DE, M–C, FP	IN for all
Kus and Raharijaona 1990	Contemporary and historic Madagascar	Betsileo groups	A–D, BP	SP for both
Larick 1987	Contemporary North Kenya	Loikop cattle pastoralists	PP	CT
Markell and others 1995	Vergelegen Plantation, Capetown, South Africa; 18th century	Dutch colonists and indigenous Africans	A–D; M–I	SP for both
Sterner 1989	Contemporary North Cameroon	Sirak Bulahay	DE, M–C	SP for M–C; CT for DE
Washburn 1989	Contemporary Zaire and Rochester, NY	Female Bakuba and Laotian (refugee) weavers	DE	SP
Wiessner 1983	Contemporary Kalahari Desert in eastern Botswana and northwestern Namibia	Kalahari San groups	PP	SP
Wiessner 1984	Contemporary Kalahari Desert in eastern Botswana and northwestern Namibia	Kalahari San groups	PO	CT

* Case study is supportive (SP), cautionary (CT), or inconclusive (IN) for identification of ethnic, cultural, or migrant group.

Table 2.3 - continued

Source	Context	Cultural Groups	Material Markers	Results*
Americas				
Armstrong 1990	Drax Hall Plantation, Jamaica; 18th and 19th centuries	Anglo plantation owners; Afro-American slaves	FP, M–C	SP for both
Arnold 1989	Yucatan, Mexico; contemporary	Ticul potters in patrilocal descent system	DE, M–C	SP for M–C; CT for DE
Baker 1980	Andover, Massachusetts; late 18th–early 19th centuries	Afro-Americans	A–D, FP	SP for both
Becker 1977	Northeastern U.S.; 17th and 18th centuries	Swedish and Dutch settlers	M–W	SP
Cheek and Fried-lander 1990	Washington D.C.; early 20th century	Afro-Americans	FP	SP
Costello and Walker 1987	Santa Barbara Presidio, California; late 18th and early 19th centuries	Hispanics and Native Americans	PO	CT
Croes 1987	Prehistoric Northwest Coast in U.S.; 3000 bp–historic era	Salishan, Wakashan, and Chimakuan groups	M–T	SP
Deagan 1983	St. Augustine, Florida; 18th century	Europeans (Spanish and British), *criollos*, Native Americans, Afro-Americans	FP, A–D, M–C, PO, BP	IN for all
DeBoer 1990	Ucayali Basin in the Peruvian Amazon; contemporary	Panoan (including Shipibo-Conibo) groups, Arawak and Tupi speaking tribal groups	DE, PP, M–C	SP for all
DeFrance 1996	Southern Peru; 16th century	Colonial Spanish (Iberians) and Incas	FP	SP
Diehl and others 1998	Tucson, Arizona; late 19th and early 20th centuries	Chinese	FP	SP
Evans 1980	California; about 1850–1900	Chinese	M–I, FP, RG	SP for all
Ferguson 1992	Southeastern U.S.; 18th and 19th centuries	Afro-Americans	A–D, M–C, FP, DE	SP for all
Handler 1996	Plantation at Barbados, West Indies; late 1600s or early 1700s	Afro-American slaves	BP	SP

* Case study is supportive (SP), cautionary (CT), or inconclusive (IN) for identification of ethnic, cultural, or migrant group.

[20]

Table 2.3 - *continued*

Source	Context	Cultural Groups	Material Markers	Results*
Isajiw 1984	20th-century Alberta	Migrant Ukrainians	A–P, FP	SP for both
Jordan and Kaups 1989	American 'backwoods' frontier regions; about A.D. 1640–1875	Northern Europeans	M–W, A–D	SP for both
Kimmel 1993	19th-century Virginia farmstead	Afro-American households	A–D, M–I	CT for both
Klingelhofer 1987	Slave quarters at Garrison Plantation, Maryland; 19th century	Afro-American slaves	M–L, DE	SP for both
Langenwalter II 1980	Chinese store in Madera County; California	Chinese	FP, M–C, DE	SP for all
Lister and Lister 1974	Colonial Spanish America	Hispanics and Native Americans	DE, M–C	CT for both
Lyons 1987	19th- and 20th-century highland Peru	14 ethnic groups, including 4 linguistic groups	PP	CT
McGuire 1982	19th-century Tucson, Arizona	Anglo, Hispanic, Chinese groups	FP, A–D, M–C	SP for all
McLaughlin 1987	19th-century U.S. Midwest	Plains Indians	DE, PO	SP for both
Newton 1974	Central Brazil; 19th–20th centuries	Krikati and Pukobye tribes of the Timbara	M–T	SP
O'Shea 1984	Prehistoric and early historic Great Plains	Omaha and closely related Arikara and Pawnee Plains tribes	BP	IN
Otto 1980, 1984	Cannon's Point Plantation, Georgia; late 18th–early 19th centuries	Afro-American slaves, and Anglo plantation owners and overseers	FP	IN
Russell 1997	Hermitage near Nashville, Tennessee; 19th century	Afro-American slaves	RG, DE, PO	SP for all
Stine and others 1996	Plantation sites from South Carolina and Georgia; 18th and 19th centuries	Afro-American groups	PO	SP
Towner and Dean 1992	U.S. Southwest; early Historic period	Native American groups in northeastern Arizona and northwestern New Mexico	A–D, M–W	SP for both
Underhill 1944	Historic U.S. Southwest	Navaho and Hopi groups	M–T	SP

* Case study is supportive (SP), cautionary (CT), or inconclusive (IN) for identification of ethnic, cultural, or migrant group.

Table 2.3 - continued

Source	Context	Cultural Groups	Material Markers	Results*
Wegars 1991	North American mining and railroad-construction sites; late Historic	Italian immigrants	M–I, M–W; FP	SP for all
Wilkie 1996	Oakley Plantation, Louisiana; 1840–1930	Afro-American groups	M–L	SP
Williams 1992	Contemporary U.S.	Afro-American groups	PO	SP
Asia and the Pacific				
Barth 1969	Contemporary Swat, Pakistan	Pathan, Kohistani, Gujar groups	SS	CT
Burley 1995	Contemporary Tonga	Polynesians	BP	CT
Cummins 1984	Prehistoric and early historic Hawaii	Indigenous Polynesian-speaking Hawaiian polities	PO	CT
Dothan 1982	Early Iron Age Palestine	Philistines	DE, M–C	SP for both
Earle 1990	Historic Hawaii	Hawaiian complex chiefdoms	PO, BP	CT for both
Emberling 1997	Mesopotamia; early 3rd millennium B.C.	Various Mesopotamian groups	DE, BP	SP for both
Esse 1992	Early Iron Age Palestine	Prehistoric Israelites	M–C	SP
Graves 1994	Contemporary Philippines	Philippines; Kalinga	DE	IN
Green 1987	Historic and prehistoric Polynesia	Polynesian ethnic groups	M–G	SP
Kramer 1977	Northern Mesopotamia; early 2nd millennium B.C.	Hurrians	DE	CT
Ninsheng 1989	Yunnan, China; about 1st century B.C. and contemporary China	Dian kingdom under Western Han Empire and same geographic area in the modern era	PO	SP
Europe				
Davis 1985	Feudal England, Japan; Greece, about 800–400 B.C.	Feudal societies	PO, DE	CT for both
Greene 1987	Late Roman Era	Ostrogoths and Visgoths	PO	IN
Pálóczi-Horváth 1989	Hungary; 13th–16th centuries A.D.	Cumanians	A–D, SS	SP for both

* Case study is supportive (SP), cautionary (CT), or inconclusive (IN) for identification of ethnic, cultural, or migrant group.

CHAPTER THREE

The Salado and the Tonto Basin

During the Classic period, A.D. 1200–1450, the Tonto Basin was an important region with respect to the Salado archaeological horizon in the American Southwest as defined by the distribution of Salado polychrome pottery. This distribution encompasses 130,000 square kilometers (50,000 square miles) in Arizona, New Mexico, and northern Mexico (Crown 1994: 1), including the Anasazi, Hohokam, Mogollon, and Sinagua culure areas as they have been traditionally defined by archaeologists (Fig. 3.1). Explanations for the widespread distribution of Salado polychrome vessels include exchange, imitation, and migration, and the definition of the Salado horizon has changed with every major paradigm shift in the discipline. Debate continues as to the character of the horizon and the extent to which it was the result of internal developments or external factors such as population movement (Dean 2000). For these reasons, the Salado represents an ideal research context in which to study migration.

By summarizing previous Salado research and archaeological investigations in the Tonto Basin, this chapter sets the stage for the case study in Chapter 4. Relevant highlights from the pre-Classic sequence in the basin are discussed to provide a historical background for the analysis, which focuses on the Classic period. Recent fieldwork in the eastern portion of the basin has thoroughly documented the development and collapse of a prehistoric community that endured for more than 500 years. Because few areas in the Southwest have been subjected to such intensive investigation, this portion of the basin provides a unique opportunity to assess the scale and impact of migration at high resolution.

THE SALADO

At various times, the Salado has been described as a puebloan migration (Gladwin and Gladwin 1935); a hybrid of Hohokam, ancestral puebloan, or Sinaguan cultures (Haury 1945; Schroeder 1953); a product of Mesoamerican contact and influence (Di Peso 1976); an indigenous development from the pre-Classic Hohokam (Doyel 1976); a religious cult (Crown 1994); or simply a question (Nelson and LeBlanc 1986: 1–14). These divergent views permit little common ground among the various researchers as to the character of the Salado. At the most general level, the Salado can be defined as an archaeological horizon, a term relatively devoid of interpretation that refers to the temporal and spatial dimensions of a widely distributed style or suite of artifacts. The temporal dimension of the Salado horizon is approximately A.D. 1250 to 1450. The spatial dimension includes central and eastern Arizona, southern New Mexico, and the northern portions of Sonora and Chihuahua, Mexico. The only consistent horizon marker across this broad region is Salado polychrome pottery, in particular the type Gila Polychrome, which has one of the widest distributions of any decorated ceramic type in the prehistoric Southwest.

The Salado as Migrants

Prior to defining the Salado as a horizon, decorated pottery that later would be called Salado polychrome was recognized by Adolph Bandelier during his western explorations, which included the Tonto Basin (Bandelier 1892; Lange and Riley 1970). Subsequently this polychrome pottery, which was initially referred to as "Lower Gila Polychrome," was also recovered from sites in southern and central Arizona (Fewkes 1912; Hough 1907; Kidder 1924). Erich Schmidt, working in the Phoenix Basin, noted that this polychrome pottery only co-occurred with Hohokam Buff Ware in the uppermost stratigraphic levels of investigated sites, leading him to suggest a "dual occupation" late in the prehistoric sequence (Schmidt 1928). Schmidt linked groups using red-on-buff pottery with cremation burial practices and groups using "Lower Gila Polychrome" with extended primary inhumation.

Working out of Gila Pueblo in Globe, Arizona, Harold and Winifred Gladwin first used the term 'Salado' in reference to prehistoric groups associated with

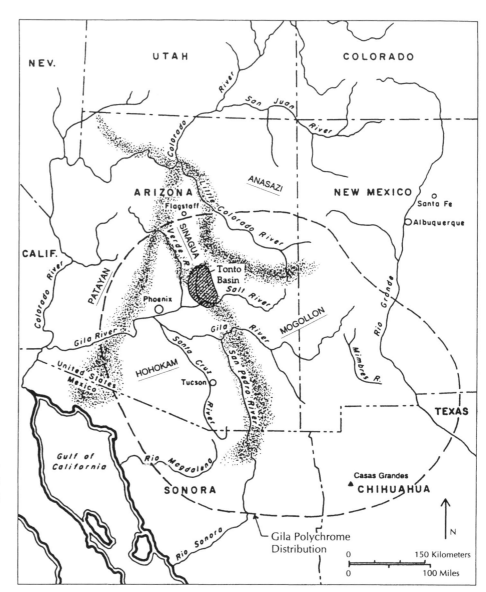

Figure 3.1. The Tonto Basin and pre-historic culture areas (underlined) in the American Southwest (adapted from Stark and Elson 1995, Fig. 1.1).

"Lower Gila Polychrome" (Gladwin and Gladwin 1930b). In the prevailing Culture Area paradigm of the 1930s, the distribution of this polychrome pottery was thought to define a culture that was centered in the Tonto Basin–Globe area (Gladwin and Gladwin 1930b: 3). The Gladwins defined the three basic Salado polychrome types, in chronological order: Pinto, Gila, and Tonto, with significant temporal overlap noted between the last two types. Gila Polychrome is by far the most widely distributed of the Salado polychromes (Crown 1994, Fig. 1.1). Pinto Polychrome, the earliest type in the series (about A.D. 1275–1325), has a more limited range, restricted to central and southeastern Arizona, with the highest density in and around the Tonto Basin.

Harold and Winifred Gladwin (1935) subsequently developed a scenario in which migrants from the Little Colorado River valley entered the Tonto Basin around A.D. 1000. The previous inhabitants of the basin, Hohokam groups associated with red-on-buff pottery, were thought to have abandoned the region prior to this migration. The immigrants evolved into a distinct ethnic group, the Salado, over the course of the next century and eventually settled in the Salt and Gila river valleys beside Hohokam groups. These initial migrants were associated with Pinto Polychrome, the earliest of the Salado polychrome types. During the Roosevelt phase (about A.D. 1250–1325), migrants from the Four Corners region in northeastern Arizona allegedly entered the Tonto Basin in another migration episode, bringing with them puebloan architecture and Gila Polychrome pottery.

The Gladwins' influence on Emil Haury's conception of the Salado is apparent in Haury's publication (1945) of Cushing's 1887–1888 excavations at Los Muertos in the Phoenix Basin. The excavations documented a consistent pattern of cremation burial outside compound walls and extended inhumation in specially designated burial areas within compounds. Most of the residences were associated with both cremation and inhumation burial areas. Haury interpreted this pattern as reflecting the presence of two different ethnic groups that lived side by side in the village. Cremations were associated with the indigenous Hohokam and extended inhumations with Salado migrants. Haury placed the origins of the Salado in the Mogollon and Anasazi regions, with a stronger connection to the latter. The migrants passed through the Tonto Basin, where they resided for an interval of sufficient length to become a unique cultural manifestation. Albert Schroeder (1953) proposed another variant of the 'cultural blend' theme with the Salado produced by intense contact between the Hohokam and Sinaguan regions, resulting in a unique hybrid culture. These early conceptions of the Salado horizon set the course for subsequent research, and archaeologists currently working in central and southern Arizona continue to define their positions with respect to these early migration hypotheses (Dean 2000).

Processual Archaeology and an Indigenous Salado

With the advent of processual archaeology in the early 1960s, Salado research was taken in new directions. Previous explanatory frameworks emphasizing migration were eclipsed by the new paradigm. New explanations for the Salado horizon in southern and central Arizona emphasized connections with the pre-Classic Hohokam and deemphasized puebloan migration (Steen 1962; Wasley 1966). Although influence from the puebloan world was recognized, this influence was attributed largely to exchange between Hohokam and puebloan groups or imitation of the former by the latter, especially in decorated ceramic manufacture. This position was adopted by a number of researchers (Doyel 1976; Hohmann and Kelley 1988; Rice 1985; Wasley and Doyel 1980; Weaver 1976; Wood 1985, 1989; Wood and Hohmann 1985; Wood and McAllister 1980, 1982). Doyel's work (1978) in the Miami Wash area on the southeastern margin of the Tonto Basin defined the Miami phase (A.D. 1150–1250) that spanned the hiatus

proposed by the Gladwins between pre-Classic and Classic period settlement in the basin. This phase was an attempt to establish a direct link between pre-Classic Hohokam groups living in pit houses and the Classic period inhabitants of the region residing in masonry compounds.

Proponents of the migration hypothesis persevered through this interval, resulting in two widely divergent views of the Salado horizon. This divergence is evident in the proceedings of the 1967 Salado Red Ware conference. Various participants listed Western Pueblo, Mogollon, Sinagua, Little Colorado, and Hohokam as possible cultural antecedents to the Salado (Lindsay and Jennings 1968: 4). Basic agreement could not be reached as to whether or not the Salado horizon even represented a cultural tradition. In an attempt to find common ground, the horizon was described in increasingly vague terms as a phenomenon, a problem, or merely a question.

The Casas Grandes Connection and an "Eastern Salado"

Charles Di Peso brought yet another perspective to Salado research. He argued for a strong Mexican influence in the production of Gila Polychrome. Di Peso believed that Paquime (Casas Grandes) became a regional production center for Gila Polychrome when the indigenous population was joined by Mesoamerican *puchteca,* or state-sponsored merchants, from the Toltec region in the mid-eleventh century (Di Peso 1976). Using controversial tree-ring dates, Di Peso argued that Gila Polychrome was first produced in northern Mexico during the mid-eleventh century, 250 years earlier than its appearance in central Arizona. This claim called into question the Globe-Tonto Basin area as the center of Salado polychrome production, shifting the core area of the horizon to the south and east.

Reevaluation of tree-ring dates from Casas Grandes casts doubt on a Chihuahuan origin for Gila Polychrome (Dean and Ravesloot 1993). This reanalysis places the majority of contexts associated with Gila Polychrome in the fourteenth and fifteenth centuries, roughly 150 to 200 years later than Di Peso's beginning date for Gila Polychrome. The revised chronology temporally realigns Gila Polychrome in northern Mexico with Gila Polychrome in the American Southwest and constitutes a strong argument against a north Mexican origin for the horizon.

Regardless of the dating of Gila Polychrome, significant Mexican influence is apparent in the Salado of western New Mexico and portions of southeastern Arizona (Lekson 1992; Nelson and LeBlanc 1986). This influence may have included population movement from Paquime into areas such as the Mimbres Valley at the end of the thirteenth century (Nelson and LeBlanc 1986: 11–12). The extent of influence from north Mexico differentiates this "Salado of the East" (Lekson 1992) from the western portion of the horizon in central and south-central Arizona.

Awareness that the area encompassed by the horizon was even larger than previously defined occurred at the same time that debate on the cultural composition of the Salado intensified. Included in the expanded Salado horizon were late prehistoric sequences in the Safford Basin (Brown 1973) and the San Pedro River valley in southeastern Arizona (Franklin and Masse 1976), the Mimbres and Cliff River valleys in southwestern New Mexico (Fitting 1972; LeBlanc and Nelson 1976; Lekson 1978; Mills and Mills 1972), and areas proximal to the U.S.–Mexican border (Johnson and Thompson 1963; McCluney 1962, 1965; Mills and Mills 1969). At this stage, use of "Salado" had become so inconsistent that researchers debated whether the term served any meaningful purpose. Indeed, differences between puebloan, Hohokam, and north Mexican models for the origins of the Salado appeared irreconcilable.

The first Salado Conference in 1976 attempted to reach a consensus among these divergent views. A primary objective of the conference was to derive a cultural definition of the horizon (Doyel and Haury 1976). However, the results were generally inconclusive, with Mexican and puebloan models for Salado cultural origins each vulnerable to criticism. With the exception of Salado polychrome pottery, a common artifact assemblage could not be defined for the Salado across the broad geographic region encompassed by the horizon (Cartledge 1976; Gumerman and Weed 1976; Weaver 1976).

Recent Research

Cultural Resource Management projects in the Tonto Basin and work in the Mimbres region (Nelson and LeBlanc 1986) has greatly expanded the Salado database over the past two decades. Publication of Erich Schmidt's investigations at several large Salado sites in central Arizona also represents an important addition to this database (Hohmann and Kelley 1988). A second Salado Conference (Lange and Germick 1992) was held to discuss these new developments in the context of ongoing fieldwork in the Tonto Basin. Conference pa-

pers with a synthetic orientation adopted a "wait and see" attitude in consideration of the immense, and yet unanalyzed, body of data that was currently being generated by the Bureau of Reclamation's Roosevelt Dam project (Doyel 1992).

Patricia Crown's (1994) Salado polychrome study represents the most systematic attempt to date to define the Salado horizon. Crown (1994: 213–217, 223–225) links the production and circulation of Salado polychrome pottery to the spread of the "Southwest Regional Cult." This cult was an egalitarian religious institution that promoted the flow of goods, services, information, and people across political and ethnic boundaries. Crown concludes that the rise of the Southwest Regional Cult may have been related to migrations across the area and this institution would have facilitated the integration of culturally diverse communities generated by these movements (see Adams 1991 for a similar view).

Despite these recent efforts, current conceptions of the Salado continue to run the entire gamut of explanations that have been offered since the Gladwins first defined the horizon more than 70 years ago (Dean 2000). In the Tonto Basin, several recent researchers have emphasized the importance of migration in any explanation of the Salado horizon (Whittlesey and Reid 1982; Whittlesey and Ciolek-Torrello 1992: 318; Whittlesey and Ciolek-Torrello 2000). They argue that much of the complexity of the Tonto Basin archaeological record in the Classic period can be attributed to a pluralistic society generated by puebloan migration. Indeed, Ciolek-Torrello (1997: 553) suggests that local populations in portions of the basin may have been entirely replaced by puebloan immigrants during the late Classic period (A.D. 1325–1400).

Conversely, Hohmann and Kelley (1988: 155) emphasize the indigenous character of the Salado and continuity across the pre-Classic to Classic interval. Although puebloan influence is recognized, it is attributed primarily to contact rather than migration. Near the beginning of the Roosevelt Dam Project, Rice (1990a) also proposed a model of indigenous Salado development based on polity interaction with groups in the Phoenix Basin (Renfrew and Cherry 1986). Rice initially viewed the Tonto Basin Salado as a veneer of material culture associated largely with Hohokam elites in the Classic period. However, by the end of the project, Rice (1998) had accorded migration an important role in the development of the Salado horizon. The position of Wood (2000) and his colleagues (Wood and McAllister 1982) has remained essentially unchanged throughout the past two decades. They attribute the emergence of the Salado in the Tonto Basin to internal development that can be traced back into the pre-Classic period and relegate migration to an inconsequential role. As researchers continue to disagree at such a fundamental level, the need for an objective means of assessing the scale and impact of population movement becomes increasingly apparent.

Considering the divergent views on the significance of puebloan migration in the Salado of central and southeastern Arizona, this area represents an ideal context from which to draw case studies for assessing migration using the approach developed in the previous chapter. The central role of the Tonto Basin in the history of Salado research and the vast database currently available from this region make the basin an obvious choice among the numerous river valleys within the geographic territory of the horizon.

THE TONTO BASIN

Situated in a transitional environmental zone, the Tonto Basin is bounded by high, rugged mountain ranges to the east and west, plateau uplands to the north, and the semiarid Sonoran Desert to the south. The local environment of the basin is dominated by the perennial Salt River and the near-perennial Tonto Creek (Fig. 3.2). Thus, the basin is generally well watered and would have contained abundant natural resources amenable to prehistoric settlement. The proximity of the Mazatzal Mountains to the west and Sierra Ancha to the north would have provided ready access to diverse ecological settings with riparian, Sonoran Desert, and upland piñon-juniper zones all within a day's walk. The Tonto Basin, which is part of the Tonto National Forest, can be divided into four basic subregions: (1) the Salt River arm of the lower Tonto Basin defined by the Salt River floodplain and adjacent terraces between Pinal Creek to the east and Tonto Creek to the west; (2) the Tonto Creek arm of the lower basin defined by the Tonto Creek floodplain and adjacent terraces between Hardt Creek to the north and the confluence with the Salt River to the south; (3) the upper Tonto Basin along Tonto Creek and major side drainages south of Payson and north of Hardt Creek; and (4) high elevation areas surrounding the above three zones, including the eastern slopes of the Mazatzal Mountains and the southern and western slopes of the Sierra Ancha.

Roosevelt Lake represents an obstacle to contemporary archaeological research in the area. The lake covers more than 6,800 hectares (17,000 acres) of irrigable floodplain and numerous archaeological sites. Roosevelt Lake was created in 1911 with the construction of Theodore Roosevelt Dam near the confluence of Tonto Creek and the Salt River. The archaeological record beneath the lake is known only from accounts of early explorers and brief glimpses of the lake bottom during periods of low precipitation. Several large sites in the basin, including Armer Ranch, are within the inundated area. The only part of the Salt River floodplain that is currently available for archaeological investigation is in the extreme eastern portion of the basin.

History of Tonto Basin Archaeology

The Tonto Basin has had a long history of archaeological investigation and, as noted above, has played a prominent role in Salado research (Elson and Craig 1992; Lekson and others 1992; Macnider and Effland 1989; Stark and Elson 1995; Wood and others 1989). Well-preserved ruins have attracted archaeologists to the area for more than 100 years. In 1883, Bandelier spent two weeks mapping and recording several large habitation and platform mound sites, including Oak Creek and Pyramid Point, which are briefly described in his journals (Lange and Riley 1970: 108–121). Although the following years saw a number of visits by archaeologists and other explorers, formal archaeological work in the Tonto Basin did not begin until 1925, when Eric Schmidt, employed by the American Museum of Natural History, investigated several large platform mound sites and pueblos. Schmidt's work focused on the site of Togetzoge in the Globe-Miami area. He also tested several of the largest Classic period sites in the lower Tonto Basin, including Armer Ranch Ruin, Schoolhouse Point, and the Rock Island platform mound (Fig. 3.2; Hohmann and Kelley 1988).

Schmidt was followed by archaeologists from Gila Pueblo, who conducted extensive surveys and several excavations in the Tonto Basin and vicinity (Gladwin and Gladwin 1930a, 1934, 1935). In the eastern Tonto Basin, Gila Pueblo conducted limited work at Meddler Point, which the Gladwins designated the type site for Gila Polychrome pottery. These studies formally defined the Hohokam and Salado cultures and set the tone for later research and debate.

The most extensive excavation during this early period took place in 1930 when Gila Pueblo excavated Roosevelt 9:6, a pit house settlement in the eastern portion of the basin that was considered the type site for the Hohokam Colonial period (Haury 1932). In 1929

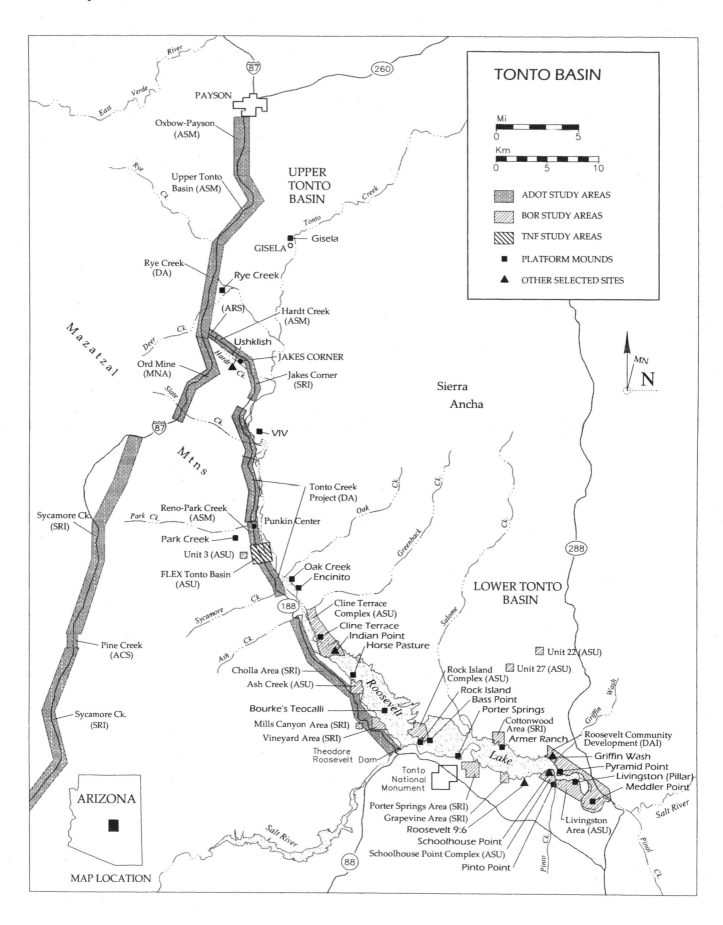

and 1930, archaeologists from Gila Pueblo also carried out limited excavations at Rye Creek Ruin, a large Classic period platform mound community in the Upper Tonto Basin (Craig 1992; Gregory 1995a; Haury 1930). Several cliff dwellings in the Sierra Ancha and nearby Canyon Creek were also investigated by Gila Pueblo archaeologists during the early 1930s (Ciolek-Torrello and Lange 1990; Haury 1934).

The next four decades saw only limited archaeological investigation in the Tonto Basin. One notable project during this period was the extensive excavation and stabilization effort at the Tonto Cliff Dwellings by archaeologists from the National Park Service (Steen 1962). During the early 1960s, the VIV platform mound and several associated compounds on the Tonto Creek arm were excavated by Jack and Vera Mills (Mills and Mills 1975). In the 1970s, several highway salvage projects were conducted in the upper basin (Hammack 1969; Huckell 1978), along Tonto Creek (Haas 1971; Huckell 1973; Jeter 1978), and along Miami Wash to the southeast of the basin (Doyel 1978). These projects were the vanguard of the massive Cultural Resource Management (CRM) efforts to follow.

The era of large CRM projects in the basin began in the mid-1980s and has continued through 2000. Over the past fifteen years an immense effort has been expended on Tonto Basin archaeology, largely as a result of highway and dam construction in the region (Fig. 3.2). Much of this effort has been funded by the Arizona Department of Transportation (ADOT) and the United States Bureau of Reclamation (BOR). The case study used in this monograph is based on work accomplished during the Roosevelt Dam Project of the BOR during the late 1980s and early 1990s. ADOT-sponsored projects included efforts in the upper basin (Ciolek-Torrello 1987; Elson and Craig 1992) and along Tonto Creek (Clark and Vint 2000; Hohmann 1985; Rice 1985). Other excavations were conducted for the Tonto National Forest as part of the Federal Land Exchange (FLEX) program, including areas along Tonto Creek (Cameron 1997) and in the Payson area north of the basin (Lindauer and others 1991; Redman 1993). This impressive amount of work has elevated the Tonto Basin from a poorly documented area to one of the most intensively investigated regions in the Southwest.

←

Figure 3.2. The Tonto Basin, showing major water courses and archaeological project areas (adapted from Clark and Vint 2000, Fig. 1.1).

As part of the Roosevelt Dam Project, the lower Tonto Basin was subjected to an intensive data recovery effort. The fieldwork was accomplished prior to raising the dam by 12 meters (40 feet). All archaeological sites that might be impacted by the raised water level or by recreational use of the new shoreline were available for investigation and many of them were either tested or intensively excavated. This fieldwork was divided among three organizations: the Office of Cultural Resource Management at Arizona State University (ASU) in Tempe and Desert Archaeology, Inc. and Statistical Research, Inc., two contract archaeology firms in Tucson.

ASU had the largest share of the contract. It was charged with investigating Classic period platform mound communities throughout the lower basin, including those associated with the Livingston (Pillar) and Pinto Point platform mounds and Schoolhouse Point, interpreted by ASU workers as a platform mound; the Rock Island complex, including the Bass Point platform mound, in the central portion of the lower basin; and the Cline Terrace mound along lower Tonto Creek in the western portion of the basin. Several upland test study areas were also investigated by ASU. Chronological focus was on the Roosevelt and Gila phases of the Classic period, about A.D. 1250 to 1450. This interval is roughly contemporaneous with the Salado horizon in the Tonto Basin.

The primary objective of Desert Archaeology's effort was to reconstruct the prehistoric sequence of the eastern portion of the lower basin. Their Roosevelt Community Development (RCD) project investigated 27 sites in the area. Statistical Research studied several areas adjacent to the Salt River that were less densely populated during the prehistoric period. These combined field efforts produced a wealth of data that has just recently been published. Synthesis of this database is only in its initial stages (Dean 2000; Elson, Stark, and Gregory 1995; Rice 1998), and future researchers will find abundant material from which to reinterpret the Tonto Basin archaeological record or to provide additional insight on existing interpretations.

The Meddler Point Community in the Eastern Tonto Basin

Most of the fieldwork for the Roosevelt Dam project was conducted in the eastern portion of the lower Tonto Basin, hereafter the eastern Tonto Basin (Fig. 3.3). Desert Archaeology's RCD project and work by ASU in the Livingston and Schoolhouse Point Mesa portions

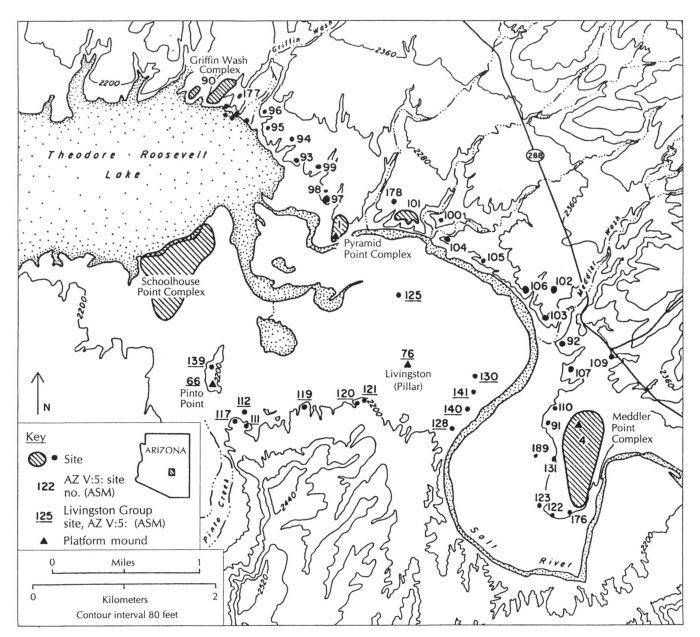

Figure 3.3. Sites investigated by the Roosevelt Dam Project in the eastern Tonto Basin (adapted from Stark and Elson 1995, Fig. 1.4).

of their project area resulted in the detailed reconstruction of the development and collapse of a community during an interval of nearly 600 years (A.D. 750–1325). This community grew up around a village at Meddler Point that was established at the beginning of the sequence.

The Meddler Point community is only one of several small communities that have been defined in the lower basin based on settlement pattern and hypothesized irrigation networks (Fig. 3.4). Our knowledge of other

Tonto Basin communities varies considerably. Only limited work has been conducted in many of the communities in the upper basin such as Rye Creek and Gisela and in areas inundated by Roosevelt Lake such as Armer Ranch. Classic period settlement on Cline Terrace has been intensively examined by ASU (Jacobs 1997; Oliver and Jacobs 1997), but the pre-Classic settlement in this area remains poorly documented. The Meddler Point community represents the best example within the region for evaluating migration because both

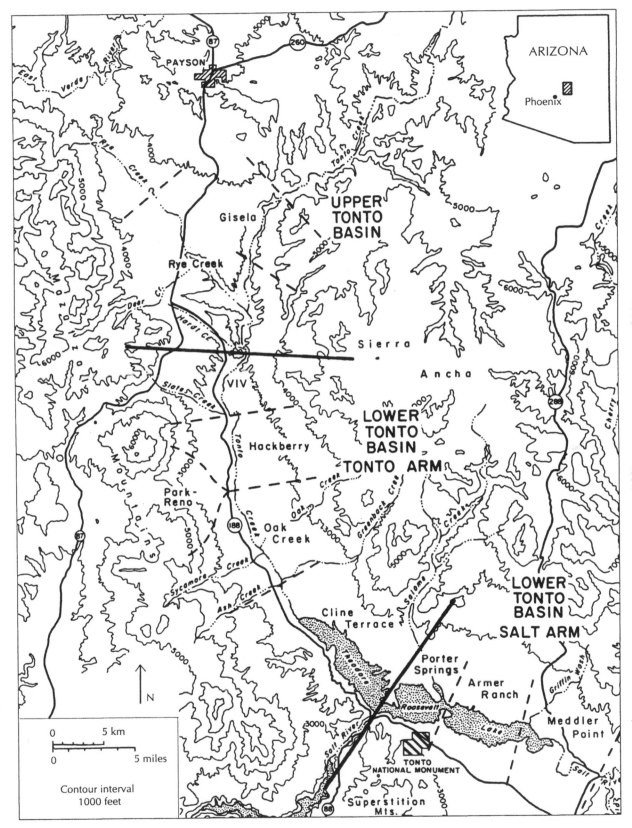

Figure 3.4. Hypothesized Classic period communities in the Tonto
Basin (adapted from Elson, Stark, and Gregory 1995, Fig. 14.3).

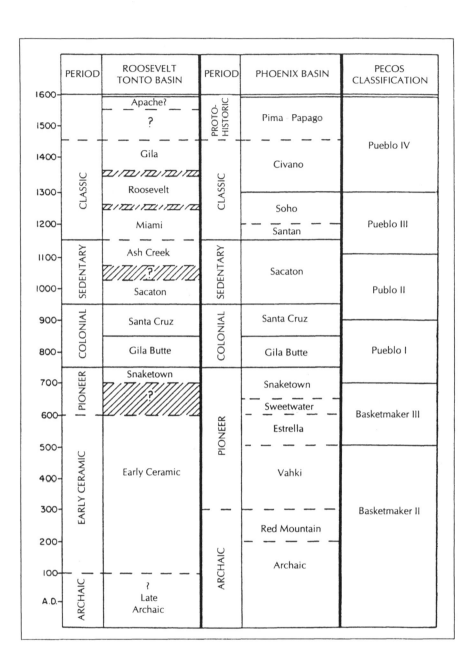

PERIOD	ROOSEVELT TONTO BASIN	PERIOD	PHOENIX BASIN	PECOS CLASSIFICATION
CLASSIC	Apache?	PROTO-HISTORIC	Pima Papago	Pueblo IV
	?			
	Gila		Civano	
	Roosevelt	CLASSIC	Soho	Pueblo III
	Miami		Santan	
SEDENTARY	Ash Creek	SEDENTARY	Sacaton	Publo II
	Sacaton			
COLONIAL	Santa Cruz	COLONIAL	Santa Cruz	Pueblo I
	Gila Butte		Gila Butte	
PIONEER	Snaketown	PIONEER	Snaketown	Basketmaker III
	?		Sweetwater	
			Estrella	
EARLY CERAMIC	Early Ceramic		Vahki	Basketmaker II
		ARCHAIC	Red Mountain	
			Archaic	
ARCHAIC	? Late Archaic			

Figure 3.5. Lower Tonto Basin phase sequence correlated with Phoenix Basin and Pecos classification systems (from Elson 1995, Fig. 2.1).

the interval of interest, the Classic period, and the preceding pre-Classic period are well documented.

The territory of the Meddler Point community extended to Griffin Wash and Schoolhouse Point to the west and to where the Salt River emerges from a restricted canyon east of Meddler Point. There is a 3–km (1.9–mile) gap in Classic period settlement between the Meddler Point community and its nearest neighbor to the west, Armer Ranch. Within the Meddler Point community, a trajectory of internal development can be traced throughout much of the sequence, from roughly A.D. 750 to 1250, although a reorientation of exchange contacts from the south to the northeast is evident by A.D. 1100. This interval includes the Colonial period, Sedentary period, and Miami phase of the early Classic period (Fig. 3.5). In the opening decades of the 1300s (start of the Gila phase), the community essentially collapsed and much of the eastern basin was abandoned. The preceding 75–year interval (A.D. 1250–1325), the Roosevelt phase, is critical in understanding the processes and events that were responsible for this collapse. The Roosevelt phase was a brief interval of accelerated sociocultural change marked by population increase, platform mound construction, and the appearance of Salado polychrome pottery in the region. It is during this interval that the evidence for migration into the area is assessed.

Pre-Classic Community Development

To set the stage for the Roosevelt phase case study, the pre-Classic sequence in the eastern basin requires consideration. Examination of this earlier interval allows us to describe the artifact assemblage associated with the local inhabitants so that we may differentiate immigrant groups from local residents during the Roosevelt phase. A summary of the pre-Classic also provides information on the character and tempo of community development before migration, thus providing a baseline to measure the impact of later population movement.

Following the Tonto Basin chronology, the late pre-Classic sequence in the lower basin is subdivided into the Colonial period (A.D. 750–950) and Sedentary period (950–1150; Fig. 3.5). The Colonial period is further subdivided into the Gila Butte phase (750–850) and Santa Cruz phase (850–950) and the Sedentary period into the Sacaton phase (950–1050) and Ash Creek phase (1050–1150). The Ash Creek phase was defined during the course of the RCD project and during this phase the Tonto Basin sequence diverges from that of the Phoenix Basin. A detailed summary of this sequence is discussed by Elson (1996). The following summary is derived from Stark, Clark, and Elson (1995), Gregory (1995b), and Elson, Gregory, and Stark (1995).

Early Ceramic Period
(About A.D. 100–600)

One Early Ceramic period settlement, Eagle Ridge Locus B (AZ V:5:104 ASM), was investigated in the RCD project area north of the Salt River (Elson and Lindeman 1994). This settlement was situated on a narrow ridge that overlooked the Salt River floodplain. Fifteen small pit houses and a large communal structure were excavated, and extensive trenching indicated that as many as sixty structures may have been present. On the basis of radiocarbon age determinations, the Early Ceramic occupation at Eagle Ridge dates between A.D. 100 and 600 and represents the only village from this period that has been intensively excavated in the Tonto Basin to date. Only plain brown ware vessels with simple forms were associated with the Early Ceramic pit structures. Most vessels were neckless "seed jars"

(Stark 1995a: 255), and other forms recorded include hemispherical and incurved bowls.

The ceramic assemblage, pit house morphology, settlement structure, and communal architecture associated with the Early Ceramic period at Eagle Ridge is comparable to contemporaneous Early Ceramic sites in the Mogollon area (Gregory 1995b: 139–146), including the Bear Ruin (Haury 1985: 139–279), the Bluff site (Haury 1985: 285–371), and Crooked Ridge Village (Wheat 1954). The first two sites are approximately 70 miles northeast of the RCD project area, and Crooked Ridge Village is roughly the same distance to the southeast.

From the abandonment of Eagle Ridge Locus B at approximately A.D. 600 until the next well-documented occupation in the RCD study area at the beginning of the Colonial period (about A.D. 750), little evidence exists for occupation along the Salt River in the eastern Tonto Basin. Considering the abundance of water and arable land, it seems counterintuitive that the eastern Tonto Basin was entirely abandoned during this roughly 150-year span, but it is difficult to establish any direct connections between the Early Ceramic inhabitants of Eagle Ridge and the Colonial period settlers of Meddler Point either in terms of artifact assemblage or settlement location. Until such links can be demonstrated, a break between the two occupations must be inferred and a continuous thread of development can only be traced back from the Classic period community to the beginning of the Colonial period.

Colonial Period
(About A.D. 750–950)

Early in the Colonial period a small village was established at Meddler Point, and evidence for eastern Tonto Basin settlement in the Gila Butte phase is largely restricted to this area (Fig. 3.6; Gregory 1995b: 158–162). From this period until the end of the Roosevelt phase, more than 500 years after its initial settlement, Meddler Point remained the principal settlement in the eastern Tonto Basin. The horseshoe bend in the Salt River around Meddler Point would have been an ideal location for canal intakes and three other favorable intake locations are in the vicinity (Gregory 1995b, Fig. 5.12). These are the first possible locations for intakes west of the point where the Salt River enters the Tonto Basin.

The original settlers of the Meddler Point village possessed a domestic artifact assemblage that can be linked with Hohokam-related groups in southern Arizona. Subrectangular pit houses with wall posts placed within

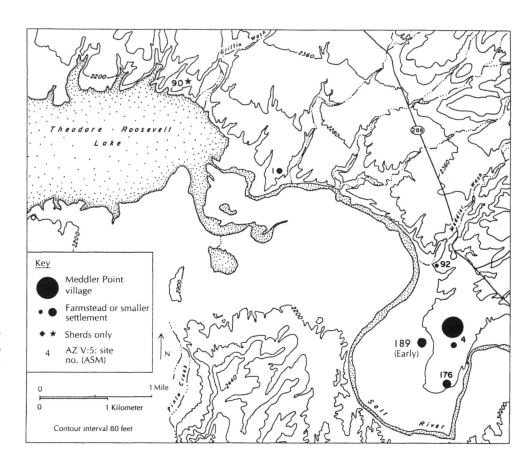

Figure 3.6. Gila Butte phase settlement in the eastern Tonto Basin (adapted from Gregory 1995b, Fig. 5.11).

the house pit were the standard residences. Roughly half the structures contained a perimeter floor or entry groove, a feature commonly associated with pre-Classic pit houses in southern Arizona.

A new element of settlement structure, the courtyard group comprised of inward facing pit houses arranged around a shared extramural area, appeared in the eastern basin during the Colonial period. Courtyard groups have been long recognized as a basic element of settlements in the Hohokam core region (Wilcox and others 1981). In the eastern basin, potential courtyard group arrangements were identified at site AZ V:5:176 and the Hedge Apple site (AZ V:5:189) on Meddler Point (Swartz and Elson 1994: 276–285; Swartz and Randolph 1994a). Single courtyard groups formed small farmsteads in the Tonto Basin, and multiple courtyard groups were probably basic elements of settlement structure at Meddler Point.

Meddler Point is the only settlement in the eastern Tonto Basin that may have approached village size during this period (Craig and Clark 1994a: 174–175). A large central plaza there contained a secondary cremation cemetery and the plaza was defined by pit house

clusters and mounded trash deposits (Fig. 3.7). Meddler Point settlement organization is reflected in three levels, with the smallest units (probably nuclear families) occupying individual pit houses, multiple pit houses forming aggregates, and multiple aggregates arranged around a central plaza and cremation cemetery. These basic elements of settlement structure continued throughout the pre-Classic period. The Meddler Point structure is virtually identical to that observed in other Hohokam pre-Classic villages in southern Arizona.

The Colonial period utilitarian ceramic assemblage was influenced heavily by Hohokam technological traditions. A large proportion (more than 70 percent) of utilitarian ceramics recovered from the Colonial period was produced using micaceous-schist temper that was obtained from a source outside the basin. Temper compositional analysis (Stark, Vint, and Heidke 1995) shows that these ceramics were probably made in the Phoenix Basin. Flare-rimmed bowls, diagnostic of Hohokam ceramic assemblages (Stark 1995b: 352–355), comprised roughly one-fourth of all plain ware bowls recovered from Colonial period contexts in the eastern basin. Local utilitarian ceramic vessels were manufac-

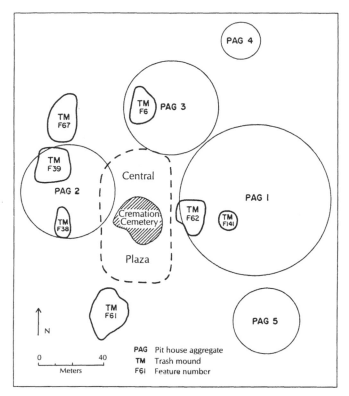

Figure 3.7. Pre-Classic structure of Meddler Point village, AZ V:5:4 ASM (adapted from Gregory 1995b, Fig. 5.13).

tured using a paddle and anvil technique that denotes further Hohokam influence. Finally, 93.7 percent of the Colonial period decorated assemblage was comprised of imported Hohokam buff ware vessels (Heidke 1995, Table 6.2), indicating extensive contact between the inhabitants of the Phoenix Basin and initial residents of Meddler Point.

The secondary cremation cemetery in the central plaza of the Meddler Point settlement also suggests ideological links with Hohokam groups in the realm of mortuary practices. The cemetery contained at least 14 secondary cremations that dated to the Colonial period (Swartz and others 1995, Table 22.1). Five of the Colonial period cremations contained carved schist palettes and three contained carved stone bowls or censers. These ritual artifacts are commonly associated with the Hohokam mortuary complex.

One facility commonly associated with the pre-Classic Hohokam, the ballcourt (Wilcox and Sternberg 1983), is notably absent from the Tonto Basin. The lack of ballcourts may indicate some degree of divergence from the Phoenix Basin Hohokam. Alternatively, low population levels in the basin may have precluded the need for these or other integrative facilities.

Domestic and ritual artifacts from Meddler Point, including architecture, ceramics, and mortuary paraphernalia bear an unmistakable "Hohokam" stamp, indicating that the initial settlers of Meddler Point were probably immigrants from the Phoenix Basin or middle Gila River valley. Later in the Colonial period, several pit house farmsteads were established west of Meddler Point on either side of the Salt River, although Meddler Point continued as the principal settlement (Fig. 3.8). Apparently the smaller settlements "budded" from the main village (Gregory 1995b: 164-168).

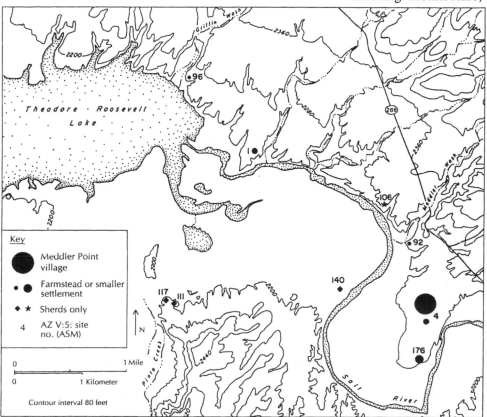

Figure 3.8. Santa Cruz phase settlement in the eastern Tonto Basin (adapted from Gregory 1995b, Fig. 5.13).

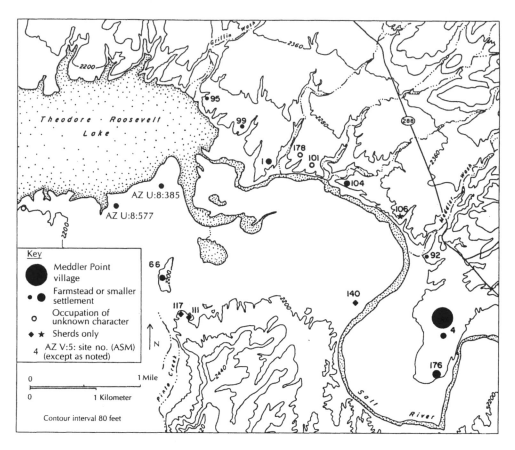

Figure 3.9. Early Sedentary period settlement in the eastern
Tonto Basin (adapted from Gregory 1995b, Fig. 5.14).

Sedentary Period
(About A.D. 950–1150)

The Meddler Point community continued to develop
and expand during the Sedentary period (Fig. 3.9). The
Meddler Point village remained the primary settlement
in the region throughout the late pre-Classic period, but
now several new farmsteads were settled along promon-
tories to the west of Meddler Point, including a settlement at Eagle Ridge Locus A (AZ V:5:104) that was
intensively investigated (Fig. 3.10; Elson and Lindeman
1994). This farmstead represents a clearcut example of
a courtyard group. Other Sedentary period pit house
farmsteads composed of courtyard groups include site
AZ U:8:385 (Lindauer 1997: 237–241) on Schoolhouse
Point Mesa and site U:8:577 (Lindauer 1997: 293–299)
immediately west of Schoolhouse Point.

Sedentary period domestic architecture and utilitarian
ceramic assemblages indicate continuity with the preceding Colonial period. For the first time, evidence
exists for widespread ceramic manufacture in the Tonto
Basin. The range of utilitarian vessel forms remained
stable from the late Colonial through the Sacaton phase
(Stark 1995b: 352–355, 360–361), but Tonto Basin potters
adopted new surface treatments of slipping and smudging late in the Sedentary period (Heidke and Stark
1995). Source areas for these technological innovations
were south of the Tonto Basin for slipping and north of
it for smudging. Smudging, a hallmark trait of the
Mogollon (Haury 1985: 221–223; Lucius 1983; Roberts
1929; Wilson 1988), could have been introduced by in-
marrying potters or through imitation.

Similar to the preceding period, there were no locally manufactured decorated ceramics. Imported Hohokam Buff Ware continued to dominate the assemblage
throughout the Sacaton phase, although it was replaced
by imported Cibola White Ware during the succeeding
Ash Creek phase. As indicated by trash mound and pit
house fill deposits at Locus A of Eagle Ridge, this transition was gradual and may have taken place over the
course of approximately fifty years (Elson and Lindeman 1994, Table 3.11, Fig. 3.23).

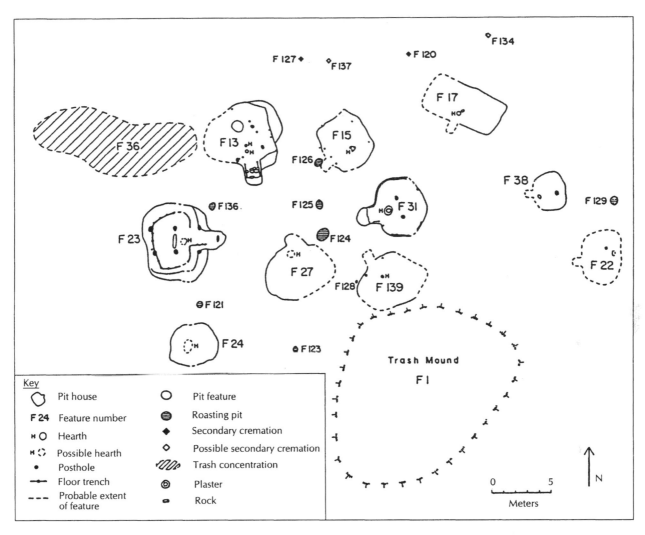

Figure 3.10. Sedentary period pit house settlement at Eagle Ridge Locus
A, AZ V:5:104 ASM (adapted from Elson and Lindeman 1994, Fig. 3.3).

Evidence for mortuary behavior during the Sacaton phase also suggests continuity with the Colonial period, including continued use of the secondary cremation cemetery at Meddler Point (Swartz and others 1995). A few secondary cremations were also recovered at Eagle Ridge Locus A. Although cremation continued throughout the Sedentary period, few cremations dating to the Ash Creek phase contained schist palettes or carved stone bowl censers. In addition, at least a segment of the eastern basin population adopted extended inhumation as a burial practice during the Ash Creek phase (Swartz and Elson 1994: 229–233). These lines of evidence suggest Hohokam influence in mortuary behavior was declining by the end of the Sedentary period.

Overall, there is considerable evidence for continuity between the Colonial and Sedentary periods. Changes in decorated ceramics and burial practices near the end of the period indicate contacts with puebloan groups north and east of the basin. These influences were probably the result of exchange, and there is little evidence for migration at this early juncture.

Early Classic Period
(A.D. 1150–1325)

During the early Classic period (Miami and Roosevelt phases), settlements of detached pit houses were replaced by multiroomed residential units built with masonry. Although the Miami phase remains poorly documented in the eastern basin, there is little evidence for a hiatus in settlement between the pre-Classic and early Classic periods as originally proposed by the Gladwins (1935).

By the Roosevelt phase (A.D. 1250–1325), several other settlements in the eastern basin rivaled Meddler Point in population, including the occupation at School-house Point Mesa and a village that rapidly developed on the ridges overlooking Griffin Wash (Fig. 3.3). Nearly every ridge overlooking the Salt River contained evidence of early Classic settlement, varying from a farmstead to a small hamlet. Thus, a mature community was in place in the eastern basin by the Roosevelt phase.

Meddler Point village continued to be the primary settlement in the eastern Tonto Basin during the early Classic period (Craig and Clark 1994a). Meddler Point Locus A, which directly overlay the earlier pit house settlement, was comprised of seven residential units arranged around a platform mound compound (Compound 1; Fig. 3.11). By the Roosevelt phase, a substantial settlement comprised of five residential units had also formed at the southern tip of Meddler Point (Locus B). Limited work at Locus B precludes definitive statements about earlier pit house settlement in the area, but it is possible that the southern tip of Meddler Point was continuously occupied beginning in the Colonial period. It is unlikely that all 13 residential units associated with both loci were occupied contemporaneously. In addition to Locus A and B, three isolated settlements were along the western edge of Meddler Point (AZ V:5:122 ASM, V:5:91, and V:5:110; Fig. 3.3).

Following Lindauer (1997), the early Classic component of Schoolhouse Point Mesa contained 16 residential units that were dispersed across a square kilometer area (Fig. 3.12). Considering the evidence for Sedentary period occupation in the area, it is likely that the early Classic village also overlay a substantial pit house settlement. One notable difference between the Meddler Point and Schoolhouse Point villages is the apparent absence of a platform mound compound at Schoolhouse Point. The large central room block (AZ U:8:24) contained several elevated rooms and has been called a platform mound by the excavator (Lindauer 1996), but this component dates primarily to the late Classic or Gila phase and any Roosevelt phase configuration within it is difficult to isolate.

→

Figure 3.11. Early Classic period settlement at Meddler Point, AZ V:5:4 ASM (adapted from Craig and Clark 1994a, Fig. 7.1, from map and computer cartography by GEO-MAP, Inc., 1993).

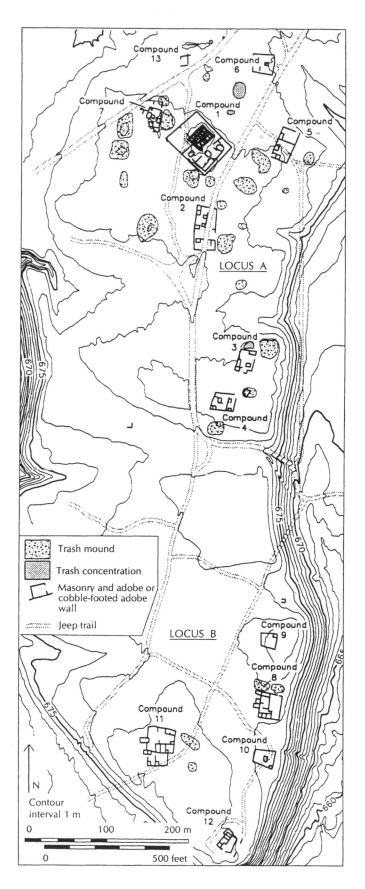

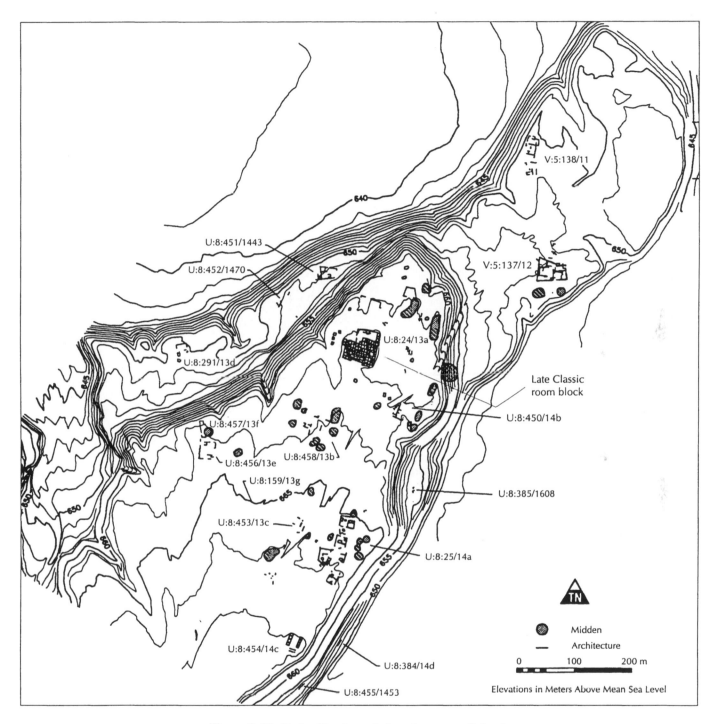

Figure 3.12. Early Classic period settlement at Schoolhouse Point Mesa (from Lindauer 1997, Fig. 1.8).

The village that developed rapidly on the ridges
overlooking Griffin Wash during the Roosevelt phase is
discussed in detail in the next chapter because of the
likely puebloan origins of its inhabitants. A small hamlet formed at Pyramid Point to the west of Griffin Wash

(Fig. 3.13; Elson 1994) that included three small residential units and another large unit that contained a
small platform mound (Elson 1994: 282–290).

The first Salado polychrome (Pinto) appears in the
archaeological record of the basin during the Roosevelt

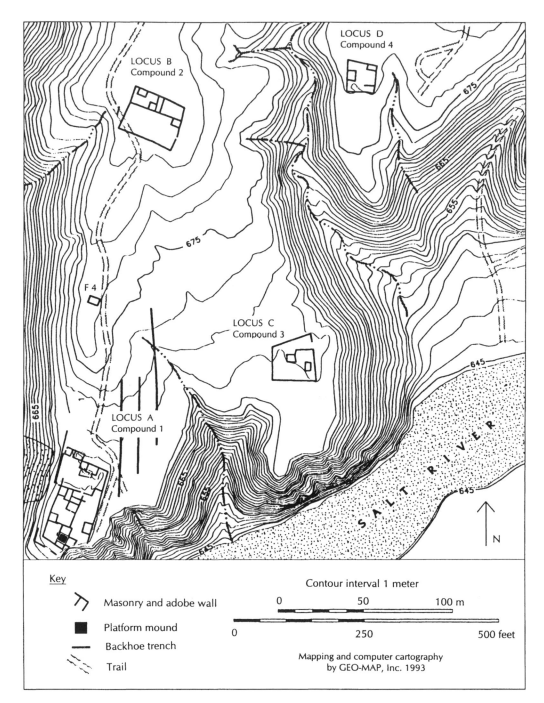

Figure 3.13. Early Classic period settlement at Pyramid Point, AZ V:5:1 ASM (adapted from Elson 1994, Fig. 8.2).

phase and is found in nearly every settlement that was occupied during this interval. Indeed, the Tonto Basin has one of the highest densities of Pinto Polychrome and Pinto Black-on-red pottery in the entire Southwest. Hence the Roosevelt phase can be considered the beginning of the Salado horizon in the region. An assessment of population movement into the eastern basin during this interval bears directly on the issue of migration in the development of the horizon and is the focus of the following chapter.

CHAPTER FOUR

The Case for Migration

To assess the scale and occurrence of migration into the eastern Tonto Basin during the Roosevelt phase, we turn to a study of domestic spatial organization and technological styles embedded in architectural construction and utilitarian ceramic manufacture. As discussed at length in Chapter 2, these are reliable indicators of migration, particularly when intrusive styles co-occur in a specific locus within a settlement or community. Domestic spatial organization is emphasized because the archaeological expressions of it in the basin are well-dated and it provides a robust set of data. Many settlements in the area were abandoned near the end of the early Classic period and were neither disturbed nor covered by later occupations. I also examine architectural construction and utilitarian ceramic manufacture to determine if they support arguments for migration based on spatial organization.

DOMESTIC SPATIAL ORGANIZATION

Domestic spatial organization may be the most reliable indicator of migration because it reflects culturally specific aspects of social organization (Ferguson 1996; Hillier and Hanson 1984) and cosmology (Ferguson 1992; Kus and Raharijaona 1990). These deeply embedded principles are typically conservative and hence more likely to be resistant to assimilation in co-residence contexts following migration. The organization of domestic space is not severely constrained by technological level or functional requirements, leaving ample room for stylistic variability as defined by Sackett (1977, 1985, 1990). The only technological requirement is the ability to partition space by building walls that restrict access and visibility. For the archaeologist, traces of these walls must remain in order to reconstruct architectural plans. Unlike ceramics, spatial organization is an intrinsic property of any settlement and on-site production can be assumed.

In the eastern Tonto Basin, the transition from the Sedentary period to the Classic period (A.D. 1100–1200) coincides with the architectural transition from pit houses to above ground masonry structures. By the Roosevelt phase (A.D. 1250–1325), these structures were typically connected by walls to produce multi-room architectural units. Because we are faced with the challenge of differentiating local groups from immigrant groups during an interval when the former were themselves building new types of architecture and using new construction techniques, we first must trace the local tradition of organizing domestic space through this period of architectural change.

Tracing Courtyard Groups from Pit House to Compound: *Gamma* Maps

As discussed in Chapter 3, pre-Classic pit house construction and layout in the Tonto Basin have strong parallels with contemporaneous settlements in southern Arizona. The concept of the courtyard group as defined by Wilcox and others (1981) is essential to understanding the layout of pit house settlements across this region, including the Tonto Basin. This basic element of settlement structure has been recognized in both small and large pre-Classic sites in the Hohokam region (for example, Craig 2000; Doyel 1991; Gregory 1987; Haury 1976). The courtyard group is defined as a cluster of pit houses, each facing inward onto a common courtyard area. The number of contemporaneous pit houses in each group varied considerably, but was typically two to four structures. In settlements of long duration, there is evidence for extended use of courtyard groups by related social groups. The ubiquity and persistence of this basic building block of settlements suggest that it was the locus of residential activities for some fundamental social unit.

Settlements organized into courtyard groups appeared in the eastern Tonto Basin during the Colonial period (about A.D. 750–950). Hedge Apple (AZ V:5:189 ASM), a small Gila Butte phase settlement near Meddler Point, apparently was organized into two courtyard groups, particularly Locus B (Swartz and Randolph 1994a). Plain ware and decorated ceramic assemblages (Stark,

Vint, and Heidke 1995; Wallace 1995) indicated that the Colonial period inhabitants in the eastern Tonto Basin, including the occupants of Hedge Apple, had strong ties with groups from the Phoenix Basin or middle Gila River valley. At site AZ V:5:176, a Colonial period settlement near Hedge Apple, the inward orientation of several pit houses onto a common open area revealed the presence of at least one courtyard group (Swartz and Elson 1994, Fig. 6.26).

Site Roosevelt 9:6 (Gila Pueblo), located about 5 km (3 miles) southwest of the RCD project area (see Fig. 3.2), is the only other Colonial period settlement in the eastern Tonto Basin that has been intensively investigated (Haury 1932). Sequential occupation and the incomplete excavation of the site make settlement layout difficult to reconstruct, but available evidence points to several courtyard groups there. At the Deer Creek site (AZ O:15:52 ASM), an early Colonial period settlement in the upper Tonto Basin, early and late components revealed the transition from pit houses oriented in a common direction (southeast) to pit houses facing inward onto a courtyard (Swartz 1992). Thus, the courtyard group appears to have been a common element in Tonto Basin settlements during the Colonial period.

Small settlements composed of courtyard groups continued throughout the Sedentary period (A.D. 950–1150) in the eastern Tonto Basin. Locus A of the Eagle Ridge site (see Fig. 3.10; Elson and Lindeman 1994), site AZ U:8:385 (Lindauer 1997: 237–241) on Schoolhouse Point Mesa, and site AZ U:8:577 (Lindauer 1997: 293–299) immediately west of Schoolhouse Point are Sedentary period settlements with pit houses arranged in one or two courtyard groups. At Locus A of Meddler Point village, the large pre-Classic occupation was represented by multiple pit house aggregates that may have been arranged in courtyard groups. These aggregates encircled a large, open plaza that contained a secondary cremation cemetery used throughout the pre-Classic period (see Fig. 3.7). This arrangement is similar to the layout of Hohokam villages excavated in the Phoenix Basin and elsewhere in southern Arizona (Craig 2000; Wilcox and others 1981).

To trace common threads of spatial organization through changes in architectural form and construction during the transition from the Sedentary period to the Classic period, a level of abstraction is required that simplifies settlement layout. One such method, developed by Hillier and Hanson (1984: 147–155), uses *gamma* maps as schematic representations of architectural plans that depict symmetry and depth in building circulation patterns with respect to the external world.

Gamma maps illustrate the degree to which access is distributed among enclosed spaces, rooms, or unroofed areas. An underlying assumption of *gamma* analysis is that domestic space is organized by the construction of walls and doorways that regulate encounters. Circulation pattern determines where encounters take place, who is encountered, and, to a certain extent, the frequency of encounters.

The following diagrams are variants of Hillier and Hanson's *gamma* maps. In these diagrams, circles represent separate spatial domains either internal or external to the residential units. Open circles represent unroofed areas, shaded circles denote probable habitation structures, and half-shaded circles depict auxiliary structures such as ramadas or storage rooms. Lines connecting circles indicate access between these spaces. The external space immediately surrounding the residential unit (carrier space) is marked by a circle with a cross. All external entries are shown originating from carrier space, which is located at the bottom of justified *gamma* maps. Depth of circulation with respect to carrier space is represented in ascending order. Only residential units with sufficient evidence to reconstruct the circulation pattern with little or no ambiguity are considered here, and inferred accesses are denoted by dashed lines. Feature numbers (if they were assigned) are listed next to each separate spatial domain.

To illustrate fundamental relationships in circulation patterns, Figure 4.1A shows a symmetrical relationship between rooms *a* and *b* with respect to *c* (carrier space): *a* is to *b* as *b* is to *a* from the perspective of an individual in *c*. It also depicts a distributed relationship because there is more than one access from *a* to *b*, including that passing through *c*. Figure 4.1B depicts a nondistributed symmetrical relationship; by definition, noncontiguous rooms are nondistributed. In Figure 4.1C, the relationship is asymmetrical and nondistributed because *a* and *b* differ with respect to *c*, with *a* controlling access between *b* and *c*. With an equal number of definable spatial domains, symmetrical patterns tend to be branching and asymmetrical patterns are more linear with greater circulation depth.

In an idealized pit house courtyard group containing three structures, external access to the central courtyard is possible through gaps between structures and each of the structures can be accessed from the courtyard area (Fig. 4.2). From the perspective of someone standing in the courtyard, the structures are symmetrical and nondistributed in terms of circulation pattern. To gain access to each structure, one would have to pass through the courtyard area.

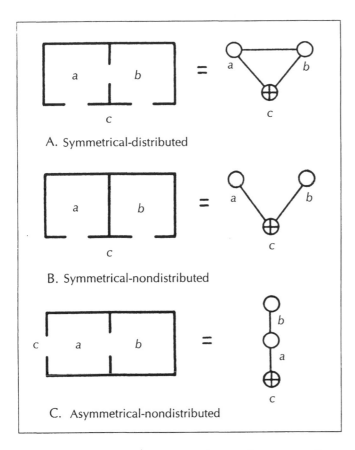

Figure 4.1. Simple building plans and corresponding justified *gamma* maps depicting symmetrical-asymmetrical and distributed-nondistributed relationships.

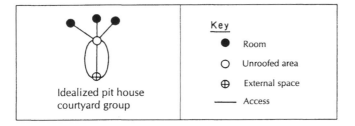

Figure 4.2. An idealized pit house courtyard group.

Figure 4.3 presents *gamma* maps of several early Classic compounds from the eastern Tonto Basin. Most of the examples contain only one or two enclosed extramural areas and no more than four rooms. Similar to pit house courtyard groups, the circulation pattern for these simple compounds is also symmetrical and nondistributed. Remodeling and rebuilding in these residential units were typically minimal.

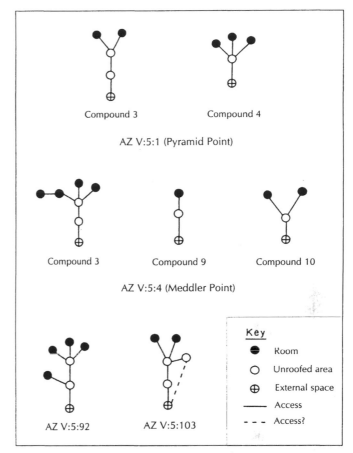

Figure 4.3. Justified *gamma* maps depicting circulation patterns of simple compounds in the eastern Tonto Basin (for plan views, see Figures 3.11, 3.13, and 4.4).

Simple compounds constituted the majority of early Classic residential units in the eastern Tonto Basin and many of the compounds were abandoned before the end of the period. Note that simple compounds have circulation patterns identical to those of pit house courtyard groups, from the perspective of someone in the courtyard area. The areal extent of these units is also comparable to that of pit house courtyard groups (Gregory 1995b: 138), suggesting occupation by social groups of similar size and composition. However, the addition of a compound wall made simple compounds considerably less permeable to the external setting than were earlier pit house settlements.

Some typical early Classic period residential units are shown in Figure 4.4; masonry surface rooms are shaded and bounded extramural spaces are unshaded. These units have dispersed room arrangements with few contiguous rooms. In each example, walls were built between rooms to form an enclosed compound.

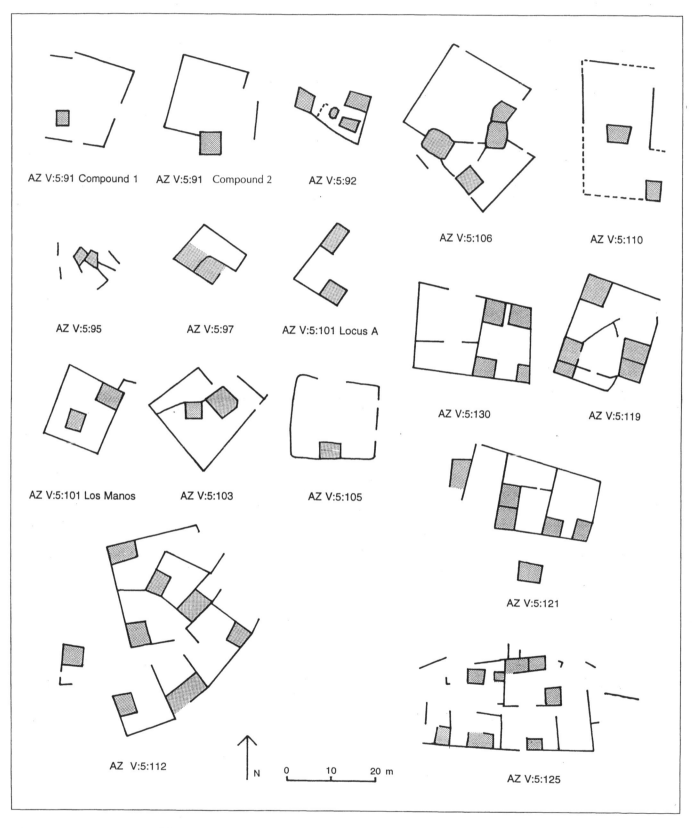

Figure 4.4. Examples of early Classic period compounds in the eastern
Tonto Basin (for other examples, see Figs. 3.11, 3.12, and 3.13).

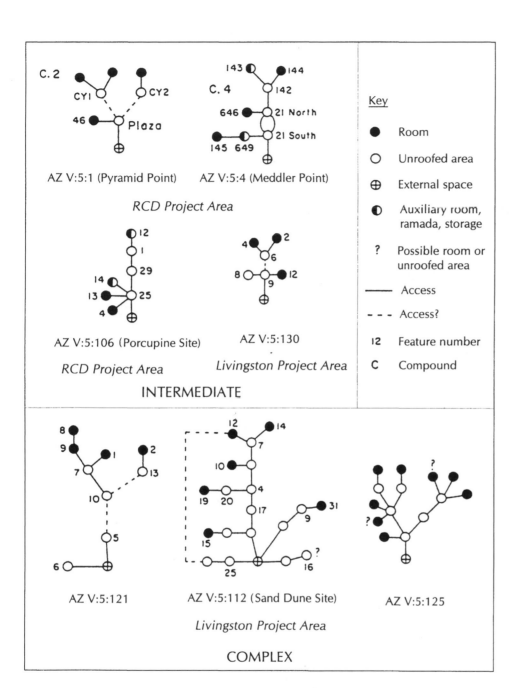

Figure 4.5. Justified *gamma* maps depicting circulation patterns of intermediate and complex compounds in the eastern Tonto Basin (for plan views, see Figs. 3.11, 3.13, and 4.4).

Several residential units shown in Figures 3.11, 3.13, and 4.4 have more rooms than do typical simple compounds. Such units, defined here as intermediate and complex compounds, are differentiated from simple compounds by the number of enclosed extramural spaces or courtyards in each unit. Figure 4.5 depicts justified *gamma* maps of examples of intermediate and complex compounds in the eastern Tonto Basin. These plots clearly illustrate the presence of a recurring element, arranged both symmetrically and asymmetrically, in more complex compounds. This element is made up of one to three nondistributed rooms in an enclosed courtyard, providing a circulation pattern equivalent to that of simple compounds and, except for an enclosing wall, reminiscent of earlier pit house courtyard groups. In two cases where archaeologists have reconstructed the building episodes for complex or intermediate compounds, it is clear that the final configurations resulted from simple compound precursors with one or more simple compound equivalents added to the existing configuration during each episode (Fig. 4.6). Simple, intermediate, and complex compounds,

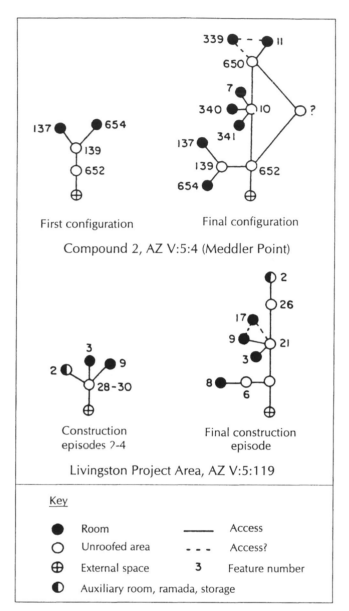

First configuration   Final configuration

Compound 2, AZ V:5:4 (Meddler Point)

Construction   Final construction
episodes 2-4   episode

Livingston Project Area, AZ V:5:119

Key

● Room   —— Access
○ Unroofed area   - - - Access?
⊕ External space   **3** Feature number
◐ Auxiliary room, ramada, storage

Figure 4.6. Justified *gamma* maps depicting circulation patterns of compound construction episodes (for plan views, see Figs. 3.11 and 4.4).

thus, can be placed in a single developmental sequence with more complex forms generated by either the addition of new courtyards or the partitioning of extant courtyards.

In summary, the basic social units represented by courtyard groups do not appear to have changed as households in the eastern Tonto Basin shifted from pit houses to masonry compounds during the early Classic period. In terms of spatial organization, the simple compound can be regarded as a pit house courtyard

group transferred above ground and conforming to rectilinear architecture. A temporal trend from simple to complex compounds suggests that resident households were beginning to aggregate near the end of the early Classic period. Throughout this sequence, however, these households maintained a conception of ordering domestic space that minimized room contiguity and numbers of rooms per courtyard area.

Evidence for continuity in settlement location through this architectural transition from pit house to compound is present at several of the intensively investigated sites in the eastern Tonto Basin, including Meddler Point (Compound 4), the Sand Dune site (AZ V:5:112), site AZ V:5:130 (Jacobs 1994: 335–391), and several compound sites on Schoolhouse Point Mesa (Lindauer 1997, Figs. 4.3, 5.32). In these cases, compounds spatially overlapped with late Sedentary period pit house settlements and several contained or overlay architectural forms that were transitional between pit houses and masonry rooms. These relationships indicate a close connection between the late pre-Classic and early Classic inhabitants of these settlements, a connection that is also evident in sites that contain both Sedentary and early Classic period components elsewhere in the Tonto Basin (Doyel 1978; Lindeman and Clark 2000) and southern Arizona (Sires 1984, 1987).

Differentiating Compounds from Room Blocks: The Room Contiguity Index

In defining the local tradition of organizing domestic space represented by compounds, I was purposefully selective in the residential units I discussed and illustrated in the previous section. I focused on units with dispersed room arrangements and, in more complex examples, segmented layouts. However, early Classic residential units in the eastern Tonto Basin exhibited a high range of variability in spatial organization. Much of this variation may be expressed in terms of room clustering tendencies or extent of settlement nucleation. Variability in room clustering differentiates two basic forms of residential architecture in the Southwest, the open compound or *ranchería* and the room block or *pueblo* (also *caseron*, following Wood 2000: 117–118). Differences between these two settlement types are a fundamental part of Hillier and Hanson's (1984: 78–79) analysis, and they differentiate the "clump growth process" (room blocks) from the "central space growth process" (compounds and courtyard groups). Dispersed and nondistributed room arrangements emphasize either the separation of activities that took place in these structures or the segregation of the social units that resided in them. Contiguous room arrangements, particularly those with distributed circulation, suggest greater integration and interaction between households, hence a more developed sense of community (Flannery 1972; Hegmon 1989).

To assess variability in clustering tendencies within eastern Tonto Basin residential units during the early Classic period, I developed a quantitative measure of room contiguity, the Room Contiguity Index (RCI). This index is calculated by dividing the number of room walls by the number of rooms within a residential unit. If rooms within a unit share a wall, this wall is counted only once. The resulting RCI is the ratio of total walls to total rooms, a number that can vary only between 2.0 and 4.0 in rectilinear architecture. As a rule, the greater the number of rooms that share walls in a unit (higher contiguity), the lower the RCI obtained. For example, a value of 2.0 represents an infinitely large, square arrangement of contiguous rooms where only two walls are counted per room. On the other hand, a value of 4.0 represents a completely noncontiguous arrangement (each room has four unshared walls). Linear arrangements of contiguous rooms tend to generate values near 3.0, with three walls counted per room. With these assignments, one would expect compounds to have values close to 4.0 and room blocks would have RCIs in the 2.0 to 3.0 range.

Several potential sources of ambiguity arise when calculating RCIs, particularly in cases where several smaller rooms abut a larger room or where rooms do not meet at corners. In the former case, the walls of smaller rooms that form one wall of a larger room are not combined, but counted separately. Where rooms do not meet at corners, the number of walls are maximized, thus obtaining the highest possible RCI value (erring toward noncontiguity) for contiguous room arrangements.

RCIs are dependent on the total number of rooms in a residential unit only to a moderate degree. For example, in linear arrangements of contiguous structures, three rooms yield an RCI of 3.3; 10 rooms, 3.1; 100 rooms, 3.01. The minimum RCI for a line of rooms is 3.0, with longer lines of rooms approaching, but never reaching, this value. Similarly, 2.0 is the minimum RCI for a square of contiguous rooms, and the largest room blocks in the Southwest generally yield values in the 2.4 to 2.5 range. The highest possible RCI (lowest contiguity) for a room block in a literal sense is 3.0 for a simple square of four rooms. Thus, the RCI values of

room blocks and lines of rooms will vary between 2.4 and 3.3. At the other extreme, a one-room settlement will always have an RCI of 4.0.

I calculated RCIs for all early Classic period residential units (n = 51) in the eastern Tonto Basin for which there were accurate plan views obtained either by intensive excavation or wall clearing (Table 4.1). Because accurate plan views are necessary for RCIs, the calculation was not attempted for units that were largely dismantled or that were only mapped from survey. Figure 4.7 presents RCI frequency distributions for early Classic residential units in the eastern Tonto Basin community. When a single residential unit had a range of RCIs because of indeterminate room assignments, I used the range midpoint.

The distribution of RCIs clusters into three groups. Forty-four of the 51 evaluated units fall within the 3.5 to 4.0 range, indicating that most of the early Classic residential units were compounds containing noncontiguous room arrangements. More than half of the residential units in this group have values of 4.0, indicating that all rooms were noncontiguous. All of the Meddler Point Locus A residential units can be classified as compounds, along with three of the five units in Locus B. At Schoolhouse Point Mesa, all settlements but one (site AZ U:8:454) can be classified as compounds. Finally, nearly all the isolated units between Meddler Point and Schoolhouse Point on both sides of the Salt River yield RCI values in the compound range.

Of the remaining seven residential units, four yielded RCIs in the 2.8 to 3.0 range. This range is at the high end expected for rectilinear arrangements of contiguous rooms or room blocks, and it indicates that nucleated settlements or room blocks, though rare, were present in the eastern Tonto Basin during the early Classic period. Room blocks are represented only by Locus A and Locus C at Griffin Wash (Figs. 4.8, 4.9), Saguaro Muerto (Fig. 4.9), and perhaps "Compound" 8 at Meddler Point Locus B (see Fig. 3.11). The final three examples have RCIs of 3.3, at the high end of the range for linear arrangements of contiguous rooms. This group includes "Compound" 12 at Meddler Point Locus B, an isolated unit (site AZ V:5:96; Fig. 4.9) near the Griffin Wash site complex, and site AZ U:8:454 on Schoolhouse Point Mesa (Fig. 4.9), which is a square U-shaped arrangement of rooms that resembles the residential portion of a "unit type pueblo" (Prudden 1903, Fig. 6). This intermediate group is of particular interest because it contains units with fewer rooms than room blocks, but the rooms are arranged differently than those in compounds. It is possible that these units

Table 4.1. Room Contiguity Indices (RCIs) for Roosevelt Phase
Residential Units in the Eastern Tonto Basin

Site (ASM site no.) Locus Compound	Total Number of Rooms	Room Contiguity Index	Comments
RCD Project Area			
AZ V:5:1 (Pyramid Point)			
Locus B	4	3.8	
Locus C	2	4.0	
Locus D	2–3	4.0	
AZ V:5:4 (Meddler Point)			
Locus A			
Compound 2	7–8	3.9	Remodeled compound
Compound 3	3–4	3.7–3.8	
Compound 4	4	4.0	Early Roosevelt phase abandonment
Compound 5	4	3.8	
Compound 6	1	4.0	Early Roosevelt phase abandonment?
Compound 7	4?	4.0	Western portion destroyed by vandalism; probably more than 4 rooms
Locus B			
Compound 8	8–10	2.8–3.1	Room block
Compound 9	1	4.0	Early Roosevelt phase abandonment?
Compound 10	2	4.0	Early Roosevelt phase abandonment?
Compound 11	9–11	3.5–3.8	
Compound 12	4–5	3.1–3.5	Line of rooms
AZ V:5:90 (Griffin Wash)*			
Locus A	48	2.8	Room block
Locus B	15?	3.5?	Partially dismantled
Locus C	26	2.9	Located on a narrow ridge, no enclosing wall
AZ V:5:91	1	4.0	
AZ V:5:95	2?	3.5	
AZ V:5:96	3	3.3	Line of rooms
AZ V:5:97	1?	4.0	Only 1 room positively defined
AZ V:5:101 (Las Manos)			
Locus C	2?	4.0	
Locus D	3	3.7	No enclosing wall
AZ V:5:103	2	4.0	
AZ V:5:105	1	4.0	
AZ V:5:106 (Porcupine site)	4	3.8	
AZ V:5:110	2	4.0	
AZ V:5:123	2	4.0	No enclosing wall, includes large roasting area surrounded by circular cobble alignment
Livingston Project Area			
AZ V:5:112 (Sand Dune site)	8	4.0	
AZ V:5:119	5	3.6	Final configuration
AZ V:5:121	4	3.8	
AZ V:5:125	6–8	3.9–4.0	
AZ V:5:128 (Saguaro Muerto)	13–18	2.9	Room block
AZ V:5:130	5–6	4.0	
AZ V:5:139	12	4.0	4–5 compounds near Pinto Point platform mound; several are partially dismantled
AZ V:5:141	6	4.0	No enclosing wall

Table 4.1.
(Continued)

Site (ASM site no.) Locus Compound	Total Number of Rooms	Room Contiguity Index	Comments
Schoolhouse Point Mesa			
AZ V:5:137	12	3.7	
AZ V:5:138	4	4.0	
AZ U:8:25			
Locus A	3	4.0	
Locus B	2	4.0	
Locus C	1	4.0	
Locus E	2	4.0	
Locus F	4	3.8	
AZ U:8:152	3	4.0	
AZ U:8:291	2	4.0	
AZ U:8:450	4	3.8	
AZ U:8:451	2	4.0	
AZ U:8:452	1	4.0	Poorly preserved
AZ U:8:453			Poorly preserved compound
AZ U:8:454	10	3.3	U-shaped line of rooms
AZ U:8:456 and U:8:457	3	4.0	
AZ U:8:458	2?	4.0	Poorly preserved, probably more than 2 rooms

* Plan view maps for Griffin Wash Locus D and the submerged residential units immediately below Griffin Wash are not of sufficient detail to determine room contiguity indices. The available evidence suggests that these units would have indices within the range for residential compounds.

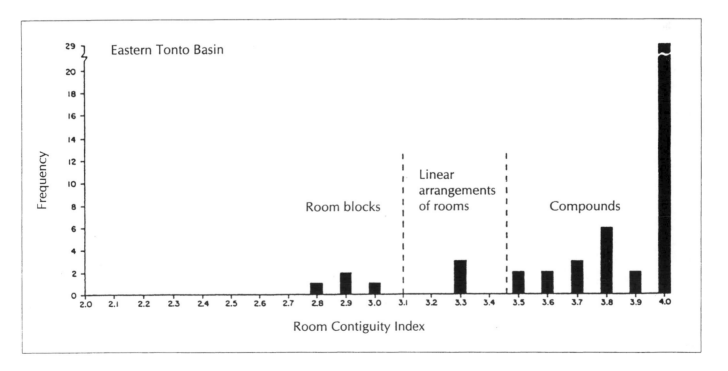

Figure 4.7. Room contiguity indices for early Classic period residential units in the eastern Tonto Basin.

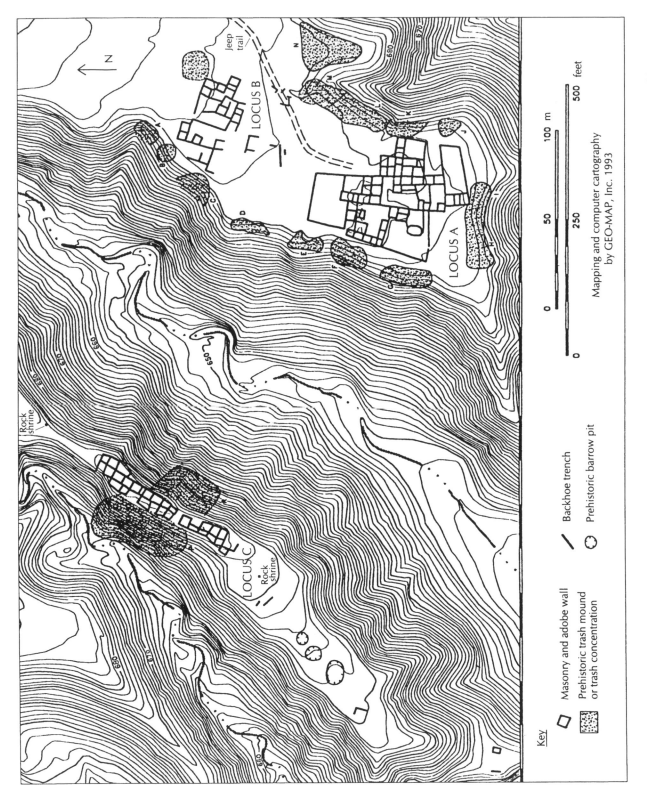

Figure 4.8. Plan of the Griffin Wash site complex (AZ V:5:90 ASM), modified from Figure 9.1 in Swartz and Randolph 1994b.

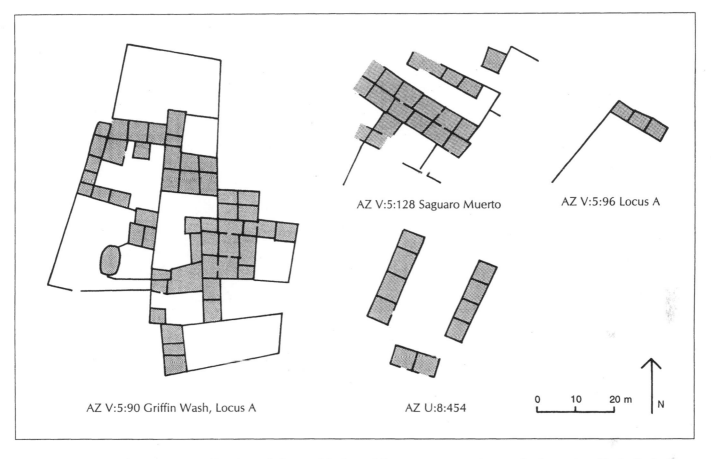

AZ V:5:128 Saguaro Muerto

AZ V:5:96 Locus A

AZ V:5:90 Griffin Wash, Locus A

AZ U:8:454

0 10 20 m

N

Figure 4.9. Examples of early Classic period room blocks and linear room arrangements in the eastern Tonto Basin.

would have developed into room blocks but they were abandoned in an early stage of development.

In the eastern Tonto Basin, the two distinct RCI groups (compounds and room blocks) suggest that two different modes of domestic spatial organization existed within the same community. The majority of units were compounds that can be linked in terms of spatial organization and, in a number of cases, settlement continuity with pre-Classic settlements in the area. The question remains as to whether room blocks were occupied by an immigrant population who possessed a different tradition of organizing domestic space or by local groups who were changing their own tradition for a variety of reasons, including population increase (Doelle 1995) or a heightened concern for security (LeBlanc 1998).

To gain a broader perspective on this issue, I calculated RCIs for a number of contemporaneous settlements across the Southwest and compared them with the eastern Tonto Basin. A sample of sites containing multiroomed residential units and dating within the A.D. 1100 to 1300 interval were selected from southern and northern Arizona,

southern Colorado, and western New Mexico (Table 4.2, Fig. 4.10). Several late eleventh-century examples were included from Chaco Canyon and the Mimbres River valley. The regions depicted in Figure 4.10 are defined primarily by previous research boundaries and do not necessarily coincide with meaningful prehistoric boundaries. The primary criterion for site selection in each region was the availability of a nearly complete architectural plan view, preferably generated by excavation rather than survey. Of necessity, in regions where few habitation sites from this time span have been excavated (for example, Rio Abajo), I did use plan views generated by survey. To avoid overemphasizing those regions that have been thoroughly investigated, only three or four sites per region were chosen. In areas where a number of settlements were available that met the above criteria (like Chaco Canyon), I selected sites that were representative of the group. Although the resulting data set is far from exhaustive, it is a reasonable sample of residential units in Arizona, southern Colorado, and western New Mexico from A.D. 1100 to 1300.

Table 4.2. Period of Occupation and Room Contiguity Index (RCI) for Pueblo II–Pueblo III and Early Classic Sites in the Macroregional Study

Area, Site (AZ = ASM site no.) *(See map, Fig. 4.10)*	Primary Period of Occupation (A.D.)	No. of Rooms	RCI
Mimbres River (MI)			
1. NAN Ranch Ruin	Late Pueblo II–early Pueblo III	43+	2.8
2. Galaz Ruin	Primarily late Pueblo II–early Pueblo III	About 125	2.6
3. Swarts Ruin	Primarily late Pueblo II–early Pueblo III	About 113	2.7
Chaco Canyon (CC)			
4. Pueblo Alto through Stage 5	Late Pueblo II (about 1050–1075)	About 78 + 4 kivas	2.7
5. Wijiji	Late Pueblo II–early Pueblo III (about 1075–1115)	About 106 + 2 kivas	2.4
6. Kin Kletso, east	Early Pueblo III (about 1115–1140)	26 + 1 kiva	2.9
Rio Abajo Province, Rio Grande (RA)			
7. Bowling Green Pueblo	Late Pueblo III	20+	3.0
8. La Hija del Nido	Late Pueblo III	43+	3.1
9. Piedras Negras	Primarily late Pueblo III	About 150	2.9
Tularosa–Quemado (TQ)			
10. Sandstone Hill Pueblo Ruin	Primarily Pueblo III	18	2.5
11. Mariana Mesa, Site 481	Early Pueblo III	34 + 1 kiva	2.6
12. Higgins Flat Pueblo	Late Pueblo III	22+	2.6
13. Starkweather Ruin	Pueblo II–III	12	2.7
Mesa Verde (MV)			
14. Sand Canyon Pueblo	Late Pueblo III (about 1250–1285)	About 420 + at least 95 kivas	2.8[a]
15. Green Lizard	Primarily late Pueblo III	About 19	3.1
Kayenta (KA)[b]			
16. Betatakin	Late Pueblo III	117+	2.7
17. Kiet Siel	Late Pueblo III	About 157	3.2
18. Swallow's Nest Cliff Dwelling	Late Pueblo III	18+	2.5
Silver Creek Drainage (SL)			
19. Broken K Pueblo	Pueblo III	91 + 2 kivas	2.7
20. Carter Ranch Pueblo	Pueblo III	About 38	2.5
21. Tla Kii Ruin	Early Pueblo III	24+	2.8
White Mountains (WM)			
22. Chodistaas	Late Pueblo III	18	2.9
23. AZ P:6:10	Primarily late Pueblo III	5	3.0
San Carlos (SC)			
24. Turkey Creek Pueblo	Late Pueblo III	314+	2.4
25. AZ W:10:37 (Point of Pines area)	Pueblo III	26+	2.7
Safford Valley (SV)			
26. AZ V:16:10	Early Pueblo III	62+	3.4
27. AZ V:16:8 (Unit 1)	Early Pueblo III?	9	3.2
28. Goat Hill	Late Pueblo III	36 + 1 D-shaped kiva	2.9
Tonto Rim (TR)			
29. Shoofly Village	Primarily Pueblo III	72	3.4
30. Mayfield Canyon	Primarily late Pueblo III?	About 34	3.0
31. Risser Ranch	Late Pueblo II–Pueblo III	About 47	3.4
Lower and Middle Verde River (LV)			
32. Roadhouse Ruin	"Middle Classic" (post-1200–pre-Gila phase)	13	3.9
Middle Gila River (MG)			
33. Sacaton 9:6 (Gila Pueblo)	Late Sedentary–early Classic	About 10	3.5
34. Las Fosas	Late Sedentary–early Classic	13	4.0
35. Escalante Ruin	Early Classic component, about 1200–1280	11 (2 compounds, Sidewinder Ruin & AZ U:15:22)	4.0
36. Columbus Site	Early Classic, about 1150–1300	About 6	3.8
Santa Cruz River Valley, Tucson Basin (ST)			
37. Cerro Prieto	Early Classic	232	4.0
38. Sabino Canyon Ruin	Early Classic	23+	3.9
39. Loma Alto	Early Classic	About 26	3.9
40. Whiptail Ruin	Early Classic	About 36	3.8
41. Gibbon Springs	Mid 1200s–early 1300s	24	4.0
Phoenix Basin (PB)			
42. Pueblo Grande	1250–1275 to 1325–1350 component[c]	About 79 in 14 habitation areas, many of which are individual compounds	3.7
43. Tres Pueblos–AZ U:9:14	Late Soho component	4	4.0
44. Casa de Piedras	Early Classic	12	4.0

a. Excavated room blocks only.

b. Cliff walls + edges were counted as walls where they defined rooms.

c. Civano phase following Abbott and others 1994 or late Soho phase following Craig 1995a.

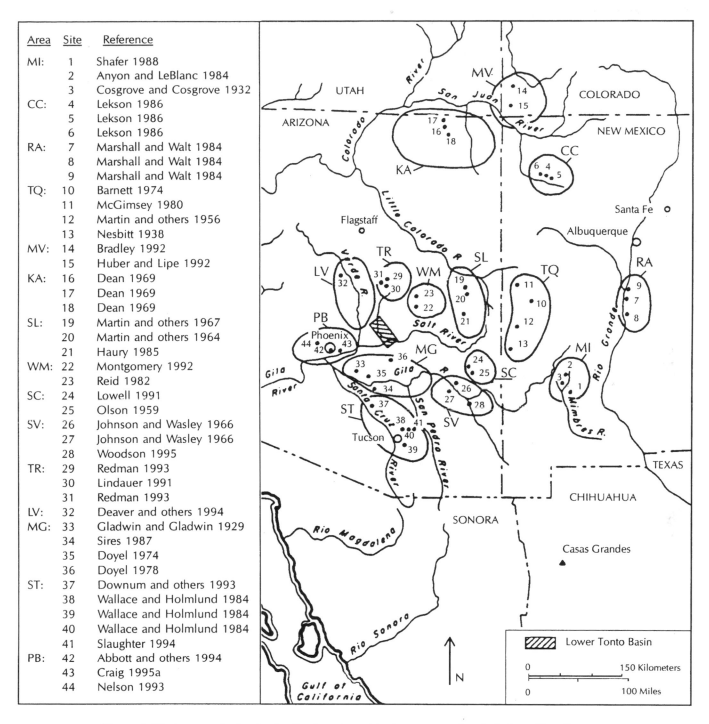

Area	Site	Reference
MI:	1	Shafer 1988
	2	Anyon and LeBlanc 1984
	3	Cosgrove and Cosgrove 1932
CC:	4	Lekson 1986
	5	Lekson 1986
	6	Lekson 1986
RA:	7	Marshall and Walt 1984
	8	Marshall and Walt 1984
	9	Marshall and Walt 1984
TQ:	10	Barnett 1974
	11	McGimsey 1980
	12	Martin and others 1956
	13	Nesbitt 1938
MV:	14	Bradley 1992
	15	Huber and Lipe 1992
KA:	16	Dean 1969
	17	Dean 1969
	18	Dean 1969
SL:	19	Martin and others 1967
	20	Martin and others 1964
	21	Haury 1985
WM:	22	Montgomery 1992
	23	Reid 1982
SC:	24	Lowell 1991
	25	Olson 1959
SV:	26	Johnson and Wasley 1966
	27	Johnson and Wasley 1966
	28	Woodson 1995
TR:	29	Redman 1993
	30	Lindauer 1991
	31	Redman 1993
LV:	32	Deaver and others 1994
MG:	33	Gladwin and Gladwin 1929
	34	Sires 1987
	35	Doyel 1974
	36	Doyel 1978
ST:	37	Downum and others 1993
	38	Wallace and Holmlund 1984
	39	Wallace and Holmlund 1984
	40	Wallace and Holmlund 1984
	41	Slaughter 1994
PB:	42	Abbott and others 1994
	43	Craig 1995a
	44	Nelson 1993

Figure 4.10. Areas and sites in the Southwest used in the macroregional study, with references.

Following the procedure discussed above, I plotted the distribution of RCIs of residential architecture by region (Fig. 4.11). Breaks in the distribution of values at 3.3 and 3.6 divide the residential units into three clusters, with ranges of 2.4 to 3.2, 3.4 to 3.5 and 3.7 to 4.0.

Group I contains units with RCI values between 2.4 and 3.2 and constitutes a majority of the sampled sites (28). The RCIs form a relatively normal distribution with median and modal values of 2.7, consistent with the definition of a room block. Examples of sites near the center of the distribution include Starkweather Ruin near Quemado, New Mexico (Nesbitt 1938), and Swarts Ruin in the Mimbres region (Cosgrove and Cosgrove 1932). Examples with values in the 3.0 to 3.2 range are more linear arrangements of contiguous rooms and include the Green Lizard site in the Mesa Verde area (Huber and Lipe 1992), Chodistaas Pueblo in the White

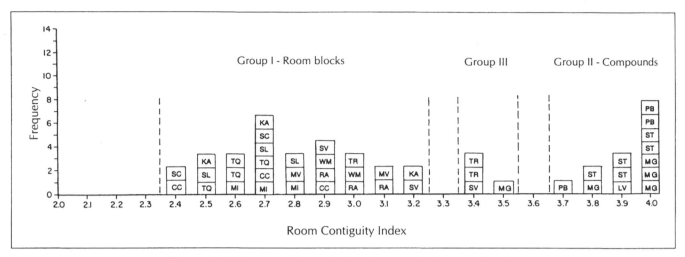

Figure 4.11. Room contiguity indices by area for sites used in the macroregional Southwest study (see Table 4.2 and Fig. 4.10).

Mountain area (Crown 1981; Montgomery 1992), and La Hija del Nido in the Rio Abajo province of the Rio Grande valley (Marshall and Walt 1984: 103). Those examples in the 2.4 to 2.5 range approach square configurations with large numbers of rooms and include Turkey Creek Pueblo in the San Carlos region (Lowell 1991) and Wijiji in Chaco Canyon (Lekson 1986: 71). Numbers of rooms per residential unit in Group I range from 5 to 420, with an average of approximately 75. Sites that make up this group are located in a geographically contiguous territory stretching from northern and eastern Arizona into eastern New Mexico and southern Colorado, approximately coeval with the spatial dimension of the Pueblo III period (Fig. 4.12). Thus, a puebloan tradition of room block architecture is lent empirical support by the distribution of Group I residential units as defined by RCIs. There are 28 cases in this group, and additional examples would probably continue to produce a relatively normal distribution of RCIs in the 2.4 to 3.2 range.

The 13 sites in Group II with RCIs in the 3.7 to 4.0 range are largely noncontiguous arrangements of rooms that fit within the RCI range for residential compounds, distinct from room blocks. Although the majority of examples contain fewer than 15 rooms, six examples contain more than 20 rooms, and two cases have more than 50 rooms, Pueblo Grande (about 79 rooms) and Cerro Prieto (about 250 rooms). In these two settlement complexes, a dispersed and segmented layout was maintained between residential units in the context of a village, suggesting that social factors played an important role in limiting the degree of aggregation in large

Group II settlements. Group II sites form a relatively cohesive geographic territory that is restricted to central and southern Arizona (Fig. 4.12). This patterning reveals a tradition of residential architecture distinct from that associated with the Pueblo III region to the north and east. In this tradition, the extent of settlement nucleation was constrained by social or economic variables.

The intermediate category with RCI values in the 3.4 to 3.5 range (Group III) contains the smallest number of cases (4) and includes two examples from the Tonto Rim, one from the Safford Basin and one from the middle Gila River valley (Fig. 4.12). This last site, Sacaton 9:6 (Gila Pueblo), produced an RCI of 3.5, slightly lower than the RCI range for compounds. The plan view of this compound depicts a row of atypically narrow rooms placed along segments of the compound wall; these rooms may have been used for storage or as part of a casemate construction (Gladwin and Gladwin 1929). Otherwise, the unit has a typical compound spatial layout and should probably be included within the architectural tradition of southern Arizona.

Three of the six cases from the Tonto Rim and the Safford Valley region fit in this intermediate category. The other three examples from these regions are in the high RCI range for room blocks, including the Goat Hill site in the Safford Valley. At Goat Hill, the circular arrangement of contiguous rooms contains a D-shaped kiva and the settlement has been interpreted as a Kayenta-Tusayan intrusion into the region (Woodson 1995, 1999). The two examples in the Tonto Rim region with RCIs of 3.4 are Shoofly Village and Risser

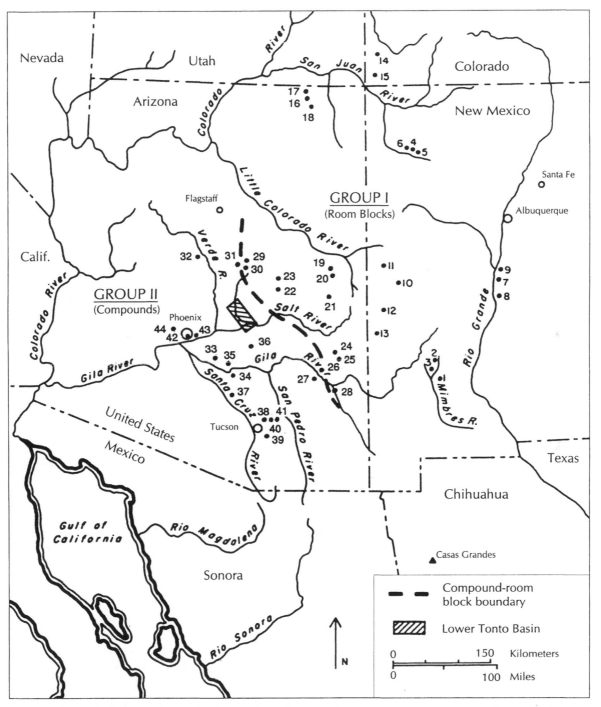

Figure 4.12. Geographic distribution of Group I (room block) and Group II (compound) residential units as defined by the Room Contiguity Index (see Table 4.2 for identification of numbered sites).

Ranch Ruin. Both are unique in that they contain distinctly separate room block and noncontiguous room components that probably overlapped temporally (Redman 1993: 49, 68–69). Comparable settlement layouts formed by agglomerates of noncontiguous and contiguous room units were not encountered elsewhere in this sample of sites. These unique room block-compound hybrids are in a region that straddles the boundary between Group I (room block) and Group II (compound) residential units (compare Figs. 4.10 and 4.12). Thus, they may represent settlements in which groups from both traditions co-resided (Redman 1993: 171–172).

A number of environmental and social factors may have influenced the patterning of the early Classic–Pueblo III period residential architecture depicted in Figure 4.12. Environmental factors may have included average ambient temperature and ecological variables that affected the length of settlement duration. In terms of social factors, degree of household autonomy, variability in the use of domestic space, and basic differences in social organization may have influenced the degree of settlement clustering.

Regardless of the causes for these macroregional patterns in domestic spatial organization, the vast expanse of territory encompassed by each architectural tradition indicates that this patterning reflects some high order social boundary. The region in which compounds are the prevalent architectural form corresponds roughly to the area where courtyard groups were the primary elements of spatial organization in pre-Classic pit house settlements. It also corresponds roughly with the Hohokam culture area as it has been traditionally defined. Recent conceptions of this region suggest it was occupied by multiple ethnic groups that were linked primarily by their participation in a common integrative ideology (Wallace and others 1995; Wilcox 1979). The territorial expanse defined by room blocks subsumes a number of regional manifestations associated with the late Pueblo II and Pueblo III periods. These include Chaco, Mimbres, Tularosa, Pinedale, Anasazi, and Western Pueblo, which have been characterized in the literature variously as culture areas, regional systems, polities, stylistic horizons, strong patterns, or simply phenomena (Gladwin and Gladwin 1929, 1930a, 1935; Haury 1936; Judge 1991; Lekson 1992; Tainter and Plog 1994; Wilcox 1979). Nevertheless, these manifestations are linked by a tradition of room block architecture that has been labeled "ancestral puebloan." The general patterns in residential architecture presented here certainly suggest two different traditions of organizing domestic space at a level well beyond that of community, district, and ethnicity.

During the early Classic and Pueblo III periods, the two architectural traditions began to overlap in the interstitial areas (Fig. 4.12). The Tonto Basin can be included in this area of overlap near the end of this interval, although compound residential units continued to predominate until A.D. 1300. Comparison of RCI distributions of Group I (room blocks) and Group II (compounds) with the RCI distribution of eastern Tonto Basin residential units indicates a higher degree of var-

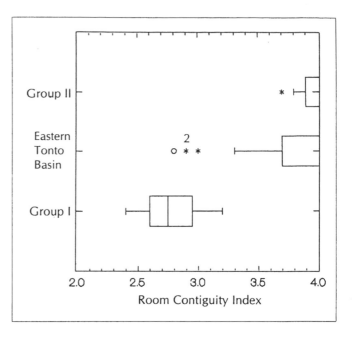

Figure 4.13. Box-and-whiskers plot of Room Contiguity Index distributions of Group I (room blocks) and Group II (compounds) for Southwestern sites in the macro-regional study and residential units in the eastern Tonto Basin.

iability in the eastern Tonto Basin than in either the Group I or Group II macroregions (Fig. 4.13). Groups I and II RCI distributions in the macroregional analysis do not overlap, and the RCI distribution for the large majority of eastern Tonto Basin residential units roughly coincides with the distribution for Group II units in southern and central Arizona. The four room block outliers in the eastern Tonto Basin RCI distribution (Griffin Wash Locus A and Locus C, Saguaro Muerto, and "Compound" 8 at Meddler Point) overlap with the central portion of the Group I RCI distribution from the macroregional study, suggesting an affinity between the two groups. The tailing of the eastern Tonto Basin RCI distribution can be attributed to the linear arrangements of contiguous rooms like those at site AZ U:8:454 on Schoolhouse Point Mesa, "Compound" 12 at the southern tip of Meddler Point, and site AZ V:5:96, a small residential unit near the Griffin Wash complex.

To conclude, RCI analysis isolated two distinct forms of domestic spatial organization in the eastern Tonto Basin community: compounds that represent the large majority of residential units and room blocks or linear arrangements of rooms that were in the minority. Compounds with dispersed room arrangements and segmented layouts are linked to the pre-Classic pit house tradition in the area. Room blocks represent a new form of settlement layout that appeared in the eastern Tonto Basin during the Roosevelt phase. The macroregional RCI study demonstrated that room blocks with similar layouts were built throughout the puebloan region north and east of the Tonto Basin for several centuries prior to their appearance in the basin. Hence, the evidence suggests that Tonto Basin room blocks were built by immigrants who originated from the puebloan region and that limited migration by puebloan households took place during the early Classic period. Subsequently these migrants co-resided with local groups living in compounds. However, domestic spatial organization constitutes only one line of evidence, and the sections that follow lend additional support to this assessment.

DOMESTIC CONSTRUCTION AND UTILITARIAN CERAMICS

Evidence of migration can also be found in various artifact classes and attributes that reflect the technological traditions of their producers, such as architectural construction and the manufacture of everyday domestic items like utilitarian ceramics. If room blocks were built by puebloan immigrants, then artifacts recovered from them should reveal intrusive technological styles that can be linked to regions north and east of the Tonto Basin. Compounds, on the other hand, should contain evidence of local technological traditions that can be traced back to the pre-Classic sequence in the area.

Architectural Construction

In addition to domestic spatial organization, the techniques and materials used in the construction of domestic architecture reveal the cultural affinity of the builders. Although environmental factors weigh heavily in the selection of raw materials and construction methods, these decisions are also influenced by cultural background, particularly in societies employing non-industrial technologies (see Chapter 2; Becker 1977; Jordan and Kaups 1989; Rapoport 1969; Towner and Dean 1992). In all but the most barren environments, sufficient materials are available to allow some freedom of choice in selecting and combining materials to erect walls, rooms, and buildings. In traditional societies, much of the knowledge of building is passed from generation to generation within the household, settlement, or community. Hence, there should be differences in architectural construction between newly arrived migrants and local groups, particularly in the earliest construction episodes following migration.

Wall Construction

The normative pre-Classic residence in the eastern Tonto Basin was a semisubterranean pit house constructed with post-reinforced brush and packed earth walls (Chapter 3). There is little evidence for the use of puddled adobe in the eastern Tonto Basin until the early Classic period. Pit house depressions were usually sloping and shallow and seldom deeper than 50 cm. The transition from subsurface pit house to above ground architecture in the Tonto Basin took place sometime between A.D. 1100 and 1250. Wall construction techniques also changed from post-reinforced packed earth to masonry and adobe during this interval.

The two main masonry wall construction techniques in the eastern Tonto Basin during the Roosevelt phase (A.D. 1250–1325) were post-reinforced adobe with an upright cobble footer (hereafter, cobble-footed adobe and jacal) and coursed cobble and adobe masonry (Fig. 4.14). Masonry in cobble-footed adobe and jacal walls

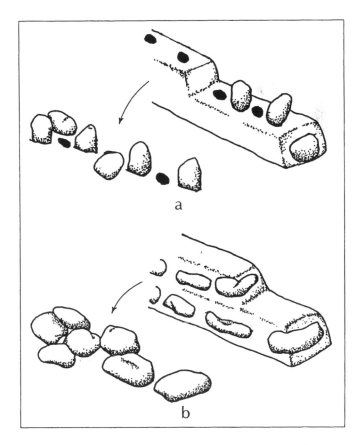

Figure 4.14. Types of masonry wall construction in the eastern Tonto Basin and their archaeological remnants: *a*, post-reinforced adobe with upright cobble footer (cobble-footed adobe and jacal) and *b*, coursed cobble masonry.

was generally confined to the base of the wall, where cobbles were placed upright in the ground at regular intervals to anchor the footer. Occasionally, cobbles were placed randomly in the upper portions of these walls. Mesquite and juniper posts placed between the upright cobbles extended up the entire height of the wall, roughly 1.8 m, as indicated by a fully preserved example in the Meddler Point platform mound (Elson, Fish, and others 1995: 258–260; Holmlund and others 1994, MP–2 Wall 28). Footed adobe and jacal walls have been called rock-reinforced walls by other researchers in the eastern Tonto Basin (Rice 1990b: 10–12).

In coursed cobble and adobe walls, unmodified river cobbles were set horizontally, either end-to-end or side-by-side, into an adobe matrix. Height of the coursed masonry in preserved or reconstructed examples varied from 1 m to 2 m. In the case of low walls, upper portions may have been coursed adobe. Many of the preserved portions of these two types of walls had adobe plaster facing, typically 2 cm to 5 cm thick (Holmlund and others 1994).

Two other types of masonry walls appeared in early Classic contexts, although in much lower frequency. We found dry-laid stacked-cobble walls only in the Meddler Point platform mound, where they were used as partitions between mound cells and never as free-standing walls (Holmlund and others 1994, MP–2). In the eastern Tonto Basin coursed masonry walls made with cut sandstone and siltstone blocks were encountered in isolated contexts; a few examples were at Griffin Wash Locus A, in the inner courtyard of the compound at the Sand Dune site (AZ V:5:112; Jacobs 1994: 338), and at Meddler Point.

I seriated early Classic residential units comprising the Meddler Point village to establish temporal relationships between the two predominate masonry techniques: footed adobe and jacal and coursed cobble and adobe (Clark 1997: 316–347). The multiple lines of chronological evidence in this seriation included stratigraphy, chronometric dates (archaeomagnetic and tree-ring), architectural data, and diagnostic ceramics recovered from compound interiors and associated trash mounds. This seriation divided Meddler Point compounds into three groups: (1) units abandoned in the early Roosevelt phase or perhaps earlier; (2) inconclusively dated units; and (3) units abandoned near the end of the Roosevelt phase (see Fig. 4.16).

The earliest compounds at Meddler Point were built primarily with cobble-footed adobe and jacal (see Fig. 4.16, *top*). These simple compounds had been abandoned in an early stage of development, prior to the construction of additional courtyards and rooms. In compounds occupied throughout extended intervals where construction sequences could be determined, early portions were built more often with cobble-footed adobe and jacal walls and later portions were built with more coursed cobble and adobe walls (see Fig. 4.16, Late Roosevelt phase compounds). When the total lengths of walls constructed with each masonry type are calculated for each seriated group of compounds, a temporal trend is readily apparent between masonry wall types (Fig. 4.15). However, in several late compound construction episodes both techniques were used, arguing for temporal overlap between the two forms. During this period of overlap, room walls were more likely to be constructed with coursed cobbles and adobe, whereas compound walls were more often built with cobble-footed adobe and jacal.

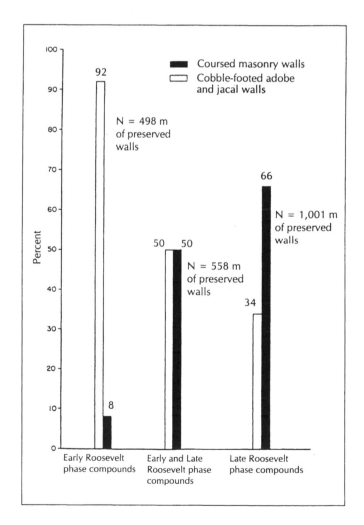

Figure 4.15. Percentages of masonry wall types in seriated compound groups at Meddler Point.

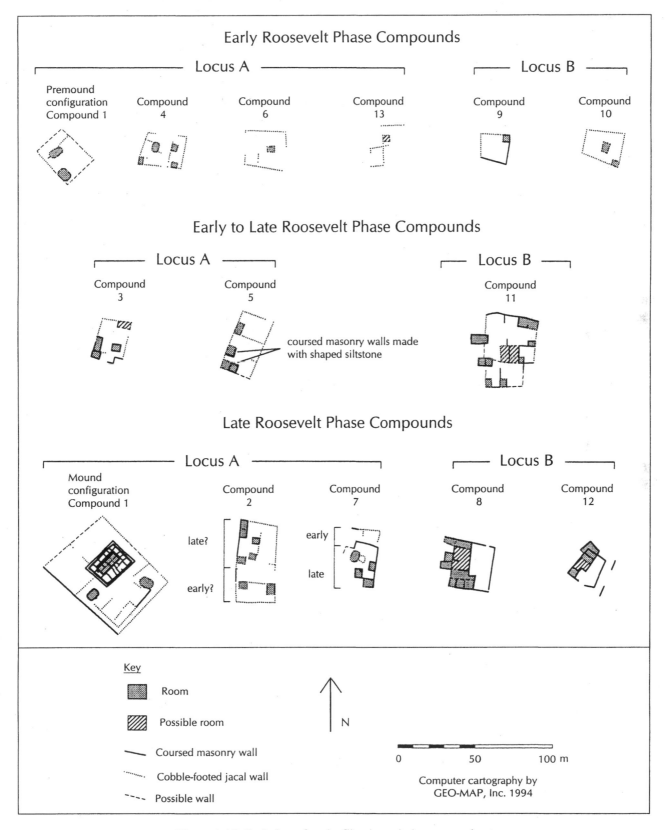

Figure 4.16. Seriation of early Classic period compounds at the Meddler Point site (adapted from Clark 1997, Fig. 5.7).

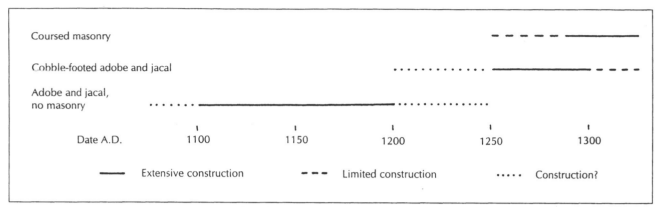

Figure 4.17. Time line for wall construction types in the eastern
Tonto Basin through the late pre-Classic and early Classic periods.

The results of the seriation and evidence from other compounds suggest the time line for wall construction techniques within the eastern Tonto Basin presented in Figure 4.17. Some time shortly after A.D. 1100, puddled adobe replaced packed earth as the primary material used to construct pit house walls in the eastern Tonto Basin, although posts continued to be the principal means of reinforcement (Clark 1997: 307–311). The first adobe structures were shallow pit houses with simple doorways instead of the protruding entries commonly associated with earlier pit houses. These structures represent transitional forms between pre-Classic pit houses and early Classic surface rooms.

The first cobble-footed adobe and jacal walls were built by the mid-thirteenth century, if not earlier. The degree to which both footed and nonfooted adobe and jacal walls overlapped in the first half of the thirteenth century is uncertain. The distinction between these two techniques may be insignificant, because seemingly the addition of an upright-cobble footer to a post-reinforced adobe and jacal wall does not represent an appreciable change in wall construction technology. Cobble-footed adobe and jacal walls were apparently a direct development from pre-Classic wall construction techniques used in pit house construction.

Coursed cobble and adobe became widely adopted at some point during the mid-to-late thirteenth century. By the end of the early Classic period, coursed masonry had nearly replaced cobble-footed adobe and jacal as the primary wall construction technique in the eastern Tonto Basin, a fairly rapid transformation occurring over the course of a generation or two. Both in terms of tempo and technology, coursed masonry techniques represent a dramatic departure from the early tradition of wall construction in the region.

Of the 44 units defined as compounds by RCI values in the eastern Tonto Basin, all but two (sites AZ U:8:456 and V:5:138 on Schoolhouse Point Mesa) contained cobble-footed adobe and jacal wall segments. The relative percentages of cobble-footed adobe and jacal walls varied substantially within these units from less than 5 percent to 100 percent. Some of this variability may be due to the differences in compound construction dates, considering the temporal relationship between cobble-footed and coursed masonry wall types. In addition, the relative proportion of room wall length to compound wall length may also influence this proportion, because rooms tended to be built with more coursed masonry than compound walls. Regardless of temporal and functional considerations, this local cobble-footed adobe and jacal construction technique is ubiquitous among compounds, residential units that can also be linked to pre-Classic settlements in terms of spatial organization. The highest proportions of footed adobe and jacal walls are recorded for the earliest compounds at Meddler Point, which was the pre-Classic center of the eastern Tonto Basin community where local traditions would have persisted.

The first room blocks and linear arrangements of rooms in the eastern Tonto Basin were constructed during the second half of the thirteenth century, including Saguaro Muerto (see Fig. 4.9), Griffin Wash Locus A and Locus C (see Fig. 4.8), and "Compound" 8 at Meddler Point Locus B (see Fig. 4.16). Linear arrangements of rooms include site AZ U:8:454 at Schoolhouse Point, "Compound" 12 at Meddler Point Locus B, and site AZ V:5:96 near Griffin Wash. At Saguaro Muerto, only one wall segment was built with cobble-footed adobe and jacal. This segment was situated outside the room block and may have been part of an earlier unit that

Figure 4.18. Sandstone block wall at Griffin Wash Locus A.

predated room block construction (Lindauer 1994a: 444). The remainder of Saguaro Muerto was constructed exclusively with coursed cobble and adobe masonry. At Griffin Wash Locus A, the only identified cobble-footed jacal wall segment was beneath the room block and was also associated with an earlier residential unit (Swartz and Randolph 1994b: 369–372). The Locus A room block was built exclusively with coursed masonry techniques. Of the remaining room blocks and linear arrangements, Griffin Wash Locus C, site AZ V:5:96 adjacent to Griffin Wash, site AZ U:8:454 on Schoolhouse Point Mesa, and "Compound" 12 at Meddler Point Locus B were built exclusively with coursed masonry. "Compound" 8, also at Meddler Point Locus B, was the only residential unit defined as a room block or linear room arrangement in the eastern Tonto Basin that was not built entirely with coursed masonry. In this case, only 5 percent of the walls by length were constructed using cobble-footed jacal, an amount considerably lower than that for other compounds in the Med-

dler Point settlement. With only this one minor exception, room block and linear room arrangements as a group were constructed, start to finish, with coursed masonry techniques.

At Griffin Wash, the original enclosure of Locus A, the largest of the room block settlements, was built with cut sandstone-siltstone blocks to a height approaching 2 m (Fig. 4.18). Elsewhere in the eastern Tonto Basin, this technique appeared only at the Sand Dune site (AZ V:5:112; Jacobs 1994: 338) and in several wall segments at Meddler Point Locus A, including one platform mound cell. Use of this technique in the initial construction episode at Griffin Wash Locus A demonstrates that the founders of the settlement possessed a developed coursed masonry tradition that was relatively foreign to the region. Such traditions existed in the puebloan world north and east of the Tonto Basin for two or more centuries prior to the construction of Griffin Wash Locus A (Barnett 1974; Haury 1985: 1–133; Lekson 1986). In this light, the few sandstone-siltstone walls constructed in eastern Tonto Basin compounds may reflect some mixing between local and immigrant populations within residential units, especially at the Sand Dune site where this technique was used extensively. This site also contained other indicators of the presence of puebloan groups in the form of slablined fireboxes (Jacobs 1994: 344–355, 360–365). Fireboxes were present in both compound rooms and underlying pit houses that immediately preceded compound construction, suggesting a close connection between the inhabitants of both components. In the eastern Tonto Basin, the only other example of this type of domestic installation was found at Saguaro Muerto (Lindauer 1994a: 442).

Walls built later in the Griffin Wash Locus A room block were composite constructions of tabular stone and unworked river cobbles, and ultimately cobbles became the sole masonry material. Apparently the coursed masonry tradition of the original inhabitants was soon adapted to accommodate the more locally available and abundant river cobbles in the immediate vicinity. The sequence at Griffin Wash Locus A from cut sandstone-siltstone blocks to coursed cobble and adobe masonry contrasts with the sequence of footed adobe and jacal to coursed cobble and adobe in many of the compounds, particularly units comprising the Meddler Point Locus A settlement. Although the inhabitants of Griffin Wash Locus A and Meddler Point Locus A ultimately adopted the same construction technique, this convergence came from opposite technologies, Meddler Point with local antecedents and Griffin Wash with a foreign tradition.

One possible explanation for the widespread adoption of coursed masonry in both compounds and room blocks by the end of the early Classic period is that construction of post-reinforced walls taxed local wood resources during the Roosevelt phase (for evidence of over-exploitation of locally available woods, see Elson, S. Fish, and others 1995: 259–260). However, examples of compounds built or remodeled later in the Roosevelt phase (for example, Compounds 1 and 2 at Meddler Point) demonstrate that footed adobe and jacal walls continued to be built until the end of the thirteenth century, after room block construction began at Griffin Wash and Saguaro Muerto. Neither functional nor environmental factors adequately explain the near-absence of the local tradition of wall construction in early Classic period room blocks. More likely, the inhabitants of these units were newcomers to the eastern Tonto Basin and possessed a different technological tradition of wall construction that did not include cobble-footed adobe and jacal.

Construction Wood

Wood was used as a construction material throughout the pre-Classic and Classic periods in the eastern Tonto Basin. Posthole patterns of pre-Classic period pit houses indicate that posts placed at regular intervals supported the walls of the structure. Smaller posts and perhaps cactus ribs, placed between these posts, were often anchored in a shallow groove that ran along the inner perimeter of the structural pit. Large posts supported the roofs, which were constructed of big poles that were spanned by increasingly smaller elements in a cross-hatch pattern. Local pre-Classic preferences in construction were generally restricted to locally available low elevation woods, especially mesquite and cottonwood, and mid-elevation species, such as juniper (Elson, S. Fish, and others 1995, Fig. 22.11). Juniper grows on the slopes of the Sierra Ancha and other surrounding ranges and was readily accessible to the inhabitants of the Tonto Basin.

Early Classic period wall construction techniques featured coursed cobble and adobe and footed adobe and jacal, but only the footed adobe and jacal incorporated wood. In cases where posts were recovered in situ from footed adobe and jacal walls, juniper was the predominant species. Wood was also used extensively in the support and construction of room ceilings throughout the early Classic period. In general, wood assemblages recovered from both room blocks and compounds in the eastern Tonto Basin were comparable to wood assemblages retrieved from pre-Classic pit houses (mesquite, cottonwood, juniper), with the exception of eight investigated rooms (Elson, S. Fish, and others 1995: 259–260; Dering 1994: 871; Dering 1997, Tables 14.4, 14.5). These rooms contained the only evidence of the use of high elevation species such as ponderosa pine, Douglas-fir, and white fir for construction (Elson, S. Fish, and others 1995: 259, 260, Fig. 22.11). Two of these rooms were at Meddler Point Locus A and the other six were at Griffin Wash Locus A. A small amount of "generic" pine, either ponderosa or piñon, was recovered from Pyramid Point.

The two structures at Meddler Point containing high elevation species appear to have had specialized or ceremonial functions (Craig and Clark 1994b): the southern room on top of the platform mound and an oval pit room in the center of Compound 7. At Griffin Wash Locus A, assemblages of ponderosa pine, Douglas-fir, and white fir were found in six of the excavated rooms, which represent 50 percent of the investigated structures at the site. The co-occurrence of these species in-

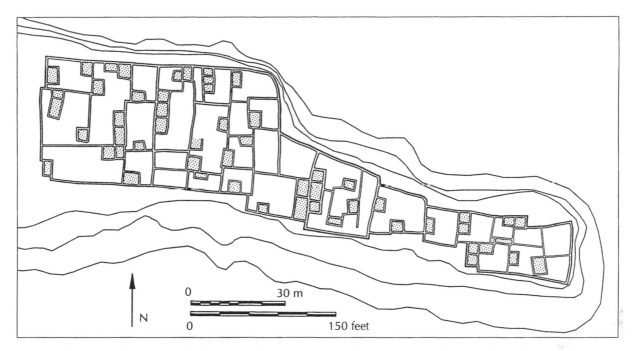

Figure 4.19. Plan of the Sycamore Creek site (adapted from map produced by Joseph Crary).

dicates selective use of high elevation woods. Both intensively investigated areas at Locus A (Areas I and III) had the highest ubiquity for fir in the entire eastern Tonto Basin, more than double that obtained from Meddler Point. Wall construction in the Griffin Wash Locus A room block was exclusively coursed masonry, so the high elevation woods were used as roof beams or roof supports rather than wall posts.

The ubiquity and co-occurrence of high elevation woods at Griffin Wash Locus A suggest that these elements were not procured as driftwood from the Salt River or its tributaries. Both Douglas-fir and white fir grow only at elevations of 2,200 m (7,000 feet) or more. At present, the closest source for these species is more than 25 km (15.5 miles, straight-line distance) north of the eastern Tonto Basin. The acquisition of these woods must have been expensive in terms of labor, requiring at least a two-day excursion. The persistent preference for these woods rather than for locally available species strengthens the argument for high elevation origins of the Griffin Wash Locus A inhabitants.

With the exception of Saguaro Muerto, evidence of construction wood in other early Classic room blocks is limited, including "Compounds" 8 and 12 at Meddler Point Locus B, Griffin Wash Locus C, site AZ V:5:96 near Griffin Wash, and site AZ U:8:454 on Schoolhouse Point Mesa. Only low elevation woods were used

as roof beams and supports in Saguaro Muerto, an expected adjustment to local resources that the new arrivals at Griffin Wash Locus A apparently did not make.

Building Episodes

Based on regularities in settlement layout and circulation patterns mentioned above, I placed simple, intermediate, and complex compounds in a single developmental sequence. The basic building block of each of these residential types was comprised of an enclosed courtyard area containing one to four rooms in a nondistributive arrangement (see Figs. 4.3, 4.4). Compound development was modular with new courtyards added in conjunction with room construction. Hence, the final layout of compounds with long settlement histories was highly segmented (see Fig. 4.5). This model of growth is supported by known compound construction sequences from the eastern Tonto Basin (Fig. 4.6), and it reflects a stable pattern of organizing domestic space that can be traced back to pre-Classic pit house courtyard groups. The spatial rules guiding compound development place constraints on settlement nucleation. The Sycamore Creek site in the western basin is perhaps the best example in the region of social groups attempting to aggregate following compound spatial rules (Fig. 4.19). The resulting configuration is still recognizable as a compound, albeit highly segmented.

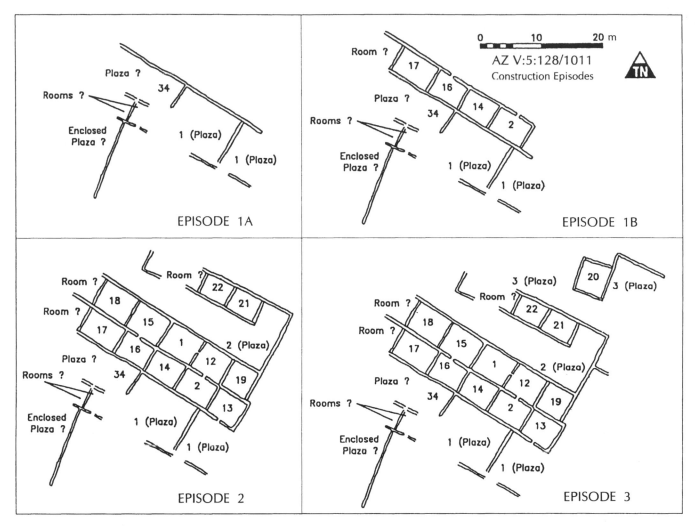

Figure 4.20. Construction sequence of Saguaro Muerto (adapted from Lindauer 1994a, Fig. 12.29).

The question remains, however, whether or not room blocks should be placed at the end of the compound developmental sequence. At some time in the settlement history of these units, perhaps external social factors or topographic constraints forced local residents of compounds to fill in existing courtyards with rooms rather than add new courtyards (Wood 1985). If so, then intermediate and complex compounds should be recognizable in the initial construction stages of room blocks.

Reconstructing room block building sequences from wall bond-abut patterns is tricky, requiring careful and complete excavation of complex sites. These sequences were partially or fully determined in three of the seven room blocks or linear room arrangements defined by RCI values in the eastern Tonto Basin.

Saguaro Muerto is the only room block identified by the RCI analysis south of the Salt River. About 60 per-

cent of the preserved portion of the site was excavated and a construction sequence was identified (Fig. 4.20; Lindauer 1994a). Limited evidence of a residential unit that predated the construction of the main room block (Episode 1A) was reported. According to the excavators, the room block was built in two major episodes (1B and 2). In each case, lines of four to five contiguous rooms formed the basic elements that were added to the previous configuration. A similar sequence is indicated for site AZ U:8:454, the U-shaped line of rooms on Schoolhouse Point Mesa, with the eastern line of three to four rooms constructed first, followed by a line of similar length to the west (see Fig. 4.9; Lindauer 1997: 193–194). At Griffin Wash Locus A, the largest early Classic room block in the area, the sequence can be reconstructed only on a general level, except for Area III (Fig. 4.21). Following Swartz and Randolph

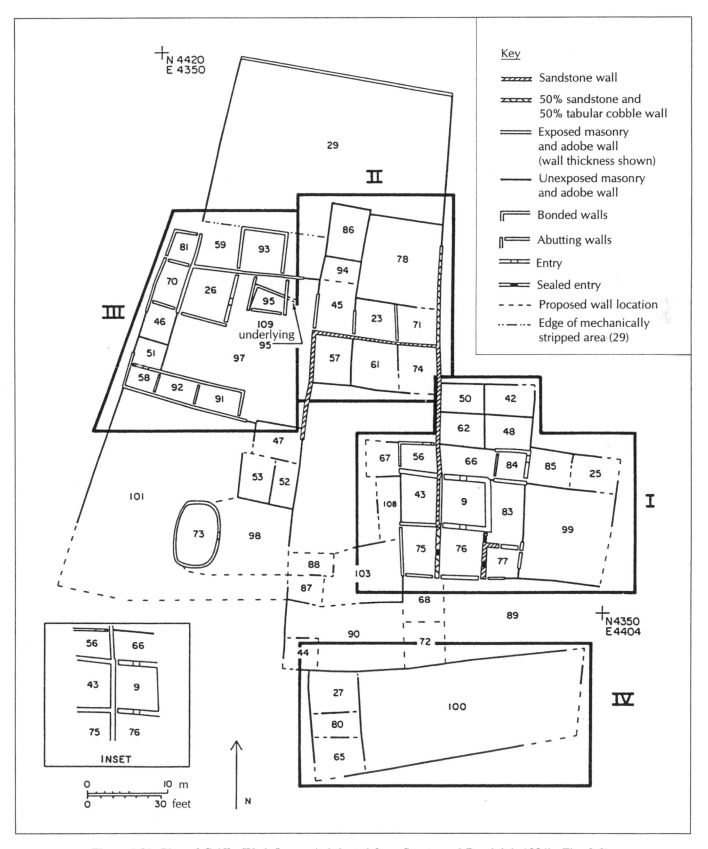

Figure 4.21. Plan of Griffin Wash Locus A (adapted from Swartz and Randolph 1994b, Fig. 9.2).

(1994b: 407–410), the available wall bond-abut relationships show that the original settlement was constructed within the confines of the inner sandstone block wall, including the southern line of rooms in Area II (Features 57, 61, and 74) and the line of rooms in Area I formed by Features 56, 43, and 75. The construction sequence in the original enclosure cannot be further determined with reasonable confidence. Feature 9 had a specialized artifact assemblage and was probably a two-story room. Based on the amount of wall collapse in the vicinity, Feature 43 also may have had a second story. All excavated rooms associated with residential compounds were single-story, and these two features are the only possibilities for two-story rooms in the eastern Tonto Basin during the early Classic period.

Wall bond-abut relationships in Area III indicated that the L–shaped configuration of rooms formed by Features 91, 92, 58, 51, 46, 70, and 81 was built either in the same construction episode or in two separate episodes, each composed of a line of three or four rooms. This arrangement is comparable to the portion of Area II in the enclosed area to the north of the sandstone wall (Features 71, 23, 45, 94, and 86). In Area III, rooms were subsequently added on the north side to form a square U–shape similar to the final configuration of site AZ U:8:454 on Schoolhouse Point Mesa (see Fig. 4.9). Finally, rooms (Features 26 and 95) were added inside the plaza area (Feature 97). Feature 109, a room constructed with cobble-footed jacal walls underlying Area III, may have been part of an earlier residential unit. However, its stratigraphic position and anomalous orientation with respect to Area III indicate that this room was never an integral part of the room block and was probably abandoned before the initial room block was constructed. Area IV may have been the last addition to Griffin Wash Locus A, and the three rooms identified there were built in a contiguous line.

These lines of evidence indicate that Roosevelt phase room block construction in the eastern Tonto Basin occurred in episodes involving the addition of contiguous lines of three to five rooms, with or without walls enclosing adjacent extramural areas. These room chains were built in isolation (such as site AZ V:5:96, "Compound" 12 at the Meddler Point site, and Area IV at Griffin Wash Locus A) or were added to existing linear arrangements to form blocks (Saguaro Muerto) or L–shaped and square U–shaped configurations (site AZ U:8:454; Areas II and III at Griffin Wash Locus A). These basic architectural building elements differ substantially from the basic elements forming compounds. From initial construction to final abandonment, room blocks and compounds in the eastern Tonto Basin were constructed with different architectural building blocks. It is improbable that the two forms of residential architecture belong in the same developmental sequence.

Utilitarian Ceramics

Manufacturing processes associated with basic utilitarian items can vary among traditional societies because technological knowledge is passed from one generation to the next within localized contexts (Chapter 2). Technological style is an especially powerful methodological tool in assessing migration because it identifies the cultural background of the artifact manufacturer from an "etic" vantage point, circumventing the need to interpret symbols or decode stylistic messages intentionally conveyed in more conspicuous media. In addition to architecture, artifact classes potentially rich in technological style include utilitarian ceramics and ground and flaked stone tools. Considering the frequency and ubiquity of utilitarian ceramics at most archaeological sites, it is an optimal artifact class to examine.

Throughout the pre-Classic period, plain ware bowls and jars dominated the utilitarian ceramic assemblage recovered from the eastern Tonto Basin (Stark 1995b). Early ceramic vessels were limited to uncomplicated forms, either deep hemispherical bowls or seed jars with simple rims (Stark 1995a). During the Colonial period, more complex forms appeared, including flare-rimmed jars and bowls and collar-rimmed jars. Locally made utilitarian vessels during this interval largely reflect Phoenix Basin technological styles (Stark 1995b: 352–355), as is consistent with other evidence of strong influences from this direction during the pre-Classic period. Many of these vessels were apparently constructed using the paddle-and-anvil technique commonly employed by prehistoric groups residing in southern Arizona.

In surface treatment, the frequency of interior and exterior burnishing and interior carbon smudging gradually increased on utilitarian vessels during the Sedentary period (Stark 1995b, Fig. 15.9). Vessel burnishing is considered part of the Hohokam ceramic technological tradition, but interior smudging is usually associated with Mogollon groups occupying the highland regions to the north and east of the Tonto Basin (Haury 1985: 221–223). Considering the paucity of other evidence for migration during this interval, the appearance of smudging on locally produced ceramics in the eastern Tonto Basin during the Sedentary period should probably be regarded as emulation of a surface treatment rather than

Figure 4.22. Tonto Corrugated vessel.

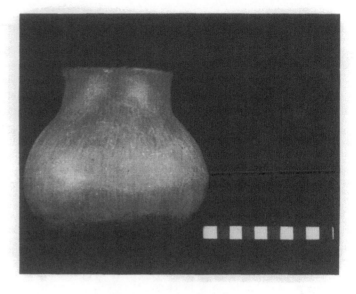

Figure 4.23. Red ware jar.

significant movement of potters from the Mogollon highlands. The frequency of red-slipped bowls and jars (red ware; Stark 1995b: 357) increased during the Sedentary period, and the direction of influence in this instance was either from the Mogollon Highlands or the Phoenix Basin.

During the early Classic period, both continuity and change is observed in manufacturing techniques, surface treatments, and vessel forms in the eastern Tonto Basin utilitarian ceramic assemblage (Stark 1995b: 356). Perhaps the most notable change was the widespread production of textured vessels, including both red-slipped (Salado Red Ware) and unslipped (Tonto) corrugated bowls and jars. On most of the slipped and unslipped corrugated vessels, the initial texturing was partially obliterated by subsequent smoothing (obliterated corrugated). As indicated by incisions between the coil joints, locally manufactured textured vessels were probably made by the coil-and-scrape method rather than the paddle-and-anvil method (Simon 1994a: 638). Both corrugation surface treatment and coil-and-scrape manufacture were common elements in the ceramic traditions throughout the Mogollon Highlands and Colorado Plateau north and east of the Tonto Basin. However, these manufacturing techniques were not a part of the technological traditions of groups in the Phoenix Basin and elsewhere in southern Arizona (Stark 1995b: 358).

In general, Salado Red Ware is similar to Tonto Corrugated, except the former has an added "raspberry" red slip. In the eastern Tonto Basin, Salado Red Ware was often more finely made and had a wider circulation than Tonto Corrugated. Salado Red Ware is discussed in detail as an important exchange commodity in the next chapter. I focus on Tonto Corrugated Ware here because its lower exchange value and more limited distribution make it a more discerning indicator of cultural background.

Corrugation techniques used to manufacture Tonto Corrugated were coarser than those used on McDonald Corrugated and Reserve Corrugated pottery produced to the north and east of the basin (Fig. 4.22). Though zoned or patterned designs are common on vessels from the Mogollon Highlands, little evidence exists for the use of corrugation as a decorative technique on Tonto Corrugated vessels (Stark 1995c: 210). In shape, however, Tonto Corrugated storage jars resemble vessels from contemporary and earlier sites in the Forestdale and Point of Pines regions. Tonto Corrugated vessels were probably thumb-indented and then smoothed to produce obliterated indented surfaces (Doyel 1978: 30) that were uneven and pebbly (Wood 1987: 20). The smoothed texturing can often be felt more easily than seen, and apparently much of the decorative aspect of corrugation has been lost.

Examining the relative proportions of Tonto Corrugated Ware in room block and compound utilitarian ceramic assemblages sheds additional light on the cultural backgrounds of the occupants of these units. In addition to red ware and Tonto Corrugated Ware, Salado Red Ware and plain ware round out these assemblages. Plain ware is excluded from this comparison because of the difficulty in sorting pre-Classic and Classic period plain

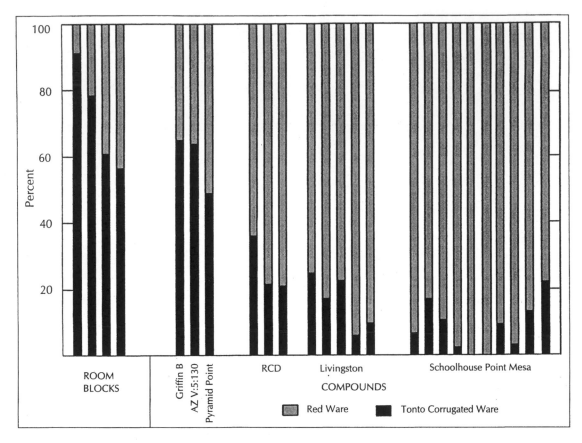

Figure 4.24. Percentages of red ware and Tonto Corrugated
Ware in eastern Tonto Basin room blocks and compounds.

ware sherds and the presence of pre-Classic pit house settlements in the vicinity of many early Classic compounds. Local red ware production in the Tonto Basin began in the Sedentary period and was influenced by similar wares manufactured either in the Phoenix Basin or in the Mogollon Highlands (Fig. 4.23). Using red ware as an index partially alleviates problems associated with temporal mixing, because it was produced in far greater quantities during the early Classic period than during the pre-Classic period.

I calculated the relative percentages of red ware and Tonto Corrugated Ware in utilitarian ware assemblages from early Classic residential units in the eastern Tonto Basin (Table 4.3). Figure 4.24 depicts the relative proportions of unslipped Tonto Corrugated ware and red ware at each site listed in Table 4.3. Only residential units from which 200 or more utilitarian sherds were recovered are included. This sample size restriction excludes many of the isolated compound farmsteads tested to the north of the Salt River as well as the two room block-linear room arrangements ("Compounds" 8 and

12), one near the south end of Meddler Point and one near Griffin Wash (AZ V:5:96). Residential units defined by RCI values as room blocks and linear arrangements of rooms are in boldface type in Table 4.3. A clear trend is indicated with room blocks and linear arrangements of rooms associated with percentages of unslipped Tonto Corrugated Ware that are at least twice those of all but three of the residential compounds (discussed below) and often are four to five times greater. Of the room block units, Saguaro Muerto yielded the highest ratio, followed in succession by Griffin Wash Locus C and Locus A, and finally site AZ U:8:454 on Schoolhouse Point Mesa.

At Saguaro Muerto, high frequencies of unslipped corrugated and use of local temper (Simon 1994b) indicate production of corrugated ware by the inhabitants of the room block and perhaps limited exchange of it throughout the rest of the Livingston project area, particularly with the nearest residential compound (AZ V:5:130). In the Griffin Wash site complex, more than 95 percent of the analyzed Locus A unslipped corrugat-

**Table 4.3. Relative Percentages of Red Ware and Tonto Corrugated Ware in
Utilitarian Assemblages from Roosevelt Phase Residential Units**

Utilitarian assemblages include red ware and plain ware (smudged and unsmudged), plain corrugated, and Salado Red Corrugated

Project Area ASM Site No. (Site Name)	Red Ware in Utilitarian Assemblage %	Plain Corrugated Ware in Utilitarian Assemblage %	Tonto Corrugated (Red Ware + Tonto Corrugated) x 100%	Sample size
RCD Project Area (subsurface deposits only)				
AZ V:5:1 (Pyramid Point)	24	23	49	3,670
AZ V:5:4 (Meddler Point), Early Classic period contexts only; percentages from Stark and Heidke 1995, Fig. 16.3	29	8	22	
AZ V:5:90 (Griffin Wash)	**15**	**24**	**62**	**18,696**
Locus A	**16**	**25**	**61**	**11,935**
Locus B	14	26	65	2,730
Locus C	**11**	**40**	**78**	**249**
AZ V:5:106 (Porcupine), Locus A	23	13	36	1,921
AZ V:5:110	19	5	21	273
Livingston Project Area *(Simon 1994a, Table 18.2)*				
AZ V:5:112 (Sand Dune)	15	5	25	13,727
AZ V:5:119	24	5	17	3,680
AZ V:5:121	17	5	23	3,566
AZ V:5:128 (Saguaro Muerto)	**4**	**41**	**91**	**14,723**
AZ V:5:130	21	37	64	2,629
AZ V:5:139	31	2	6	8,199
AZ V:5:141	65	7	10	302
Schoolhouse Point Mesa Project Area *(Simon 1997, Table 8.4)*				
AZ U:8:25*	28	2	7	24,253
AZ U:8:291	34	7	17	215
AZ U:8:450	25	3	11	24,659
AZ U:8:451	41	1	2	2,302
AZ U:8:452	29	0	0	490
AZ U:8:453	49	0	0	2,849
AZ U:8:454	**20**	**26**	**57**	**6,591**
AZ U:8:456 and AZ U:8:457	29	3	9	3,248
AZ U:8:458*	31	1	3	10,272
AZ V:5:137	26	4	13	6,696
AZ V:5:138	21	6	22	3,408

NOTE: **Bold** entries indicate room blocks and linear room arrangements. Sample size limited to 200 or more sherds. Information compiled from Craig and Clark 1994a, Table 7.2; Elson 1994, Table 8.2; Elson and Randolph 1994, Table 5.1; Simon 1994a, Table 18.2; Simon 1997, Table 8.4; Swartz and Randolph 1994b, Table 9.1.

* Buff ware counts indicate a significant pre-Classic component at this location.

ed sherds were produced using sands from the Armer-Cline petrofacies (Stark and Heidke 1995, Fig. 16.7). Although this petrofacies is large and includes several other communities, the Griffin Wash site complex is the only settlement in the Meddler Point community situated within it.

Only three units defined by RCIs as compounds have high relative quantities of Tonto Corrugated Ware com-

parable to room blocks and linear room arrangements, and all three are located close to room blocks. Griffin Wash Locus B produced the highest ratio in this group. This unit is only 40 m to the north of Griffin Wash Locus A and may have served a nonresidential function for the inhabitants of the nearby room block (Swartz and Randolph 1994b: 413). Similarly, site AZ V:5:130, the compound unit yielding the second highest ratio in this group, is the closest compound to the Saguaro Muerto room block. Pyramid Point, the third member of this group, is the closest village to Griffin Wash on the north bank of the Salt River. Based on the low percentages of Tonto Corrugated Ware recovered from the vast majority of residential compounds, proximity to room blocks and exchange of pots or potters between neighboring residential units may have been responsible for the relatively high quantities of Tonto Corrugated Ware in this group of compounds. The results of this analysis link unslipped textured ceramics with room blocks and constitute yet another compelling argument supporting migration in the region by puebloan groups during the early Classic period.

MIGRATION BEYOND REASONABLE DOUBT

The occurrence and scale of puebloan migration into the eastern Tonto Basin during the early Classic period has been assessed using multiple data sets that are considered reliable indicators of population movement (Chapter 2), with domestic spatial organization forming the baseline study. Room Contiguity Indices (RCIs) sorted early Classic settlements into segmented units with dispersed room arrangements (compounds) and nucleated units with contiguous rooms (room blocks and linear room arrangements).

Simple, intermediate, and complex compounds were constructed with the same basic building block, an enclosed courtyard containing from one to four rooms. This structural element can be linked to pre-Classic pit house courtyard groups in the area and in southern Arizona. The presence of this basic structural element, discernible in Tonto Basin settlements for more than half a millennium, indicates the persistence of a stable and relatively small social unit that organized residential space in a consistent manner. The spatial segregation observed among and in residential compounds composing the larger settlements at Meddler Point and Schoolhouse Point Mesa reveals a relatively high degree of autonomy for this social unit.

No antecedents for room block architecture were encountered in the eastern Tonto Basin. A macroregional RCI analysis of residential units throughout the eleventh, twelfth, and thirteenth centuries defines two fundamental architectural traditions in the Southwest, one dominated by room blocks in northern and eastern Arizona, western New Mexico, and southern Colorado, and one associated with compounds restricted to southern and central Arizona. The Tonto Basin is close to the boundary between the two regions defined by these architectural traditions, near the northern limit of compound architecture. These lines of evidence suggest that room blocks in the eastern Tonto Basin were built by immigrants originating from areas to the north and east of the basin.

Differences in architectural construction between room blocks and compounds corroborate this reconstruction. The examination of wall construction techniques isolated a local post-reinforced wall tradition that was traced back into the pre-Classic period. During the twelfth century, puddled adobe replaced packed earth as the primary construction material in post-reinforced walls. During the early Classic, a cobble footer was added to anchor the base. This technique was used almost exclusively in the construction of the earliest residential compounds. However, during the late thirteenth century, use of coursed masonry techniques increased dramatically in the eastern Tonto Basin. These techniques represented a dramatic departure from the local tradition, and the widespread adoption of coursed masonry coincided roughly with initial room block construction in the area.

Compounds that were occupied throughout the early Classic contained both cobble-footed adobe and jacal walls and coursed masonry and adobe walls. Room blocks and linear arrangements of rooms were built almost exclusively with coursed masonry techniques. The initial compound enclosure at Griffin Wash Locus A, the largest room block in the eastern Tonto Basin, was built with cut sandstone blocks, indicating that the inhabitants possessed a developed coursed masonry tradition that was linked to the inhabitants of areas north and east of the Tonto Basin. Additionally, the inhabitants of Griffin Wash Locus A were the only residents to use high elevation woods such as ponderosa pine and fir species on a regular basis in room construction. The nearest source of these woods is 25 km (15.5 miles) north of the eastern Tonto Basin.

In room blocks where building sequences could be reconstructed, it appears that in all stages of construction, room blocks were built using a different architectural grammar than that of compounds. Griffin Wash Locus A, Saguaro Muerto, and site AZ U:8:454 on Schoolhouse Point Mesa contained a repetitive architectural element, comprised of three to five contiguous rooms, that differed fundamentally from the architectural building block of residential compounds. Room blocks did not develop from compound precursors and the two architectural forms cannot be placed within a single developmental sequence.

Additional support for the argument that room blocks were occupied by puebloan immigrants and compounds by local groups was apparent in the utilitarian ceramic assemblages recovered from these units. Technological traditions reflected in the early Classic utilitarian ceramic assemblage indicated both continuity with and departure from pre-Classic traditions. In terms of the latter, local production of obliterated corrugated wares represented the most dramatic break with the past. Textured wares were an integral part of the ceramic traditions of groups residing in the Mogollon Highlands and Colorado Plateau. The distribution of locally produced Tonto Corrugated Ware, the unslipped and more coarsely made of the two textured wares in the basin,

was largely restricted to room blocks, and the handful of exceptions may be explained by the proximity of compounds to room blocks.

Multiple lines of evidence converge to make a compelling case that early Classic room blocks (and linear room arrangements) in the eastern Tonto Basin were occupied by puebloan immigrants who originated to the north and east of the region. The inhabitants of compounds, on the other hand, had strong connections with the pre-Classic residents of the area and constituted an enduring local population. With the scale and occurrence of migration into the eastern Tonto Basin established with reasonable confidence, I assess the impact of these thirteenth-century population movements.

CHAPTER FIVE

Migrant Origins, Motivation, and Impact

In the assessment of the occurrence and scale of Roosevelt phase migrations in the eastern Tonto Basin (Chapter 4), I differentiated immigrant enclaves from local settlements in terms of domestic spatial organization, architectural construction, and utilitarian ceramic manufacture. The immigrant population was linked to room blocks and linear room arrangements. These units were constructed almost exclusively with coursed masonry walls and associated with high frequencies of unslipped corrugated ware. Griffin Wash Locus A, the largest of the enclaves, was built using woods from high elevations and the initial walls were constructed with shaped sandstone blocks, suggesting that the inhabitants possessed a developed masonry tradition that was nonlocal in origin. Intrusive attributes associated with the enclaves indicated that the immigrants originated from somewhere within the puebloan world to the north and east of the Tonto Basin. The first migrations were limited in scale and did not disrupt the local settlement system that had been developing in the area since the early Colonial period (about A.D. 750).

With this baseline established, I discuss the motivations and consequences of migration in the region and the possible origins of the immigrants. A model of interaction between immigrants and local inhabitants is based on the Roosevelt phase archaeological record and previous settlement history in the area, and I explore the possible role played by immigrants in the collapse of the Meddler Point community in the early fourteenth century.

ORIGINS

Thus far the origins of the early Classic period immigrants have only been assigned to the broad geographic region defined by room block architecture, developed coursed masonry techniques, and textured ceramics. This region covers much of northern Arizona and western New Mexico, including the Anasazi, Mogollon, and Sinagua culture areas as they have been traditionally defined. Although differences certainly existed among groups within this vast region as reflected in domestic spatial organization (Bernadini 1998; Potter 1998), technological traditions (Futrell 1998), and iconography (Graves and Eckert 1998), it is a considerably more subtle exercise to pinpoint the homelands of immigrant groups within the puebloan world than to establish their presence among Hohokam-related groups in the Tonto Basin.

The migration process itself greatly compounds the problem of specifying immigrant origins. As discussed in Chapter 1, the discrete nature of migrant units, typically households or small groups of households in the Southwest, and point-to-point movements inevitably lead to a mixing of populations in large migration processes. A variety of outcomes is possible in each destination area targeted by migrant households, including displacement of one group by another, co-residence between local and various migrant groups, ethnogenesis, and various combinations of each. In large migration processes, these outcomes may vary from region to region and through time within the same region, resulting in an extremely complicated social map.

In the Southwest, the late thirteenth century A.D. was an interval of widespread population movement within the puebloan world, generating culturally diverse settlements and communities throughout much of the region (Adams 1991, 1996; Crown 1994; Mills 1998; Reid and others 1996). Further complicating the issue, population mixing occurred to such an extent that several archaeologists have posited that previously distinct traditions converged and new ethnic groups were formed (Crown 1998: 298; Reid 1997: 635). The Tonto Basin and other riverine settings in central and southeastern Arizona were near the end points of long routes followed by migrants. By the time immigrant groups reached the Tonto Basin, forming and reforming along the way, they may have been composed of individuals and households with diverse origins, coming from areas as near as the Sierra Ancha and as far away as the Colorado Plateau.

Although the extent of population mixing in large migration processes complicates the task of determining origins, bioarchaeological analyses can aid the archaeologist in accomplishing this goal. Relevant analyses include dental morphological trait studies (Turner 1998), DNA analysis, and bone isotope analysis (Ezzo 1991). A substantial skeletal population was recovered from early Classic sites in the eastern Tonto Basin during the course of the Roosevelt Platform Mound study (Regan and Turner 1997; Turner and others 1994) conducted by Arizona State University. Early Classic burial areas were not investigated by Desert Archaeology at sites in the Roosevelt Community Development study, including Griffin Wash. Hence the burial population from the eastern basin was obtained largely from settlements south of the Salt River, in ASU's Livingston and Schoolhouse Point Mesa project areas. An analysis of genetic-related dental traits within this population yielded results that not only lend support to early Classic migration into the eastern Tonto Basin, but also to substantial mixing between local and various immigrant groups with diverse origins (Rice 1998: 232-233; Turner 1998).

Specifically, the dental analysis indicates that epigenetic change in the eastern Tonto Basin population occurred over such a brief interval that gene flow as a result of migration is the most likely explanation for this change (Turner 1998: 159–160). Univariate comparisons with regional or site-specific skeleton populations outside the Tonto Basin suggest substantial contributions to the eastern Tonto Basin gene pool from Classic period Hohokam, Sinagua, Western Anasazi, and Mimbres populations, with the closest affinity to Sinaguan groups (Rice 1998, Fig. 11.1; Turner 1998: 160). Contributions from Mogollon populations such as those at Grasshopper and Point of Pines are relatively low.

The large majority of individuals from the eastern Tonto Basin used in this study were recovered from compounds that reflect local domestic spatial organization (Turner 1998, Table 8.17). Only three burials from suspected enclaves, two from Saguaro Muerto and one from site AZ U:8:454 (ASM) on Schoolhouse Point Mesa, had dentitions sufficiently intact to be used in this analysis. Considering the level of mixing of populations within compounds, the inhabitants of room block enclaves can be expected to have had considerably stronger genetic contributions from puebloan groups. However, which group had the highest overall contribution and the extent of variability between enclave populations are intriguing questions that remain unanswered.

Regardless of the specific origins within the puebloan world of the immigrant population and the physical distance traveled, the boundary traversed by migrant households entering the Tonto Basin was a significant one. Although this "material culture" boundary should be viewed more as a fuzzy zone than as a distinct line, it nonetheless demarcated two fundamentally different social groups that have been defined in Southwestern archaeology as 'Hohokam' and 'ancestral puebloan'. We can only speculate on the internal cohesion of these populations and their conceptions of each other, but we are on firmer ground in stating that basic differences existed in their life ways as reflected in the manner in which they made pottery, built houses, organized domestic space, and met their subsistence needs. These two life ways came together in the Tonto Basin during the early Classic period.

MOTIVATION

As discussed in Chapter 1, migration is a risky undertaking, particularly in traditional agrarian societies where transport is pedestrian. Migration will occur only if conditions elsewhere are more beneficial or local conditions have deteriorated to such an extent as to outweigh this risk. Prospective migrant groups typically conduct cost-benefit analyses in deciding whether to stay put or resettle, weighing the advantages and disadvantages of remaining in their current settlement area versus those associated with potential target destinations (Anthony 1990). Motivations for migration can be divided into pushes from current settlement areas and pulls into target destinations (Anthony 1990: 899). Push and pull factors include both environmental and social variables.

Identifying environmental pushes and pulls in the northern Southwest during the late thirteenth century is not a difficult task. One particularly strong push for groups inhabiting nonriverine areas on the Colorado Plateau during the late thirteenth century, the interval of the so-called Great Drought, was increased variability in the precipitation regime and general environmental deterioration (Dean 1996: 39). These conditions triggered movements from rain-dependent areas into valleys and basins with perennial sources of water (Adams 1996: 54; Dean 1996; Fish and Fish 1993: 101; Varien and others 1996: 104–106). Similar movements may have been taking place in high-elevation settings below the Mogollon Rim during this interval and possibly earlier (Clark and others 2000; Redman 1993).

The Tonto Basin can be considered one potential target destination for migrants from these areas, because it had an ample water supply and abundant agricultural land. Indeed, considering environmental factors only, it would be difficult to explain why immigrants from higher elevations would not have entered the basin, given its proximity to the puebloan world.

Social factors must also be considered in pushes and pulls. Possible social pushes out of previous settlements include factionalism, interfamilial feuds, and external threats (Whiteley 1988; Wilcox and Haas 1994). Social pushes may be amplified in the face of deteriorating environmental conditions (Herr and Clark 1997; Stanislawski 1973; Varien and others 1996: 104–106). Migration itself may be considered a social push as immigrants can displace local groups who otherwise would not have moved. In large migration processes, the 'snowball' effect of serial displacement can cause demographic upheaval at a scale well beyond that attributable solely to environmental variables.

A more difficult question is how immigrant groups with high elevation origins managed to penetrate into river valleys such as the Tonto Basin. In the arid and semiarid Southwest, these settings were optimal settlement zones throughout the prehistoric sequence and many were inhabited by substantial populations that were well established by the thirteenth century (Dean and others 1994; Doelle 1995, Fig. 7.8). Estimates for the Tonto Basin yield a resident population of 2,500 to 3,000 by the Roosevelt phase. In the eastern Tonto Basin, continuous settlement can be traced back from the Roosevelt phase for nearly five hundred years. However, the inhabitants of the basin were thinly spread throughout the basin in a dispersed settlement pattern of small villages, hamlets, and farmsteads. Roosevelt phase population density in the basin area (about 600 square kilometers, or 232 square miles) would have averaged only between 4 and 5 persons per square kilometer, well below the carrying capacity of the land if the floodplain was being intensively irrigated (Craig 1995b). In addition, the dispersed settlement system implies a weak or decentralized political organization that would have had difficulty mobilizing the entire population in response to all but the most serious of external threats (Rice 2000). With this loose organization and the limited scale of the first migration events, small groups of newcomers might have infiltrated the basin without triggering a coordinated response.

Previous social and economic ties with indigenous populations also factored into the selection of specific target destinations by puebloan migrants. The initial links between local groups and prospective immigrants are often provided by long-distance exchange prior to migration (Anthony 1990). Migrants originating from or near settlements that produce valued exchange goods can gain acceptance into new communities if they main-tain relations with folk "back home and access to these goods" (Adams and others 1993; Graves 1982; Triadan 1997). As discussed in Chapter 3, Hohokam buff wares were replaced by Cibola White Ware in the eastern Tonto Basin decorated ceramic assemblage by the late Sedentary period (about A.D. 1100; Heidke 1995: 17). These decorated wares were imported from sources to the north and east of the basin in the directions from which migrants subsequently did enter the basin. This reorientation of exchange contacts from south to northeast may well have paved the way for the entry of puebloan households into the Meddler Point community during the Roosevelt phase by establishing economic and social contacts at a distance.

Similar to many communities occupying river valleys in southern and central Arizona, the subsistence economy of the eastern Tonto Basin was probably focused on irrigation agriculture by the late thirteenth century (Craig 1995b). A model of subsistence in the eastern Tonto Basin during the Classic period shows that population size rather than land and water may have been the limiting variable in maximizing the irrigation agriculture potential of the area (Craig 1995b: 242). If the local population was hard pressed to expand and maintain canal systems because of insufficient manpower, migrant households may have been allowed into the community as an exploitable source of labor.

A final pull factor pertains specifically to the large immigrant enclave on the ridges above Griffin Wash. Available evidence indicates that several relatively autonomous irrigation communities had emerged in the Tonto Basin by the early Classic period, including the one reported in this case study (see Chapter 3; Elson, Gregory, Stark 1995: 466–470). Competition among these communities for prime agricultural land in the floodplain and for other resources probably climaxed during this interval when the population of the basin crested (Doelle 1995, Fig. 7.3; Rice and Oliver 1998: 103–104). Heightened tension within the basin may have led several communities to increase their numbers by accepting immigrants, hence enhancing their power by weight of numbers. In addition, immigrants may have been allowed to settle on community peripheries where they served as buffer populations (Gregory 1995b: 182). The nearest neighbor of the Meddler Point community was the Armer Ranch community, located approximately 3 km (1.9 miles) west of Griffin Wash (see Fig. 3.2). Armer Ranch contained perhaps the largest early Classic village in the lower Tonto Basin. The Griffin Wash enclave was ideally positioned to serve as a buffer against Armer Ranch, and this may

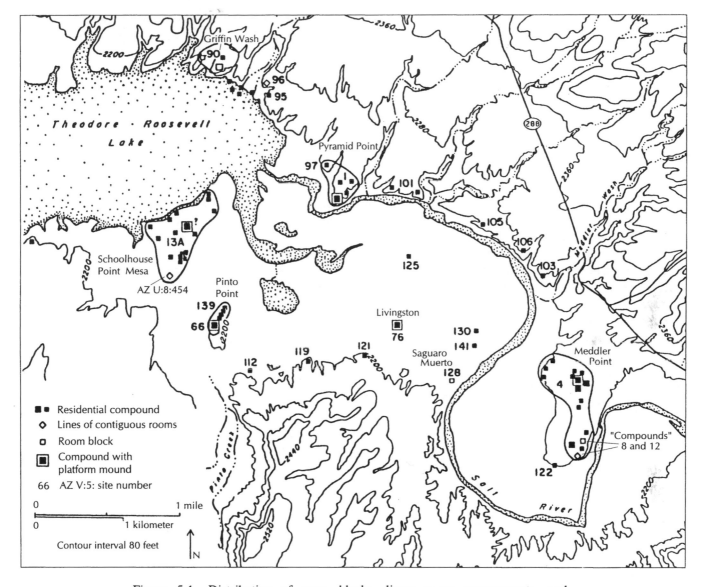

Figure 5.1. Distribution of room blocks, linear room arrangements, and compounds in the Meddler Point community (adapted from Clark 1997, Fig. 4.2)

explain why such a large enclave was allowed to form there.

MODELING INTERACTION BETWEEN IMMIGRANTS AND LOCAL RESIDENTS

Based on the number of room blocks and linear room arrangements, only 7 of the 51 (14%) residential units within the Meddler Point community were immigrant enclaves. However, these units contained an average of 16.5 rooms, a number considerably larger than the average 3.8 rooms per compound. Thus, the immigrants

may have comprised as much as 25 percent of the total Roosevelt phase population (Doelle 1995: 210–213). This figure indicates that the level of migration was limited, but not insignificant. The distribution of the room blocks and linear room arrangements with respect to compounds yields a highly informative pattern (Fig. 5.1). Not only was the early Classic community dominated by compounds, but room blocks and linear room arrangements were constructed only on the margins of the local settlement system. The enclaves were in locations that exhibited only limited occupation prior to the early Classic period, including the southern edge of Meddler Point ("Compounds" 8 and 12), the area west of Meddler Point on the opposite bank of the Salt River (Saguaro Muerto), the southern periphery of School-house Point Mesa (AZ U:8:454), and the ridges over-looking Griffin Wash on the northwest margin of the Meddler Point community. This settlement pattern pro-vides additional support for the limited scale of pueb-loan migration during the Roosevelt phase and indicates that migrant groups did not disrupt the extant commu-nity organization during this interval.

At least a segment of the migrant population re-mained a conspicuous minority in the eastern basin throughout the Roosevelt phase, inhabiting discrete resi-dential units and, in the case of Griffin Wash, entire settlements. These enclaves can be distinguished from local residences from initial construction to final aban-donment. However, the association of immigrants with room blocks and linear room arrangements and local residents with compounds should not be considered mutually exclusive. It is possible that a significant mix-ing of locals and immigrants occurred within residential units in the wake of migration. Such mixing, either as the result of intermarriage or assimilation, is supported by the analysis of dental morphological traits in burial populations recovered primarily from compounds, as discussed above (Rice 1998: 232–233; Turner 1998). Undoubtedly locals and immigrants mixed to a much greater degree than we can discern from archaeological evidence and only groups of the immigrant population that remained segregated throughout the Roosevelt phase are visible in the early Classic archaeological record. These groups are the focus of the following discussion.

Assumptions from Settlement Pattern and Settlement History

Several assumptions about interaction between immi-grants and locals can be drawn with reasonable confi-dence from the Roosevelt phase settlement pattern and our extensive knowledge of previous settlement history (Gregory 1995b). First, each immigrant enclave should be considered separately in terms of the character of its interaction with the local community. "Compounds" 8 and 12 at the southern end of Meddler Point and site AZ U:8:454 on the southern edge of Schoolhouse Point Mesa were relatively small enclaves that were located on the peripheries of local villages. It is likely that these enclaves were closely integrated into the larger settle-ments and economically dependent on them. Saguaro Muerto was a medium-sized enclave situated on the opposite bank of the Salt River across from Meddler

Point, in an area that also contained several dispersed compound farmsteads. Although the inhabitants of this room block may have been included in the Meddler Point community, the location of the settlement sug-gests its inhabitants were not as closely attached to a village as the smaller enclaves and may have had more autonomy. Finally, the large enclaves (Locus A and Locus C) on the ridges overlooking Griffin Wash ri-valed local villages in size and were farther away from the principal settlements in the local community than the other enclaves. Both size and separation suggest that the inhabitants of these two room blocks were more autonomous and less integrated into the commu-nity than the other smaller enclaves. Rapid growth of settlement in the Griffin Wash area indicates that the initial settlers were able to attract immigrant house-holds throughout the Roosevelt phase and the local com-munity did not or could not limit the rate of immigra-tion into this area.

A second assumption is based on the ideal location of Meddler Point for canal irrigation (Gregory 1995b) and the likelihood that the initial settlers at Meddler Point migrated from the Phoenix Basin or middle Gila River valley during the Colonial period (see Chapter 3). Considering this evidence and the continous sequence of occupation through the late pre-Classic period at Med-dler Point, a developed canal network probably existed in the eastern Tonto Basin by the Roosevelt phase. The level of Roosevelt Lake and minimal effort expended to date investigating the floodplain restrict our knowledge of this and other irrigation systems in the Tonto Basin. Two prehistoric canals have been identified along the south bank of the present Salt River channel near site AZ V:5:125, an early Classic compound (Waters 1998: 32). These canals were within the agricultural heartland of the Meddler Point community and it is likely that other canals were also present.

Assuming the existence of a mature canal system by the Roosevelt phase and the gradual development of the local community along internal lines for approximately 500 years prior to the arrival of the initial immigrants, a well-established system of land tenure was probably in place with respect to ownership and use of the most productive agricultural territory in the floodplain. In ethnographic accounts of traditional irrigation commu-nities, land is privately owned by participating house-holds (Mabry 1998), but canals and the water that flows in them are considered communal property and are managed by community institutions. Although these in-stitutions can be organized along consensual lines and do not require hierarchical structures, irrigation communities are usually insular and do not readily accept outsiders as partners in the subsistence economy. The location of immigrant enclaves on the margins of the Meddler Point community indicates that the extant land tenure system and community organization survived intact throughout the early Classic period. The newcomers were presumably from high-elevation settings and unfamiliar with intensive irrigation practices. Thus, the immigrants were at a marked disadvantage compared with local groups in terms of access to agricultural land and expertise with the local subsistence economy. These assumptions guide the following discussion.

Productive Specialization and Other Economic Relations

In lieu of access to optimal agricultural land, portions of the immigrant population may have pursued alternative strategies to obtain subsistence goods. The inhabitants of the small enclaves and perhaps Saguaro Muerto, which were more closely attached to the local community, may have been able to meet at least part of their subsistence needs by providing labor in the fields in exchange for a share of the harvest. As mentioned above and discussed by Craig (1995b: 242), available labor was probably the limiting variable in expanding canal systems during the Roosevelt phase. If local irrigation systems were being expanded and intensified during the late thirteenth century, the interval of the so-called Great Drought, then small groups of migrants may have been welcome additions to the local labor force. Increased interaction between locals and immigrants in the fields may have fostered close integrative ties between these groups.

The greater autonomy of the Griffin Wash enclave that allowed the settlement to grow unchecked may also have had several economic drawbacks for the inhabitants. More independence may have translated into less interaction with local groups, affording fewer opportunities for the immigrants to participate directly in the local subsistence economy. Hence, the labor-for-food arrangement potentially available to smaller enclaves may not have been a viable option for the Griffin Wash migrants. Instead, households settling in this area may have been forced to exploit less productive lands above the floodplain.

Use of marginal lands by the inhabitants of Griffin Wash Locus A is indicated by the archaeobotanical assemblage recovered from the site. There was a 100 percent ubiquity of agave remains in analyzed flotation samples from Area I (see Fig. 4.21). Agave was prob-

ably cultivated on the terraces overlooking the Salt River floodplain in areas not suitable for maize agriculture. Although agave utilization peaked throughout the eastern basin during the early Classic period, the ubiquity of agave at Area I is not matched by other investigated settlements in the area. In addition, the overall agave ubiquity for Griffin Wash Locus A is considerably higher than for other sites in the RCD project area (Elson and others 1994: 259).

Griffin Wash Locus A also had the highest maize pollen counts in the RCD project area and some of the highest counts recorded for sites in southern and central Arizona (Elson, S. Fish, and others 1995: 260). Although at first glance these counts may seem to indicate ample access to this vital subsistence resource and by extension to land in the Salt River floodplain, more careful consideration of the evidence points to other explanations. The high pollen counts suggest that unshelled maize ears with tassels still attached were regularly stored within rooms (Elson, S. Fish, and others 1995: 260). Significantly lower maize pollen counts associated with compounds indicate different storage practices by local groups that involved the shelling and detasseling of maize ears. Thus, high pollen counts at Griffin Wash Locus A cannot simply be equated with unlimited access. Indeed, intensive maize storage may suggest the opposite conclusion, that the residents were concerned with their maize supply to the extent that they created a reserve in anticipation of intervals when their access to this staple was restricted.

If the immigrants at Griffin Wash Locus A were unable to meet all their subsistence requirements by the direct procurement of resources, they may have produced nonsubsistence goods that could be traded to local groups for food. As ethnographic case studies document (Arnold 1975; Rice 1981; Sanders 1956), groups disenfranchised from agricultural land often turn to craft production on at least a part-time basis as a means to meet their subsistence requirements. In the eastern Tonto Basin, crafts that may have been commodities include ceramics and textiles.

Salado Red (Corrugated) Ware

As discussed in Chapter 4, relatively large quantities of textured wares appear in Tonto Basin ceramic assemblages during the early Classic period. These wares were apparently produced using a coil-and-scrape method, a common technique employed by puebloan potters north and east of the Tonto Basin. Within the eastern Tonto Basin, unslipped corrugated ware or Tonto Cor-

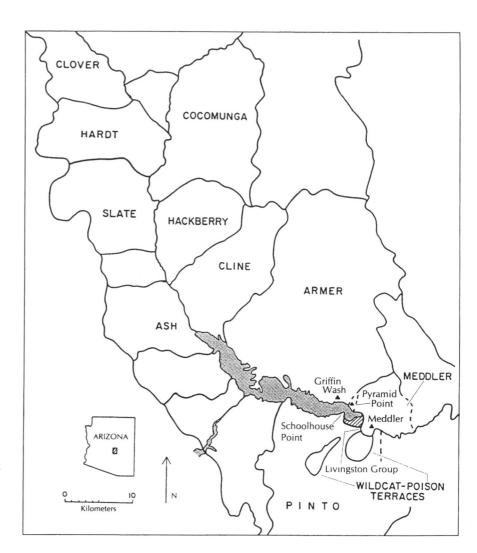

Figure 5.2. Locations of selected petrofacies in the Tonto Basin (adapted from Stark and Heidke 1995, Fig. 16.2).

rugated comprised roughly 10 percent of the early Classic ceramic assemblage (Heidke 1995: 14–16; Simon 1994a: 637; Simon 1997: 304). Tonto Corrugated Ware has an extremely uneven distribution among investigated sites and was determined to be associated largely with room block and linear room arrangements. This distribution was presented as corroborating evidence that these units were occupied by puebloan immigrants.

Salado Red (Corrugated) Ware, hereafter Salado Red Ware, is essentially a more finely made version of Tonto Corrugated, with smaller coils (Simon 1994a: 638) and a hematite-based red slip. Similarities in manufacture between the unslipped and slipped textured wares raise the possibility that Salado Red Ware was also produced by puebloan immigrants entering the region during the Roosevelt phase.

Several lines of evidence suggest that the inhabitants of Griffin Wash specialized in the production of Salado

Red Ware for trade (Stark and Heidke 1995: 386–389). Extensive petrographic studies indicate that Salado Red Ware was produced almost exclusively with diabase-rich sand temper that was collected from washes draining the Sierra Ancha to the north of the Salt River (Simon and others 1998: 109, 116). More specifically, the temper sources for Salado Red Ware are located within the large Armer and Cline petrofacies (Fig. 5.2; Miksa and Heidke 1995, Fig. 9.22). Unfortunately, the two petrofacies encompass much of the northern portion of the lower basin, including the Cline Terrace and Armer Ranch communities and a number of upland settlements. However, ceramic paste comparisons and variability in the proportion of diabase in the utilized sand temper indicate that Salado Red Ware was produced in increasing frequency within communities near the basin floor during the Classic period (Simon and others 1998: 116). Griffin Wash was the only settlement along the river in the eastern basin that lies within the Armer-Cline petrofacies and hence the only potential producer of Salado Red Ware in the Meddler Point community. Evidence for ceramic production at Griffin Wash is suggested by the high density of polishing stones recovered from Griffin Wash Locus B, particulary from one room (Swartz and Randolph 1994b: 385–386). Locus B, situated close to the Locus A room block, was an atypical unit that was "eclectically" constructed and many of the investigated rooms lacked hearths (see Fig. 4.8). The excavators concluded that this unit may have served one or more specialized, nonresidential functions for the inhabitants of Locus A (Swartz and Randolph 1994b: 413). One of the activities that occurred at Locus B may have been ceramic production. Given the concentration of textured wares at Griffin Wash, both Tonto Corrugated and Salado Red Ware may have been produced there. Unfortunately, only a portion of Locus B was investigated and other evidence for ceramic production is lacking.

In an analysis similar to that conducted for Tonto Corrugated (see Chapter 4), the relative percentages of Salado Red Ware were calculated with respect to red ware for each Roosevelt phase residential unit in the eastern Tonto Basin (Table 5.1). Only settlements with recovered assemblages of 200 utilitarian sherds or more were considered. Red ware is also largely restricted to Classic period contexts, allowing us to compare relatively contemporaneous assemblages. The relative percentages of Salado Red Ware and red ware from investigated Roosevelt phase settlements are depicted in Figure 5.3. Comparison of this graph with Figure 4.24 indicates that Salado Red Ware is more evenly distributed between room blocks and compounds than is Tonto Corrugated Ware. The most dramatic difference in the distribution of Salado Red Ware is between project areas north (RCD) and south (Livingston and Schoolhouse Point Mesa) of the Salt River. Most settlements in the RCD project area, including Griffin Wash, have relative percentages of Salado Red Ware two to three times those obtained from most of the settlements south of the river. Only three sites south of the Salt River have proportions of Salado Red Ware comparable to those north of the river: the Saguaro Muerto enclave, a compound (AZ V:5:121) in the Livingston project area, and a compound on Schoolhouse Point Mesa (V:5:138). The high figure for Saguaro Muerto is largely the result of the small quantity of red ware recovered from this site (Table 5.1). Site AZ V:5:138 is situated on the northern edge of Schoolhouse Point Mesa, directly across the river from Griffin Wash and may have had close exchange ties with the producing enclave.

Table 5.1. Percentages of Red Ware and Salado Red (Corrugated) Ware in Early Classic Period Sites in the Eastern Tonto Basin

Utilitarian wares include red ware (smudged and unsmudged), plain ware (smudged and unsmudged), and unpainted corrugated (slipped and unslipped) except for fine corrugated.

Project Area ASM Site No. (Site Name)	Red Ware %	Salado Red Corrugated %	Utilitarian Assemblage Sample Size
RCD Project Area			
AZ V:5:1			
(Pyramid Point)	23	25	3,557
AZ V:5:4			
(Meddler Point)*			
Early Classic period			
components only	29	34	N/A
AZ V:5:90			
(Griffin Wash)	*15*	*24*	*18,270*
Locus A	*15*	*23*	*11,835*
Locus B	14	26	5,395
Locus C	*11*	*32*	*251*
AZ V:5:106			
(Porcupine)	21	22	1,889
AZ V:5:110	19	2	277
Livingston Project Area			
AZ V:5:112			
(Sand Dune)	15	6	13,727
AZ V:5:119	24	3	3,680
AZ V:5:121	17	16	3,566
AZ V:5:128			
(Saguaro Muerto)	*4*	*5*	*14,723*
AZ V:5:139	31	7	8,199
AZ V:5:141	65	11	302
Schoolhouse Point Mesa			
Project Area			
AZ U:8:25*	28	3	24,253
AZ U:8:291	34	16	215
AZ U:8:450	25	8	24,659
AZ U:8:451	4	1	2,302
AZ U:8:452	29	2	490
AZ U:8:453	49	0	2,849
AZ U:8:454	*20*	*5*	*6,591*
AZ U:8:456 and			
AZ U:8:457	29	4	3,248
AZ U:8:458*	31	1	10,272
AZ V:5:137	26	13	6,696
AZ V:5:138	21	23	3,408

NOTE: **Bold** italic entries indicate room blocks and linear room arrangements. Only samples with more than 200 sherds are included.

* Substantial pre-Classic period component present.

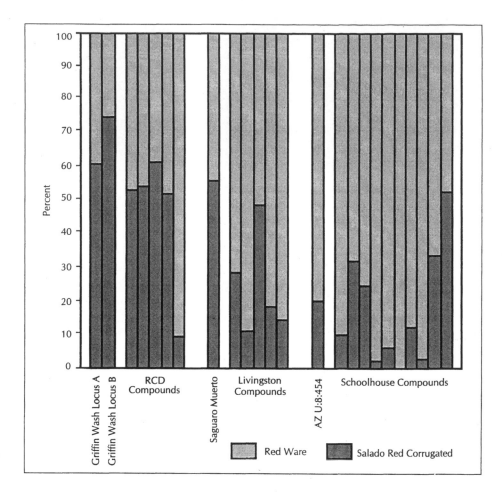

Figure 5.3. Percentages of Salado Red Corrugated Ware and red ware in ceramic assemblages from early Classic period sites in the eastern Tonto Basin.

This analysis indicates that there were only slight differences in the distribution of Salado Red Ware between compounds and room block settlements along the same side of the Salt River. If Salado Red Ware was produced largely by immigrant groups, this distribution suggests that this ware was traded to local groups on a regular basis. Salado Red Ware vessel forms are largely bowls and small jars that would have been easily transportable.

Although Salado Red Ware comprised only 8 percent of the early Classic ceramic assemblage in the eastern Tonto Basin (Heidke 1995: 14–16; Simon 1994a: 637; 1997: 304), it represented more than 20 percent of the early Classic assemblage from intensively investigated sites north of the Salt River (Table 5.1). This reflects a particularly intense level of exchange between the producers of this ware (possibly at Griffin Wash) and the local settlements at Pyramid Point and Meddler Point. With the exception of two compounds, considerably less exchange between the producers of Salado Red Ware and settlements on the south bank of the Salt River was indicated. The proximity to Griffin Wash of one of the compounds (AZ V:5:138) on the south bank that had a relatively high percentage of Salado Red Ware lends additional support to the hypothesis that Griffin Wash was a production area. The differential distibution of Salado Red Ware on each side of the Salt River supports the idea proposed by Elson (1998: 93–100) that there was an internal community boundary, demarcated by the river, between descent groups at Meddler Point and Pinto Point–Schoolhouse Point Mesa.

In summary, Salado Red Ware was an important component of early Classic ceramic assemblages throughout the lower Tonto Basin and was probably produced in multiple locations within the Armer and Cline petrofacies by puebloan immigrants entering the region during the Roosevelt phase. Available evidence points to Griffin Wash as one production source. Although we have little evidence of what products local groups exchanged with immigrants in return for these vessels, the above assumptions with respect to settlement pattern and land ownership underscore subsistence resources as the likely commodities.

Textiles

The puebloan immigrants may have also exchanged textiles with local groups for subsistence goods. The well-known Tonto Shirt, recovered from the Tonto Cliff Dwellings, attests to the high quality of Classic period textiles in the basin (Teague 1998: 80–81). The shirt appears to have been produced on a stationary three-bar frame, a kind of loom associated with puebloan textile manufacture (Teague 1998: 116). In the Southwest, the widespread exchange of textiles has been documented among the historic pueblos and between the pueblos and early European traders, including exchange for subsistence goods (Teague 1998: 162–164, 166). However, it is unclear how far this exchange can be projected back into the prehistoric past and little archaeological evidence exists for prehistoric textile trade in the Southwest (Teague 1998: 171–173). Instead, more evidence exists for the exchange of raw materials such as cotton.

Griffin Wash Locus A had by far the highest ubiquity value for cotton remains (41%) in the eastern Tonto Basin (Elson, S. Fish, and others 1995: 242). The next highest values, ranging from 21 percent to 27 percent, were obtained from platform mound settlements (Rice 1998: 238). Although cotton was undoubtedly a floodplain crop, the inhabitants of Griffin Wash Locus A had ample access to this raw material. The widespread occurrence of cotton at Griffin Wash Locus A does not necessarily indicate textile production, but there was extensive storage of this raw material within the settlement.

As the largest and most autonomous of the immigrant enclaves, Griffin Wash Locus A was perhaps confronted with the greatest challenges. To help meet subsistence requirements, the inhabitants of this enclave may have been forced to bring marginal agricultural land under cultivation. They may have produced commodities that could be exchanged to local groups for food, such as Salado Red Ware and textiles. These producers were probably independent households or small groups of households that manufactured goods within or near Griffin Wash Locus A on a part-time basis to supplement their subsistence needs.

PLATFORM MOUNDS AND INTEGRATION

The proposed model for economic interaction outlined above between immigrants and local residents is based on cooperation between the two groups. Such an arrangement was not symmetrical by any means, but heavily favored local groups who were in the majority and who had an established settlement history in the area. The indigenous groups controlled much of the best farm land and the migrant minority had to make do with marginal lands. The migrants may have attempted to obtain agricultural surpluses through trade or labor. Such an arrangement would have placed immigrants at a distinct disadvantage in the local economy, particularly during years with agricultural shortfalls. In addition to possible competition between local groups (Elson 1998: 93–100), the asymmetry of migrant-local interaction and a steady trickle of immigrants entering the basin during the Roosevelt phase were potential sources of instability to existing community organization.

These destabilizing forces may have pushed local organizational structures to or beyond the breaking point near the end of the thirteenth century. In the absence of established kinship links between immigrants and local groups, new integrative institutions may have been required that were not based on descent or familial ties. In this light, the timing of platform mound construction in the region with migration during the late thirteenth century suggests a connection between these two events. One of the functions of the mound facilities may have been to integrate neighboring groups from diverse cultural backgrounds.

Platform Mounds in the Eastern Tonto Basin

Four mounds were built within the eastern Tonto Basin during a twenty year interval, about A.D. 1280–1300 (Fig. 5.1; Craig and Clark 1994b; Doelle and others 1995; Elson 1998). This group represents the densest concentration of mounds within the entire basin. One mound was erected in the center of Meddler Point Locus A (Fig. 5.4), a mound (AZ V:5:76, Livingston) similar in construction and layout was built across the Salt River from the southern end of Meddler Point, another mound (AZ V:5:66) was built at Pinto Point, and a small towerlike mound was constructed at Pyramid Point (see Fig. 3.13). Each mound was investigated intensively during the course of the Roosevelt Dam projects. Details of mound layout and construction are discussed at length in the relevant descriptive volumes (Craig and Clark 1994a; Elson 1994; Jacobs 1994).

The Meddler Point platform mound is the most intensively investigated and securely dated of the group (Craig and Clark 1994a: 180), and it may have been the first mound constructed in the eastern basin (Fig. 5.4;

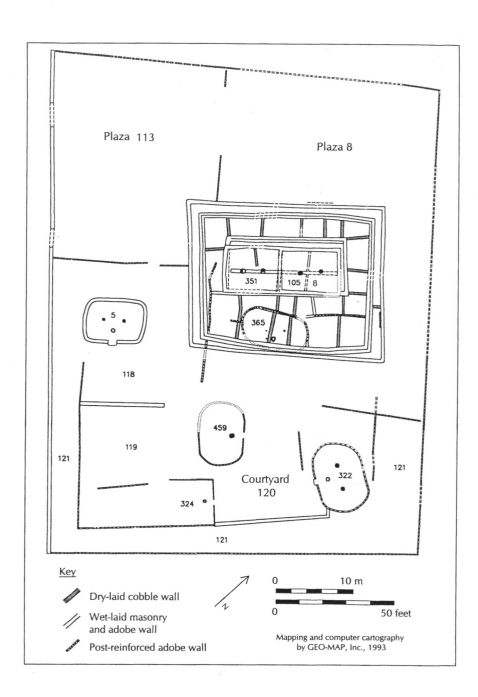

Figure 5.4. Meddler Point platform mound and associated Compound 1 (adapted from Craig and Clark 1994a, Fig. 7.39).

Elson 1998: 87–90). The platform mound was built to create an elevated surface for two contiguous rooms. Outer and inner retaining walls, an elaborate cell lattice of dry-laid cobble walls, and alternating layers of packed earth fill and cobbles in the core cells directly beneath the mound rooms indicated that the Meddler Point mound was built using a well-established technology. The complex design and engineering evident in the Meddler Point mound and the lack of developmental stages within the mound point to a technology that

was borrowed or derived from a source outside the eastern basin (Doelle and others 1995: 437–440).

Hohokam influence was evident in the early Classic component at Meddler Point Locus A in the continuation of pre-Classic marine shell networks (Vokes 1995) and cremation mortuary practices (Swartz and others 1995). The high degree of settlement continuity across the pit house to masonry-compound transition suggests that the early Classic residents were closely related to the earlier pre-Classic inhabitants. Thus, the likely source of mound building technology for the inhabitants of Meddler Point was the Phoenix Basin, where earlier platform mounds of comparable design are known and a continuous sequence of development can be traced back to smaller and less complex pre-Classic examples (Doyel 1974; Elson 1998: 8–10; Gregory 1987). Although the Meddler Point inhabitants probably used a Phoenix Basin template in building their mound, this monumental feature may have served integrative needs that were specific to the early Classic inhabitants of the eastern Tonto Basin (Craig and Clark 1994b; Elson 1998).

The Meddler Point platform mound was surrounded by a compound that contained several rooms exhibiting little evidence for domestic activities, with the exception of intramural hearths. Conspicuously absent were storage facilities of any form within the compound such as specialized storage rooms, slab-lined pits, and especially pedestaled granaries. One or more of these storage features were encountered in all of the intensively excavated residential units within the RCD project area dating to the Roosevelt phase. Early Classic settlements in ASU's Livingston and Schoolhouse Point project areas also had a high ubiquity for these features, particularly granaries (Jacobs 1994; Lindauer 1997). This trend culminated in the Gila phase with the construction of impressive storage room complexes within the Schoolhouse Point room block (Lindauer 1996). The complete absence of storage facilities within the Meddler Point mound compound suggests this facility served largely a nonresidential function. This mound and surrounding compound provided an ideal setting for rituals intended for large audiences with delineated areas for preparation, staging, and public viewing. Thus, the mound precinct probably was a locus for ceremonial activities that integrated the Meddler Point village and perhaps surrounding settlements.

A ceremonial and nonresidential function has also been argued for the Livingston (Pillar) platform mound located on the opposite bank of the Salt River, west of Meddler Point (Jacobs 1994: 112–113). The Livingston platform mound closely paralleled the Meddler Point mound in design and construction. Paramount among these similarities were two symmetrical rooms on top surrounded by a raised extramural surface (Jacobs 1994: 122, Fig. 5.11). This mound may have been built shortly after the Meddler mound, perhaps with the aid of the inhabitants of Meddler Point.

The Pinto Point platform mound, located between Schoolhouse Point Mesa and the Livingston (Pillar) mound, differed from the Meddler Point and Livingston mounds in having more rooms on top of the mound (nine) and within the compound (Jacobs 1994: 133). In general, there was more evidence for residential activity within the compound, including a ground floor room with several granary pedestals (Jacobs 1994: 207–213). However, similar to the Meddler Point and Livingston mounds, a nonresidential and ceremonial function has been inferred for the rooms on top of the mound (Elson 1998: 79). Unlike the Meddler Point and Livingston mounds, the Pinto Point mound was constructed acretionally in multiple episodes. Ceramics from the Pinto Point mound complex reveal a slightly later construction and occupation date than that for the Meddler Point or Livingston mounds (Elson 1998: 89–90).

The mound at Pyramid Point was a towerlike structure comprised of a single cell, atop which a single room had been constructed (Elson and others 1994: 279–295). It was encircled by adjoining compounds that restricted access to the mound and its surrounding precinct. The outer compounds may have been inhabited by groups that maintained the mound and organized ceremonies associated with it. Evidence for shell manufacture was recovered from one of the adjacent rooms.

There are several points of agreement among the various investigators in terms of the function of early Classic platform mounds in the Tonto Basin. Platform mounds were the loci of communal ceremonies and rituals that played an important integrative role during the Roosevelt phase. They were constructed in response to new organizational challenges that arose during the late thirteenth century.

Migrants and Mounds

The Roosevelt phase in the eastern Tonto Basin was an interval of dramatic change that can be attributed to a number of sources. In addition to external sources of change such as migration, a number of riverine communities, probably dependent on canal irrigation, had developed in the lower basin by this time (Craig 1995c; Elson and others 1995: 466–471). These communities may have laid claim to much of the optimal agricultural land in the area, straining relations among neighbors. In the absence of a central authority, internal fissioning may have occurred within communities as a result of heightened competition between descent groups (Elson 1998: 93–100) and within large settlements as a result of scalar stress (Craig and others 1998). Isolating the specific external or internal factor that was the primary impetus for platform mound construction is a difficult task, if indeed any one source is largely responsible. It is quite possible that platform mounds served multiple integrative functions.

Considering the numerous changes taking place during the Roosevelt phase, the coincidence of puebloan migration into the eastern basin with platform mound construction is not by itself a compelling argument for some connection between the two events. However, at least two lines of evidence hint at the direct involvement of immigrants in platform mound use: the distribution of White Mountain Red Ware among room blocks, compounds, and platform mounds and the use of high elevation woods in one of the rooms on top of the Meddler Point platform mound.

White Mountain Red Ware

The Roosevelt phase decorated assemblage in the eastern Tonto Basin was comprised largely of Cibola White Ware, Salado polychrome, and limited quantities of White Mountain Red Ware (Craig and Clark 1994a, Table 7.2; Elson 1994, Table 8.2; Elson and Randolph 1994, Table 5.1; Lindauer 1994b, Table 17.3; Simon 1997, Table 8.4; Swartz and Randolph 1994b, Table 9.1). Imported Cibola White Ware vessels that temporally overlap with the Roosevelt phase include Snowflake Black-on-white, Tularosa Black-on-white, Pinedale Black-on-white, and examples decorated in Kayenta and Little Colorado White Ware design styles. Unfortunately, some of these types remain either poorly dated or have wide temporal ranges that predate the Roosevelt phase. With the exception of Pinedale Black-on-white, use of Cibola White Ware as a temporal marker of the Roosevelt phase is problematic.

In the eastern basin, Salado polychrome was largely restricted to Pinto Polychrome and Pinto Black-on-red types that date to the late thirteenth and early fourteenth centuries (about A.D. 1250–1325). These two types included imported and locally produced examples (Lindauer 1994b: 625; Simon 1994b: 656–659). Vessels of later Salado polychrome types, Gila Polychrome and Tonto Polychrome, occurred in limited quantities in the eastern basin, with the exception of the Gila phase room block at Schoolhouse Point and selected contexts at Pinto Point. Because of the ubiquity of Pinto Polychrome and Pinto Black-on-red in the area, their relatively narrow temporal range, and the near-absence of later Salado polychrome from sites in the eastern basin, these two types are important diagnostics of Roosevelt phase site components.

White Mountain Red Ware ceramics recovered from Roosevelt phase contexts included St. Johns Black-on-red and St. Johns Polychrome, Pinedale Black-on-red and Pinedale Polychrome, Cedar Creek Polychrome, and Fourmile Polychrome (Heidke 1995, Table 6.1). All vessels were probably imported from source areas to the northeast and no evidence for local manufacture has been identified. The contexts from which St. Johns Polychrome and St. Johns Black-on-red (about A.D. 1175–1300) were recovered generally date to the Roosevelt phase, so these types were entering the basin relatively late in their temporal range. Cedar Creek Polychrome (around A.D. 1300–1350) and Fourmile Polychrome (A.D. 1325–1400) were also associated with Roosevelt phase components and were absent from contexts containing appreciable quantities of Gila Polychrome or Tonto Polychrome, indicating vessels of these types were being used in the basin relatively early in their temporal ranges. Thus, the White Mountain Red Ware assemblage in the Tonto Basin can be chronologically placed within a 75-year interval roughly contemporaneous with Pinto Black-on-red and Pinto Polychrome (about A.D. 1250–1325).

Similar to the use of red ware as a contemporaneous standard to measure relative proportions of Tonto Corrugated and Salado Red Ware in early Classic utilitarian assemblages, Pinto Black-on-red and Pinto Polychrome can be used to measure the relative proportions of White Mountain Red Ware in Roosevelt phase decorated ceramic assemblages. In an analysis by Stark (1995d, Table 6.1), counts of decorated ceramics were standardized with respect to counts of utilitarian ceramics from a careful selection of temporally unmixed Roosevelt phase contexts at Griffin Wash and Meddler Point. Standardized counts of Salado polychrome (Salado polychrome sherds divided by utilitarian sherds times 1000), were virtually identical (13.2) from Roosevelt phase contexts at both sites, suggesting relatively equal access to this ware by immigrant and local groups in the RCD project area. Roosevelt phase contexts at Meddler Point yielded less than half the standardized count of White Mountain Red Ware (5.9) than did similar contexts at Griffin Wash (13.5). Thus, differences in the relative proportions of White Mountain Red Ware and Salado polychrome at the two sites can be attributed to variability in the distribution of White Mountain Red Ware vessels.

Assuming this relationship existed for other sites in the eastern basin, relative percentages of White Mountain Red Ware and Salado polychrome were calculated for sites with decorated assemblages comprised of at least one hundred sherds from sites with Roosevelt phase components in the RCD, Livingston, and School-

Table 5.2. Percentages of Salado Polychrome and White Mountain Red Ware in Decorated Ceramic Assemblages Recovered from Early Classic Period Sites in the Eastern Tonto Basin

ASM site number, site name	Salado polychrome in early Classic decorated assemblages[1] %	White Mtn. Red Ware in early Classic decorated assemblages[2] %	Early Classic decorated assemblages, raw counts[3]
Roosevelt Community Development Project Area			
AZ V:5:90, Griffin Wash	10.6	10.8	1,981
AZ V:5:4, Meddler Point	9.5	4.2	2,504
AZ V:5:1, Pyramid Point	30.4	11.7	280
AZ V:5:106, Porcupine	10.9	9.5	137
Livingston Project area (Lindauer 1994b, Table 17.3)			
Platform Mound Compounds			
AZ V:5:76, Livingston	8.9	42.7	553
AZ V:5:66, Pinto Point[4]	13.3	16.9	1,579
AZ V:5:139 (compound on Pinto Point)[5]	5.9	9.6	899
Residential Compounds			
AZ V:5:112, Sand Dune site	23.5	13.5	871
AZ V:5:119	7.7	6.0	317
AZ V:5:121[6]	17.8	17.0	342
AZ V:5:130	21.9	7.2	360
Residential Room Blocks			
AZ V:5:128, Saguaro Muerto	19.1	22.9	388
Schoolhouse Point Mesa (Simon 1997, Table 8.4)			
Residential Compounds			
AZ V:5:137	15.8	5.9	424
AZ V:5:138	18.9	8.1	111
AZ U:8:25	11.6	3.2	888
AZ U:8:450	41.1	5.9	2,607
AZ U:8:456 and AZ U:8:457	9.2	7.0	228
AZ U:8:458	3.4	1.4	353

1. Salado polychrome types include Pinto Polychrome, Pinto Black-on-red, and limited quantites of Gila Polychrome and Gila Black-on-red.

2. White Mountain Red Ware types include St. Johns Polychrome and St. Johns Black-on-red, Pinedale Polychrome and Pinedale Black-on-red, Cedar Creek Polychrome, and limited quantities of Fourmile Polychrome.

3. In addition to White Mountain Red Ware and Salado polychrome, Early Classic period decorated ceramic assemblages include Cibola White Ware and limited quantities of Little Colorado White Ware. Only assemblages with sample sizes of more than 100 identified decorated sherds classified to the ware level are considered here.

4. Excludes from the Salado polychrome assemblage and raw counts 256 sherds of Gila Black-on-red, Gila Polychrome, and Tonto Polychrome that came from the late Classic occupation of the site.

5. Excludes from the Salado polychrome assemblage and raw counts 56 sherds of Gila Black-on-red, Gila Polychrome, and Tonto Polychrome that came from the late Classic occupation of the site.

6. Excludes from the Salado polychrome assemblage and raw counts 32 sherds of Gila Polychrome and Tonto Polychrome that came from the late Classic occupation of the site.

house Point Mesa project areas (Table 5.2). Hohokam Buff wares, relating to the presence of underlying pit house components, were excluded from these calculations. In assemblages where Gila Polychrome, Tonto Polychrome, or both composed at least 25 percent of the Salado polychrome recovered, counts of these late types were excluded from consideration because they denoted the presence of a significant Gila phase component (for example, site AZ V:5:121, Pinto Point platform mound, and site AZ V:5:139). Also excluded from this analysis were small samples from a number of tested compounds and several suspected immigrant enclaves (site AZ U:8:454, "Compounds" 8 and 12 at Meddler Point Locus B).

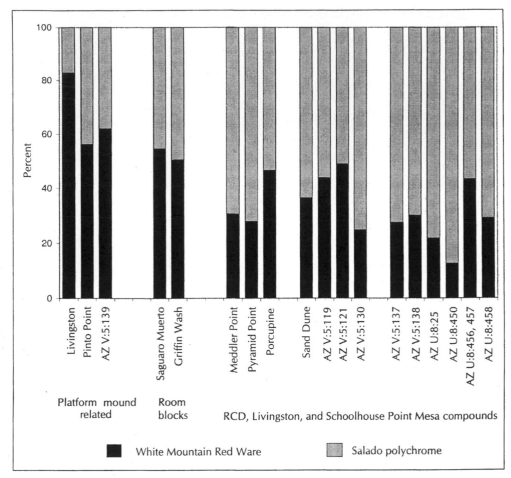

Figure 5.5. Percentages of Salado polychrome and White Mountain Red Ware in ceramic assemblages from early Classic period sites in the eastern Tonto Basin.

Figure 5.5 depicts relative proportions of the two wares recovered from platform mound precincts and from residential room blocks and compounds listed in Table 5.2. Among the residential units with samples of sufficient size, both the Griffin Wash and Saguaro Muerto room blocks yielded the highest relative percentages of White Mountain Red Ware in the eastern basin and were the only such units in the area from which more White Mountain Red Ware was recovered than early Salado polychrome. Generally, residential compounds had considerably lower relative percentages of White Mountain Red Ware. Notable exceptions included the Porcupine site (AZ V:5:106); an isolated compound in the RCD project area; site AZ V:5:121 in the Livingston project area; and sites AZ U:8:456 and 457 on Schoolhouse Point Mesa. The relative percentages of White Mountain Red Ware from these units approached the values from the two room blocks, although all three were less than 50 percent. Differences in the relative percentages of White Mountain Red Ware between compounds and room blocks were con-

siderably less dramatic than those observed for Tonto Corrugated Ware (compare Fig. 4.24 with Fig. 5.5). However, this analysis indicates that inhabitants of room blocks had somewhat greater access to White Mountain Red Ware vessels than did compound residents.

Other units associated with relatively high White Mountain Red Ware percentages included the Livingston (Pillar) platform mound precinct (AZ V:5:76), the Pinto Point platform mound precinct (V:5:66), and a series of small compounds that were adjacent to the Pinto Point mound (V:5:139). The location of the Meddler Point platform mound in the midst of a village made it difficult to isolate trash contexts that could be associated exclusively with mound use and it was not included in this analysis. The Pinto Point mound and associated compounds had White Mountain Red Ware values comparable to the two room blocks. The Livingston mound had four times more White Mountain Red Ware than Salado polychrome, far exceeding all other units. These results support the idea that White Mountain Red Ware was associated with ceremonial activities taking place within platform mound compounds.

With the relatively high percentages of White Mountain Red Ware associated with room blocks and at least two platform mound compounds, a link is proposed between immigrants inhabiting room blocks and the ceremonial activities that occurred within the mound compounds. Considering their proximity, a particularly strong connection is indicated between Saguaro Muerto and the isolated Livingston (Pillar) mound. To date, no evidence exists for local production of White Mountain Red Ware in the eastern Tonto Basin, although at least two production loci outside the basin are indicated, including one in the Pinedale-Snowflake area (Lindauer 1994b: 630, 633). As it is unlikely that potters producing these wares were entering the Tonto Basin region (in contrast to the Grasshopper area; Triadan 1997, 1998), differences between compounds and room blocks may be better explained by links between immigrant households in the eastern Tonto Basin and groups to the north and east who were producing these wares. Local groups may have obtained vessels down-the-line from immigrants (for similar views, see Adams and others 1993; Graves 1982).

High Elevation Woods

The two rooms constructed on top of the Meddler Point platform mound were associated with wood assemblages from different elevational zones. The northern room (Feature 105) contained woods from desert and foothill elevations, typical of the large majority of residential units in the eastern basin. However, the assemblage in the southern room (Feature 351) was almost exclusively comprised of high elevation woods, including Douglas-fir and white fir. These species presently grow only at elevations of more than 2,130 meters (7,000 feet; Elson, S. Fish, and others 1995: 259–260). Unfortunately, both mound rooms were heavily vandalized and Feature 351 was largely removed by a bulldozer that bladed through the mound in the 1960s.

With the exception of a charcoal fragment from a large oval pit room in Compound 7 at Meddler Point, fir species were only recovered in the eastern basin at Griffin Wash Locus A. As discussed in Chapter 4, Douglas fir was present in approximately 50 percent of the excavated rooms and white fir in 25 percent (Elson, S. Fish, and others 1995: 259–260). Although speculative, this link in wood use may mean that the inhabitants of Griffin Wash Locus A participated in ceremonies taking place within the Meddler Point platform

mound compound or even assisted in mound construction. The Griffin Wash connection is further supported by the relatively high proportion of Salado Red Ware at Meddler Point and settlements north of the Salt River. As discussed above, Salado Red Ware may have been produced by the inhabitants of Griffin Wash as an exchange commodity.

Alternatively, the dual organization of the Meddler platform mound and associated compound is mirrored in the division of the settlement at Meddler Point into two discrete loci (see Fig. 3.11). This parallel between site structure and layout of the platform mound compound suggests that space inside the mound precinct may have been partitioned between the two residential loci. If the northern and southern mound rooms were associated with the northern and southern loci respectively, then the room containing the high elevation wood assemblage could have been linked with the portion of the settlement that contained the two suspected immigrant enclaves ("Compounds" 8 and 12). These two units differed substantially from other residential compounds in the settlement with respect to wall construction and layout, and they closely resembled the early configurations of the Saguaro Muerto room block (see Fig. 4.20) and Griffin Wash Locus A (see Fig. 4.21). "Compounds" 8 and 12 were not intensively investigated and little evidence was recovered for wood use.

The Legitimizing Role of Platform Mounds

Presently, Roosevelt phase platform mounds in the eastern basin are considered to have been the loci of ceremonial activities that served a number of integrative functions (Craig and Clark 1994b; Doelle and others 1995; Elson 1998; Rice 1998: 235–237). Apparently, these platform mounds were not the private residences of elite groups and they were certainly not redistribution centers of economic resources. Many of the integrative functions associated with these mounds may have been internally focused, either alleviating scalar stress between households within a settlement (Craig and Clark 1994b) or decreasing social tension between settlements and descent groups within the community (Elson 1998).

The flurry of platform mound construction that occurred in the eastern basin shortly after the arrival of the first puebloan groups and the connections between ceramic and wood assemblages recovered from enclaves and several mounds support the idea that the migrants played some role in platform mound use and perhaps construction. In addition to serving local integrative requirements, several of the eastern basin mounds may have provided formalized settings in which local groups and newly arrived immigrants interacted. This interaction may have included exchange, feasting, social discourse, and participation in mound-related rituals. In the volatile social setting that followed migration, this interaction may have been vital in maintaining community cohesion. Integrative ceremonies occurring within mound precincts may have provided a substitute for the bonds of kinship and shared settlement history that were lacking between migrant and local households.

Economic interaction between migrants and local residents posed the greatest potential for inequality within the Meddler Point community. Local households owned the best land and were much more familiar with the local environment and prevailing subsistence economy than newly arrived migrants. But the arrival of migrants in increasing numbers during the Roosevelt phase potentially threatened the economic *status quo* that favored local households. In addition to playing an integrative role between immigrants and locals, platform mounds may have served to legitimate this asymmetrical arrangement.

The proposed model of economic relations between immigrants and local groups is based on the ownership of agricultural land in the floodplain by locals. Platform mounds would have been highly visible symbols on the landscape and ideal markers of land ownership. Association of platform mounds with local settlements and the fact that mound technology was probably borrowed from the Phoenix Basin suggest that Roosevelt phase mounds in the eastern basin were constructed under the supervision of local groups and ultimately controlled by them. Hence, immigrants would have been guests at platform mound activities hosted by local groups, and ceremonies and feasts conducted at platform mounds may have ideologically reinforced the fact that migrants were also guests within the community. In this light, integrative links between local and immigrant populations may have had a vertical dimension, with local control of mound facilities reifying local ownership of agricultural land. Economic inequality between local and immigrant groups was thus legitimized by the established history of the local population in the region, which was symbolized by platform mounds. Such attempts at legitimization may have been successful for only a short interval, because the Meddler Point community collapsed within a generation or two of initial mound construction.

COLLAPSE OF THE MEDDLER POINT COMMUNITY

Nearly all the early Classic settlements and platform mounds associated with the Meddler Point community, including Meddler Point itself, Pyramid Point, Griffin Wash Locus A, and Saguaro Muerto were abandoned in the opening decades of the fourteenth century A.D. Many of the settlements exhibited evidence of burning near the time of abandonment and several, including Griffin Wash Locus A, contained extensive floor assemblages. Available chronological evidence reveals that many of the units were abandoned within a relatively short time, probably within a decade and certainly within a generation. Most abandoned units exhibited little or no evidence of subsequent use. In the eastern basin, the succeeding Gila phase occupation, defined by the predominance of Gila Polychrome and Tonto Polychrome in the decorated ceramic assemblage, was largely restricted to the large room block or mound at Schoolhouse Point (Fig. 5.6; Lindauer 1996) and a few isolated contexts at Pinto Point (Jacobs 1994: 266). The Schoolhouse Point room block could not have accommodated the entire Roosevelt phase population in the eastern basin, suggesting that at least a segment of the population left the area in the early fourteenth century (Doelle 1995: 209–211).

The transformations taking place in the eastern basin between the Roosevelt phase and the Gila phase were so dramatic that terms such as "development" and "reorganization" do not accurately characterize their magnitude. In a few short years the dispersed community that had been developing in place for more than five hundred years *collapsed* and the focus of settlement shifted from Meddler Point to Schoolhouse Point Mesa. Tracing threads of continuity across this turbulent interval is difficult at best.

Who Lived at Schoolhouse Point?

An issue critical to our understanding of the Gila phase in the eastern basin is whether the main room block on Schoolhouse Point was inhabited by local groups who aggregated in response to some perceived threat or by puebloan groups that were part of a larger migration into the basin. A combination of both explanations is possible. Various researchers have expressed all three scenarios. Ciolek-Torrello (1997: 552) notes similarities between the artificially elevated rooms within the Schoolhouse Point room block and terraced pueblos

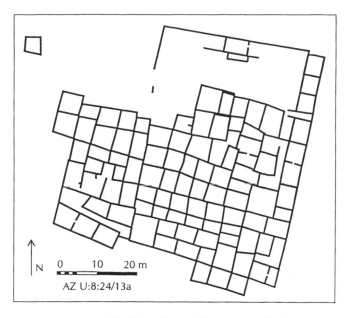

Figure 5.6. Schoolhouse Point room block (adapted from Lindauer 1996, Fig. 2.3).

in the White Mountains and Colorado Plateau. He states that the ascendancy of the immigrant tradition of room block architecture over that of local groups is a logical conclusion to draw from the puebloan layout of Schoolhouse Point, from evidence for puebloan migration during the Roosevelt phase, and from the dramatic changes in settlement pattern that occurred between the Roosevelt and Gila phases (Ciolek-Torrello 1997: 553). The excavator of the site adopts a different view (Lindauer 1996: 381), emphasizing similarities between the site and platform mounds that would link the settlement to local groups. Rice and his colleagues (1998: 70) take a central position, describing the Gila phase settlement at Schoolhouse Point as a "syncretic mound-village." This architectural form represents a melding of two earlier architectural traditions, one characterized by aggregated settlements with high elevation origins and one characterized by platform mound complexes associated primarily with riverine settings within the Tonto Basin (Rice and others 1998, Fig. 4.22). Combination of the two distinctive architectural traditions at Schoolhouse Point would seem to imply co-residence between immigrants from the mountains and local groups within one settlement.

An analysis of genetic-based dental traits from Gila phase burials associated with the Schoolhouse Point room block links the inhabitants with Classic period Hohokam populations in southern Arizona. This Gila phase population differs substantially from the more puebloan-

affiliated population of the Roosevelt phase in the eastern basin (Turner 1998: 160). However, Turner concludes that the direction of gene flow between desert floor Hohokam and Gila phase Tonto Basin populations cannot be established because of the paucity of Hohokam dentitions from the pre-Classic period. The inadequate sample is due to poor preservation of dental remains as a result of cremation burial practices. Thus, the results of this analysis are inconclusive with respect to the ultimate genetic affiliations of the Schoolhouse Point "mound" burial population.

Speculation on the Role of Immigrants

At this juncture, definitive statements as to what caused the collapse of the Meddler Point community in the early fourteenth century seem premature, if indeed this dramatic event can be attributed to one factor. Three potential sources of stress and conflict can be identified: (1) heightened tension within local settlements and between descent groups within the community (Craig and others 1998; Elson 1998), (2) competition between irrigation communities in the basin (Gregory 1995b; Rice and Oliver 1998: 103–104), and (3) conflict between immigrants and local groups at both levels.

Although the relative contributions of each potential source cannot be established, several issues concerning the possible role played by immigrants are worth mentioning. Migration should be considered a process or series of connected events that can occur over generations (Alvarez 1987: 133–138; Anthony 1990: 904). Once migrants have established a foothold within a region, it is usually to their advantage to encourage further immigration. In this regard, prior success in migration can act as a pull factor for subsequent movements (Dozier 1966; Lefferts 1977: 39; Stone 1996: 150–151). The addition of new migrants to an enclave often enhances the status of the initial immigrant households, since they are considered founding families by the newer arrivals. Hence, the status of the founding group is directly related to the size of the settlement. In a similar manner, continued immigration also enhances the power of the immigrant sector vis-à-vis local groups within the community, leading to a faster population increase among migrants than that generated by the natural birth rate of the locals. For this reason, it is typically in the best interest of local groups to limit the level of migration to some fraction of their population. As the organization of the Meddler Point community was increasingly challenged and perhaps overtaxed in the late thirteenth and early fourteenth centuries, local groups may have found it increasingly difficult to control immigration, particularly in the Griffin Wash area. Griffin Wash Locus C, which was built later (around A.D. 1300) but overlapped chronologically with Locus A (Swartz and Randolph 1994b: 412), may represent an unwelcome addition to the community, as indicated by the highly defensible location of the settlement (see Fig. 4.8).

Another consideration is the apparently burgeoning Roosevelt phase population in the piedmont and bajada zones that surrounded the riverine-oriented communities near the basin floor. Nearly 40 settlement clusters, each comprised of between 8 and 80 habitations, have been identified in the Superstition uplands, Mazatzal piedmont, and Sierra Ancha bajada encircling the basin, even though less than 50 percent of this vast area has been systematically surveyed (Germick and Crary 1992: 293). In addition to compounds, several large room blocks are included in this sample. Unfortunately, few of these sites have been intensively investigated. Much of the unsurveyed area is within the Sierra Ancha, a likely locale for immigrant settlements based on the position of this mountain range astride potential migration routes into the basin from the north and east.

Available evidence suggests only limited economic interaction occurred between groups residing near the basin floor and in upland settings during the Roosevelt phase (Rice and Oliver 1998: 96). It is likely that much of the bajada and piedmont were beyond both the economic and political control of riverine-focused irrigation communities, and immigrants may have had considerably more freedom to resettle in those areas than along the river. Upland areas near springs, major drainages, and relatively flat tracts of land where agriculture was possible would have been attractive localities to immigrant populations entering the region, particularly if many of these groups were not able to gain acceptance into local communities. The upland population represents an important, yet largely unknown, segment of the Tonto Basin population and the relatively few puebloan households that managed to penetrate the low-lying areas of the basin may be only the conspicuous tip of a much larger migrant "iceberg."

If significant proportions of the upland population were puebloan immigrants, they would have constituted a potential threat that was hovering on the edges of established irrigation communities and waiting for an opportunity to force entry into more optimal settlement areas along the river. Such an opportunity may have presented itself in the early fourteenth century as communities along the river were competing against each other and attempting to integrate increasingly large and diverse populations. Movement of the upland population down into the basin during this interval is consistent with evidence for abandonment of many upland settlements shortly after the start of the Gila phase (Rice and Oliver 1998: 90). This movement may have accelerated the collapse of local irrigation communities by delivering the coup de grace through overt conflict or by placing additional stress on community organizations and economies that were already beginning to come apart at the seams.

If immigrants both within and outside the Meddler Point community played a significant role in the collapse of this and other irrigation communities in the Tonto Basin during the early fourteenth century, then the Roosevelt phase represents a brief attempt at integrating local and migrant populations that ultimately failed. In the model I propose, the initial migrant households and local groups cooperated economically during the Roosevelt phase, although the arrangement heavily favored local groups who controlled much of the optimal agricultural land.

One integrative function of platform mounds built during this interval may have been to establish ideological links between these socially distant groups in the absence of kinship ties while at the same time legitimizing the asymmetrical economic arrangement. These asymmetries were potentially a destabilizing force in the Meddler Point community, especially as more migrants entered the region. This scenario is consistent with the available evidence, but as archaeologists continue to examine the massive database generated by the Roosevelt Dam projects and conduct fieldwork in the upland areas of the Sierra Ancha, more definite conclusions on the causes of upheaval at the end of the Roosevelt phase may be forthcoming.

CHAPTER SIX

Implications for the Salado and Beyond

The eastern Tonto Basin has provided an ideal example of limited migration and subsequent co-residence with indigenous groups. Intensive investigation of this area as part of the Bureau of Reclamation's Roosevelt Dam Project has generated a rich database that includes large samples of several attributes that are reliable markers of migration. The previous three chapters contain a detailed consideration of the evidence; I conclude with a brief summary of the argument and implications for migration research in the Southwest and beyond.

This study assessed the scale and impact of puebloan migration into the Meddler Point community during the Roosevelt phase (A.D. 1250–1325). The term 'puebloan' in this monograph refers to a variety of different social groups that by A.D. 1200 were living in masonry room blocks in the northern Southwest and were manufacturing textured ceramics using the coil-and-scrape method. Although there is a considerable degree of vagueness in this definition, the magnitude of difference between puebloan migrants and indigenous groups is sufficiently large to compensate for this ambiguity.

The Meddler Point community was originally founded by Hohokam immigrants from the middle Gila River valley or Phoenix Basin around A.D. 750. It developed along internal lines for the next five hundred years, and strong Hohokam influence continued up through the thirteenth century. However, increasing contact with puebloan groups to the north and east of the basin is indicated in the local decorated ceramic assemblages at least two hundred years prior to the Roosevelt phase. This contact may have facilitated the subsequent movement of social groups from the north and east into the Tonto Basin.

Evaluation of the extent of settlement nucleation using the Room Contiguity Index and close examination of construction sequences indicate the contemporaneous presence of two different traditions of organizing domestic space in the eastern basin during the Roosevelt phase. Groups associated with one tradition constructed lines of contiguous rooms. In the largest settlements associated with this tradition, room blocks were ultimately constructed in multiple episodes. These settlements have parallels with Pueblo III residential units in the northern Southwest and were probably occupied by migrants who originated from within this region, although the precise homelands of these groups remain unclear. It is possible that by the time the migrants reached the Tonto Basin they were comprised of mixed groups with multiple origins within the puebloan world.

Groups associated with the other tradition of organizing domestic space built walled compounds containing rooms dispersed around a central courtyard. Typically, no more than four rooms were built within a single courtyard and new courtyards were added on to existing compounds to accommodate the construction of additional rooms. The spatial rules associated with this tradition restricted settlement aggregation. Large settlements were highly segmented arrangements of abutting courtyard groups. This compound tradition can be traced back to earlier Hohokam pit house settlements in the area, suggesting that it was associated with the indigenous population during the Roosevelt phase.

This reconstruction is further supported by differences in wall construction between room blocks and compounds. A local wall construction tradition using post-reinforced adobe and upright cobbles as footers is traced back to similarly constructed pit houses of the late pre-Classic period. This technique was employed in building the earliest compounds and continued to be utilized in compound construction through the end of the Roosevelt phase. Room blocks, on the other hand, were constructed almost exclusively with coursed masonry and, at Griffin Wash Locus A, a well-developed masonry tradition is indicated in the use of dressed sandstone in the initial construction episode. This tradition is associated with contemporaneous pueblo groups living to the north and east of the basin. In addition, the ubiquity of pine and fir at Griffin Wash Locus A suggests that the builders preferred high elevation woods. The nearest sources of these species are currently 25 km (15.5 miles) to the north and east of the basin.

Finally, technological traditions reflected in Roosevelt phase utilitarian ceramic assemblages lend additional support to the scenario of puebloan migration. Locally produced Tonto (unslipped) Corrugated Ware is concentrated at room block sites in the eastern basin. This ware reflects puebloan traditions of surface treatment and probably basic forming techniques, considering the available evidence that the ware was manufactured using a coil-and-scrape method. Although any one line of evidence may be refuted, the co-patterning of three intrusive attributes that are considered reliable indicators of migration constitutes a compelling case.

Assessing the socioeconomic impact of migration is a more subjective exercise than determining the demographic scale of population movement. However, several reasonable inferences can be made from the evidence. Room blocks were by far in the minority during the Roosevelt phase and are only found on the margins of a settlement system dominated by compounds. This settlement pattern indicates that puebloan migration did not disrupt the local community, at least during the Roosevelt phase. It also implies that the migrants were at a distinct disadvantage in terms of access to optimal agricultural land; they would have had limited experience with the local environment and prevailing subsistence economy, which was probably based on canal irrigation. Considering these factors, economic relations between immigrant and local groups, although cooperative, may have heavily favored the indigenous population. Enclaves that were closely integrated within the community may have provided labor in the fields in exchange for a share of the harvest.

It is possible that the inhabitants of the large and relatively isolated Griffin Wash enclave, for better and worse, had more autonomy than the other enclaves. On the positive side, greater independence may explain why the Griffin Wash enclave was allowed to rapidly grow to a size that rivaled Meddler Point in population whereas the other enclaves remained relatively small. On the negative side, the Griffin Wash enclave probably was less integrated into the local economy and the inhabitants may have resorted to alternative strategies to meet their subsistence requirements. Archaeobotanical evidence shows that the resident households extensively utilized less than optimal lands above the Salt River floodplain by focusing on agave cultivation. They may have supplemented their subsistence base by exchanging manufactured goods for food, including textiles and ceramic vessels. Available petrographic data, the presence of ceramic production tools, and the high density of slipped and unslipped corrugated ware at Griffin Wash

suggest this settlement was a production area for Salado Red Corrugated vessels. Unlike Tonto Corrugated, which has a distribution restricted largely to room blocks, Salado Red Corrugated Ware is found in quantity throughout the lower basin, indicating it was extensively traded.

Economic inequality between migrants and local groups would have been a potential source of social and political instability as migrants continued to arrive and their numbers increased relative to the indigenous population. The construction of platform mounds at local settlements, indicating continued ties with the Phoenix Basin, may have served several integrative needs. One of these functions may have been to impress immigrants, who were invited to participate in mound-related ceremonies and activities. High elevation woods in the Meddler Point platform mound and relatively high densities of White Mountain Red Ware recovered from room blocks, from the Livingston platform mound, and from the Pinto Point platform mound and associated compounds lend support to migrant participation. Platform mounds may have functioned as impressive territorial markers and symbols of the first-comer status of the indigenous population, thereby providing ideological legitimization of asymmetrical economic relationships between local and migrant groups. Considering the dramatic collapse of the Meddler Point community at the end of the Roosevelt phase, this attempt at integration eventually failed.

If the above reconstruction is accurate, limited puebloan immigration significantly impacted the trajectory of the Meddler Point community. In the closing decades of the thirteenth century, at least two strikingly different groups came into close contact. Local groups formed residentially stable irrigation communities and had ties to the land that extended back for several centuries. Enter a migrant population who built stone houses, made pottery, farmed, and lived very differently than the local inhabitants. Puebloan migrants not only increased the cultural heterogeneity of the eastern basin population but the economic inequality as well. The unstable arrangement of socially distant and economically unequal groups residing in close proximity set the stage for accelerated change in the direction of increasing complexity. Considering the dispersed Roosevelt phase settlement pattern and absence of centralized authority, migrants who were not accepted into extant communities may have formed temporary communities in optimal bajada settings above the basin. Little is known about the inhabitants of these upland areas and this gap in knowledge stands in stark contrast to the massive database available from riverine settlements on the basin floor.

Although platform mounds, adding a new level of integration in the basin, were built by local groups to hold the community together, this attempt was apparently 'too little too late' and the brief leap toward complexity fell short of the organizational requirements of an increasingly differentiated society. By the early fourteenth century, a significant portion of the Roosevelt population had left and nearly everyone else in the eastern basin resided in a large room block at Schoolhouse Point. It is difficult to place this aggregated settlement in the same developmental sequence as the Meddler Point community, and the cultural composition of the room block inhabitants has not been clearly demonstrated. Schoolhouse Point was probably abandoned by the end of the fourteenth century and there is little evidence for subsequent prehistoric activity in the eastern basin.

FUTURE DIRECTIONS IN SALADO RESEARCH

Migration was by no means restricted to the Tonto Basin during the Classic period (Fig. 6.1). Past and recent studies highlight the late thirteenth through early fourteenth centuries A.D. as a very large spike above the general background noise of population movement in the American Southwest (Adams 1996; Dean and others 1994; Di Peso 1958; Duff 1998; Haury 1958; Lindsay 1987; Mills 1998; Reid 1989; Riggs 1998; Woodson 1999). As discussed in the previous chapter, the so-called Great Drought, an interval of increased environmental variability, provided a strong push factor for groups inhabiting the Four Corners region and other rainfall dependent areas (Dean 1996). Once initiated by the mass exodus from this region, the process of migration generated its own dynamic as the arrival of new groups pushed some groups out of and pulled others into various destination areas, triggering additional movements.

This widespread migration was not an instantaneous event, even on an archaeological time scale, but a process that took place over several generations as Kayenta and Tusayan groups from the Four Corners region moved across the Colorado Plateau and into the Mogollon highlands, mixing with and displacing indigenous populations. Ultimately, the entire northern and eastern periphery of the Hohokam region was impacted by these movements. In addition to the Tonto Basin, puebloan settlers and other migrants arrived in the Verde River valley (Ciolek-Torrello 1997: 593–594), the Safford Basin (Woodson 1999), and the San Pedro River valley

(Clark and others 2000; Di Peso 1958). Finally, puebloan migrants may have penetrated into the Phoenix Basin, as proposed by Haury (1945) more than half a century ago based on mortuary patterns at Los Muertos. There is evidence for significant population movement along segments of this corridor before this migration, during the first half of the thirteenth century and perhaps earlier (Clark and others 2000; Slaughter and Roberts 1996). Thus, late thirteenth-century migrants may have taken advantage of previous migration routes, particularly in the long-distance movements into southeastern Arizona.

The general north-to-south direction of movement can be attributed both to geography and to the common pushes and pulls motivating individual migrant groups. During this interval of environmental uncertainty, perennial water and arable land would have been important considerations for migrants in search of new homes. In Arizona, the nearest valleys with permanent rivers were generally situated to the south of mountain and plateau regions that were being abandoned. In addition to migration routes depicted in Figure 6.1, north-to-south movements from the Mesa Verde region in southwestern Colorado to the northern Rio Grande valley in New Mexico were taking place during the same interval (Duff 1998).

New approaches to migration and the recent explosion of fieldwork in the Tonto Basin and adjacent regions provide at least a partial answer to the Salado 'question'. In this explanation, migration returns to the forefront as the process that links the Classic period sequences of valleys and basins within the territorial extent of the Salado horizon, especially the western Salado of central and southeast Arizona. However, the role of migration has changed from that of cultural replacer (Gladwin and Gladwin 1935) to cultural mixer. As argued by critics of the original puebloan migration hypothesis, the Salado of central and southeastern Arizona also had an indigenous and Hohokam-influenced component that must be considered (Doyel 1976; Rice 1990b; Steen 1962; Wasley 1966; Wasley and Doyel 1980; Weaver 1976; Wood and McAllister 1980; Wood and Hohmann 1985). This local component is not only recognized in the current migration model, it is essential because of the emphasis placed on the relations that develop between socially distant groups living in close proximity as the result of population movement. Distinctive artifact assemblages associated with each co-resident group account for the complicated archaeological patterns associated with the Salado that have defied explanation in the past (Nelson and LeBlanc 1986: 1–14).

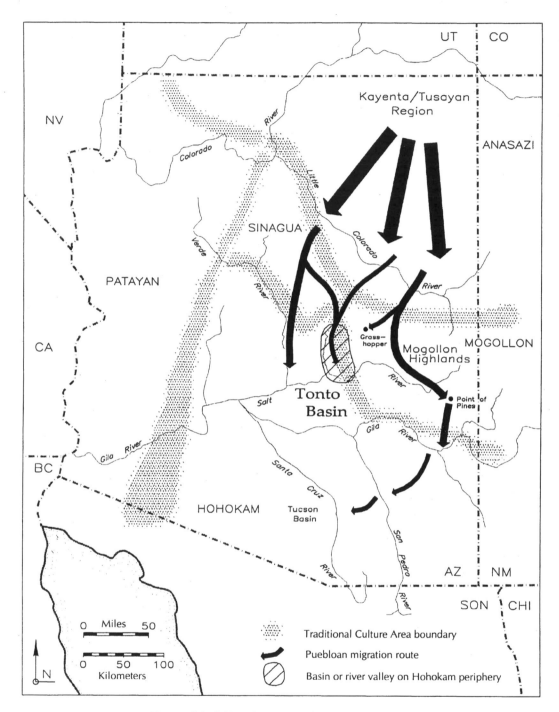

Figure 6.1. Migration routes in eastern Arizona
during the late 13th and early 14th centuries A.D.

Methodological tools are currently within reach that make sense of these patterns and, in many cases, pinpoint the habitation areas of each group if the sample is sufficiently large and resolved.

Future Salado research can proceed within the general explanatory framework provided by migration and subsequent co-residence of different social groups (Nelson 2000: 326; Whittlesey and others 2000: 260–261). The Classic period archaeological record of each river and valley in the western Salado area relates a fascinating tale as to how these groups struggled to integrate (Crown 1994) or simply struggled and left (LeBlanc

1999; Wilcox and Haas 1994). Considering the unique historical and geographic circumstances associated with each of these regions and its inhabitants, every story may have a different ending. Thus, models should be built from the bottom up, one valley and basin at a time. Instead of focusing on which group contributed more to the Salado, local reconstructions should emphasize *interaction* among the various groups. Whether based on cooperation, conflict, or both, this interaction transformed communities and dramatically altered local trajectories.

BEYOND THE SOUTHWEST

The Southwest has been called the laboratory of American archaeology because of fine-grained chronological resolution and the vast amount of fieldwork that has been accomplished. As the result of recent cultural resource management efforts, the Tonto Basin is currently one of the more intensively investigated areas within the Southwest. Hence, it represents an optimal testing ground for ideas and theories concerning small-scale agricultural societies. From the perspective of migration studies, the eastern Tonto Basin provides an ideal case study in which to apply the methodological approach for determining the scale of population movement developed in this monograph. Fine-grained chronological resolution allows us to examine the impact of these movements on a local community over the course of one or two generations. This example provides a useful source of contrast and comparison to prehistorians considering migration in less-studied regions and without such well-defined chronological sequences.

The basic approach for detecting migration that was developed in Chapter 2 is applicable to prehistoric contexts well beyond the Southwest. It can be used both to follow the movements of specific groups across the landscape or to sort out the settlements of different social groups living in close proximity as the result of migration. In this approach, material culture attributes that reflect subtle differences in the enculturative backgrounds of groups are used to track their movements. Ideally, these attributes should have *low* message potential to maximize the probability that they are simply the unconscious by-products of enculturation. Use of these distinct cultural 'fingerprints' avoids the subjective exercise of isolating specific ethnic signals in the vast array of messages intentionally conveyed in material culture. Attributes that reflect subtle nuances in enculturation between groups tend to endure in co-resi-

dence settings and are not likely to be imitated by other groups with different backgrounds.

To reduce message potential, physical and contextual visibility of the attribute should be low (Carr 1995b). Local production of the artifacts associated with these attributes must be demonstrated to exclude the possibility that these items were introduced within a region by exchange. Domestic contexts are rich in data sets that meet these criteria (Burmeister 2000: 542), including the organization of domestic space, preferences in food flavorings and preparation techniques, domestic installations, and embedded technological styles associated with the early manufacturing steps of basic utilitarian items. Relevant technological styles include cordage spin patterns in weaving, basic forming techniques in ceramic production (especially utilitarian wares), wall construction, and reductive strategies used in flaked stone and ground stone tool manufacture. The more attributes within this set that can be brought to bear on the assessment, the more convincing is the argument for migration.

This approach represents the culmination of developments in stylistic theory in anthropology over the past forty years. General highlights of this long interval include Binford's (1963) use of culture drift to explain subtle differences in lithic assemblages associated with red ochre caches in Michigan, Wobst's (1977) seminal article on 'style as information exchange', Wiessner's (1983, 1984) further refinement of this approach based on her work with the Kalahari San; and Sackett's (1973, 1977) *isochrestic* model. Carr's (1995a, 1995b) 'unified middle range theory of artifact design' is a noteworthy synthesis of the various theoretical stances that emerged from the Sackett-Wiessner debate (Sackett 1985, 1986, 1990; Wiessner 1985, 1990). In addition, the concepts of technological style (Lechtman 1977) and technological tradition (Childs 1991) and recognition of the strong cultural component in residential construction and spatial organization (Hillier and Hanson 1984; Rapaport 1969; 1990) represent specific contributions.

Dependent on the scale, migration can be viewed both as process and event. As an event or series of related events, movements of discrete migrant units can be tracked across the landscape at maximum resolution. At this microscale, a number of outcomes are possible, including co-residence between local and migration groups as well as displacement of one group by another. Migration models of the early nineteenth century emphasized displacement and the intrusive aspect of migration. Processual archaeology focused on the development of local populations and largely ignored migration.

Our new model of migration reconciles these two positions by recognizing the importance of both migrant and local populations and stressing the transformational character of interaction between the two groups.

On a macroregional level, the numerous migration events can be collapsed into lines and arrows on a map. At this scale, migration can be viewed as a directed and self-perpetuating process with predictable results when the economic and social motivations for migration are considered. In this light, the 'new migration' does not represent a paradigm of itself, but merely a valid research topic that can finally be included within the processualist paradigm. In returning to migration at the start of the new millennium, the discipline is not moving in circles but spirally in the direction of increasing resolution and theoretical sophistication. An old explanation can still be a good one, so in the spirit of Anthony's (1990) seminal article, now that the baby has returned, let's draw a fresh bath.

References

Adams, E. Charles
1991 *The Origin and Development of the Pueblo Kat-sina Cult*. Tucson: University of Arizona Press.
1996 The Pueblo III–Pueblo IV Transition in the Hopi Area, Arizona. In *The Prehistoric Pueblo World, A.D. 1150-1350*, edited by Michael A. Adler, pp. 48–58. Tucson: University of Arizona Press.

Adams, E. Charles, Miriam T. Stark, and Deborah S. Dosh
1993 Ceramic Distribution and Exchange: Jeddito Yellow Ware and Implications for Social Complexity. *Journal of Field Archaeology* 20(1): 3–21.

Adams, William Y., Dennis P. Van Gerven, and Richard S. Levy
1978 The Retreat from Migrationism. *Annual Review of Anthropology* 7: 483–532.

Agorsah, Emmanuel
1986 House Forms in Northern Volta Basin, Ghana: (Evolution, Internal Spatial Organisation and the Social Relationships Depicted). *West African Journal of Archaeology* 16: 25–51.

Algaze, Guillermo
1989 The Uruk Expansion: Cross-cultural Exchange in Early Mesopotamian Civilization. *Current Anthropology* 30(5): 571–608.

Alonso, Ana María
1994 The Politics of Space, Time, and Substance: State Formation, Nationalism, and Ethnicity. *Annual Review of Anthropology* 23: 379–405.

Alvarez, Robert R.
1987 *Familia: Migration and Adaptation in Baja and Alta California, 1800–1975*. Berkeley: University of California Press.

Anthony, David W.
1990 Migration in Archeology: The Baby and the Bathwater. *American Anthropologist* 92(4): 895–914.

Anyon, Roger, and Steven A. LeBlanc
1984 *The Galaz Ruin, A Prehistoric Mimbres Village in Southwestern New Mexico*. Albuquerque: Maxwell Museum of Anthropology and the University of New Mexico Press.

Armstrong, Douglas V.
1990 *The Old Village and the Great House: An Archaeological and Historical Examination of Drax Hall Plantation, St. Ann's Bay, Jamaica*. Urbana: University of Illinois Press.

Arnold, Dean E.
1975 Ceramic Ecology of the Ayacucho Basin, Peru: Implications for Prehistory. *Current Anthropology* 16: 183–205.
1989 Patterns of Learning, Residence, and Descent among Potters in Ticul, Yucatan, Mexico. In *Archaeological Approaches to Cultural Identity*, edited by Stephen J. Shennan, pp. 174–184. London: Unwin Hyman.

Arutiunov, Sergei A., and A. M. Khazanov
1981 Das Problem der Archaeologischen Kriterien mit Ethnischer Spezifik. *Ethnographisch-Archäogische Zeitschrift* 22: 669–685.

Baker, Vernon G.
1980 Archaeological Visibility of Afro-American Culture: An Example from Black Lucy's Garden, Andover, Massachusetts. In *Archaeological Perspectives on Ethnicity in America: Afro-American and Asian American Culture History*, edited by Robert L. Schuyler, pp. 29–37. Farmingdale, New York: Baywood.

Bandelier, Adolph F. A.
1892 Final Report of Investigations among the Indians of the Southwestern United States, Carried on Mainly in the Years from 1880 to 1885, Part II. *Papers of the Archaeological Institute of America, American Series* 4. Cambridge: University Press.

Barnett, Franklin
1974 *Sandstone Hill Pueblo Ruin: Cibola Culture in Catron County, New Mexico*. Albuquerque: Albuquerque Archaeological Society.

Barth, Fredrik
1969 Ecologic Relationships of Ethnic Groups in Swat, North Pakistan. In *Environment and Cultural Behavior*, edited by Andrew P. Vayda, pp. 362–376. Garden City, New York: The Natural History Press.

Becker, M. J.
1977 "Swedish" Colonial Yellow Bricks: Notes on Their Uses and Possible Origins in 17th Century America. *Historical Archaeology* 11: 112–118.

Bentley, G. Carter
1987 Ethnicity and Practice. *Comparative Studies in Society and History* 29(1): 24–55.

Bernardini, Wesley
1998   Conflict, Migration, and the Social Environment: Interpreting Architectural Change in Early and Late Pueblo IV Aggregations. In "Migration and Reorganization: The Pueblo IV Period in the American Southwest," edited by Katherine A. Spielmann. *Anthropological Research Papers* 51: 91-114. Tempe: Arizona State University.

Binford, Lewis R.
1963   "Red Ocher" Caches from the Michigan Area: A Possible Case of Cultural Drift. *Southwestern Journal of Anthropology* 19: 89-108.
1965   Archaeological Systematics and the Study of Culture Process. *American Antiquity* 31(2): 203-210.
1971   Mortuary Practices: Their Study and Their Potential. In "Approaches to the Social Dimensions of Mortuary Practices," edited by James A. Brown. *Society for American Archaeology Memoir* 25: 6-29.
1973   Interassemblage Variability—The Mousterian and the "Functional" Argument. In *The Explanation of Culture Change*, edited by Colin Renfrew, pp. 227-254. Pittsburgh: University of Pittsburgh Press.

Blinman, Eric, and C. Dean Wilson
1993   Ceramic Perspectives on Northern Anasazi Exchange. In *The American Southwest and Mesoamerica: Systems of Prehistoric Exchange*, edited by Jonathon E. Ericson and Timothy G. Baugh, pp. 65-94. New York: Plenum Press.

Bogucki, Peter
1987   The Establishment of Agrarian Communities on the North European Plain. *Current Anthropology* 28(1): 1-24.

Bordes, François, and Denise de Sonneville-Bordes
1970   The Significance of Variability in Palaeolithic Assemblages. *World Archaeology* 2: 61-73.

Bradley, Bruce A.
1992   Excavations at Sand Canyon Pueblo. In "The Sand Canyon Archaeological Project: A Progress Report," edited by William. D. Lipe. *Crow Canyon Archaeological Center Occasional Paper* 2: 79-104. Cortez, Colorado: Crow Canyon Archaeological Center.

Bradley, Ronna J.
1993   Marine Shell Exchange in Northwest Mexico and the Southwest. In *The American Southwest and Mesoamerica: Systems of Prehistoric Exchange*, edited by Jonathon E. Ericson and Timothy G. Baugh, pp. 121-151. New York: Plenum Press.

Braun, David P.
1995   Style, Selection, and Historicity. In *Style, Society, and Person: Archaeological and Ethnological Perspectives*, edited by Christophe Carr and Jill E. Neitzel, pp. 123-138. New York: Plenum Press.

Brown, Jeffrey L.
1973   *The Origin and Nature of Salado: Evidence from the Safford Valley, Arizona.* MS, doctoral dissertation, University of Arizona, Tucson.

Burley, David D.
1995   Contexts of Meaning: Beer Bottles and Cans in Contemporary Burial Practices in the Polynesian Kingdom of Tonga. *Historical Archaeology* 29(1): 75-83.

Burmeister, Stefan
2000   Archaeology and Migration: Approaches to an Archaeological Proof of Migration. *Current Anthropology* 41(4): 539-567.

Cadwallader, Martin
1992   *Migration and Residential Mobility: Macro and Micro Approaches.* Madison: University of Wisconsin Press.

Caldwell, Joseph
1965   Interaction Spheres in Prehistory. In "Hopewellian Studies," edited by Joseph R. Caldwell and Robert L. Hall. *Illinois State Museum Scientific Papers* 12: 133-143. Springfield, Illinois.

Cameron, Catherine M.
1991   Structure Abandonment in Villages. In *Archaeological Method and Theory*, Volume 3, edited by Michael B. Schiffer, pp. 155-194. Tucson: University of Arizona Press.
1995   [Editor] Migration and the Movement of Southwestern Peoples. *Journal of Anthropological Archaeology* 14(2).

Cameron, Catherine M., and Steve A. Tomka, Editors
1993   *Abandonment of Settlements and Regions: Ethnoarchaeological and Archaeological Approaches.* Cambridge: Cambridge University Press.

Cameron, Judi, Editor
1997   Prehistoric and Historic Archaeological Resources in the Tonto Basin: Report on the FLEX Tonto Basin Project. *Office of Cultural Resource Management Report* 93. Tempe: Office of Cultural Resource Management, Arizona State University.

Carr, Christopher
1995a   Building a Unified Middle-Range Theory of Artifact Design. In *Style, Society, and Person: Archaeological and Ethnological Perspectives*, edited by Christopher Carr and Jill E. Neitzel, pp. 151-170. New York: Plenum Press.
1995b   A Unified Middle-Range Theory of Artifact Design. In *Style, Society, and Person: Archaeological and Ethnological Perspectives*, edited by Christopher Carr and Jill E. Neitzel, pp. 171-258. New York: Plenum Press.
1995c   Mortuary Practices: Their Social, Philosophical-Religious, Circumstantial, and Physical Determinants. *Journal of Archaeological Method and Theory* 2(2): 105-200.

Cartledge, Thomas R.
1976   Prehistory in Vosberg Valley, Central Arizona. In "The 1976 Salado Conference," edited by David E. Doyel and Emil W. Haury. *The Kiva* 42(1): 95–104.

Cheek, Charles D., and Amy Friedlander
1990   Pottery and Pig's Feet: Space, Ethnicity, and Neighborhood in Washington, D.C., 1880–1940. *Historical Archaeology* 24(1): 34–60.

Childe, V. Gordon
1950   *Prehistoric Migrations in Europe*. Oslo: Aschehoug.
1956   *Piecing Together the Past: The Interpretation of Archaeological Data*. New York: Frederick A. Praeger.

Childs, S. Terry
1991   Style, Technology, and Iron Smelting Furnaces in Bantu–Speaking Africa. *Journal of Anthropological Archaeology* 10(4): 332–359.

Ciolek-Torrello, Richard S.
1987   [Editor] Archaeology of the Mazatzal Piedmont, Central Arizona. 2 vols. *Research Paper* 33. Flagstaff: Museum of Northern Arizona.
1997   Prehistoric Settlement and Demography in the Lower Verde River Region. In *Vanishing River: Landscapes and Lives of the Lower Verde River Valley*, edited by Stephanie M. Whittlesey, Richard Ciolek-Torrello, and Jeffrey H. Altschul, pp. 531-595. Tucson: SRI Press.

Ciolek-Torrello, Richard S., and Richard C. Lange
1990   The Gila Pueblo Survey of the Southeastern Sierra Ancha. *Kiva* 55(2): 127–154.

Clark, Jeffery J.
1995   Archaeological Clearance Report for the Phase 2 Data Recovery at Sites in the Punkin Center Section, ADOT State Route 188 Project, Tonto Basin, Arizona. *Technical Report* 95-17. Tucson: Center for Desert Archaeology.
1997   *Migration and Integration: The Salado in the Tonto Basin*. Doctoral dissertation, University of Arizona, Tucson. Ann Arbor: University Microfilms.

Clark, Jeffery J., and James M. Vint, Editors
2000   Tonto Creek Archaeological Project: Archaeological Investigations along Tonto Creek. *Anthropological Papers* 22. Tucson: Center for Desert Archaeology.

Clark, Jeffery J., Kyle Woodson, and Mark C. Slaughter
2000   Those Who Went to the Land of the Sun: Puebloan Migrations into Southeastern Arizona. Manuscript prepared for *Between the Hohokam and the Mimbres: Archaeology of a Land Between*, edited by Henry D. Wallace. Amerind New World Studies Series, forthcoming.

Collett, David
1987   A Contribution to the Study of Migrations in the Archaeological Record: The Ngoni and Kololo as a Case Study. In *Archaeology as Long–Term History*, edited by Ian Hodder, pp. 105–116. Cambridge: Cambridge University Press.

Cordell, Linda S.
1995   Tracing Migration Pathways from the Receiving End. *Journal of Anthropological Archaeology* 14(2): 203–211.

Cosgrove, Hattie S., and C. Burton Cosgrove
1932   The Swarts Ruin: A Typical Mimbres Site in Southwestern New Mexico. *Papers of the Peabody Museum of American Archaeology and Ethnology* 15(1). Cambridge: Harvard University.

Costello, Julia G., and Phillip L. Walker
1987   Burials from the Santa Barbara Presidio Chapel. *Historical Archaeology* 21(1): 3–17.

Craig, Douglas B.
1992   Rye Creek Ruin. In "The Rye Creek Project, Archaeology In The Upper Tonto Basin, Vol. 3: Synthesis and Conclusions," by Mark D. Elson and Douglas B. Craig. *Anthropological Papers* 11(3): 107–117. Tucson: Center for Desert Archaeology.
1995a   Archaeological Investigations at AZ U:9:14 (ASM). In "Archaeology at the Head of the Scottsdale Canal System, Vol. 1: Project Background and Site Descriptions," edited by M. R. Hackbarth, Douglas B. Craig, and T. K. Henderson. *Technical Reports* 95–1: 31–83. Flagstaff: Northland Research.
1995b   The Social Consequences of Irrigation Agriculture: A Perspective from Meddler Point. In "The Roosevelt Community Development Study: New Perspectives on Tonto Basin Prehistory," edited by Mark D. Elson, Miriam T. Stark, and David A. Gregory. *Anthropological Papers* 15: 227–249. Tucson: Center for Desert Archaeology.
2000   Rewriting Prehistory in the Hohokam Heartland. *Archaeology Southwest* 14(3): 1-4.

Craig, Douglas B., and Jeffery J. Clark
1994a   The Meddler Point Site, AZ V:5:4/26 (ASM/TNF). In "The Roosevelt Community Development Study, Vol. 2: Meddler Point, Pyramid Point, and Griffin Wash Sites," by Mark D. Elson, Deborah L. Swartz, Douglas B. Craig, and Jeffery J. Clark. *Anthropological Papers* 13(2): 1–198. Tucson: Center for Desert Archaeology.
1994b   The Meddler Point Platform Mound Complex: Demographic and Social Considerations. Paper presented at the 59th Annual Meeting of the Society for American Archaeology, Anaheim.

Craig, Douglas B., James P. Holmlund, and Jeffery J. Clark
1998   Labor Investment and Organization in Platform Mound Construction: A Case Study from the Ton-

Craig, Douglas B., James P. Holmlund, and Jeffery J. Clark (*continued*)
    to Basin of Central Arizona. *Journal of Field Archaeology* 25(3): 245-259.

Crawford, Sally
  1997   Britons, Anglo-Saxons and the Germanic Burial Ritual. In "Migrations and Invasions in Archaeological Explanation," edited by John Chapman and Helena Hamerow, pp. 45–72. *BAR International Series* 664. Oxford: Archaeopress.

Croes, Dale
  1987   Locarno Beach at Hoko River, Olympic Peninsula, Washington: Makah/Nootkan, Salishan, Chimakuan or Who? In *Ethnicity and Culture*, edited by R. Auger, M. Glass, S. MacEachern, and P. McCartney, pp. 259–283. Calgary: University of Calgary Press.

Crown, Patricia L.
  1981   *Variability in Ceramic Manufacture at the Chodistaas Site, East–Central Arizona.* Doctoral dissertation, University of Arizona, Tucson. Ann Arbor: University Microfilms.
  1994   *Ceramics and Ideology: Salado Polychrome Pottery.* Albuquerque: University of New Mexico Press.
  1998   Changing Perspectives on the Pueblo IV World. In "Migration and Reorganization: The Pueblo IV Period in the American Southwest," edited by Katherine A. Spielmann. *Anthropological Research Papers* 51: 293-301. Tempe: Arizona State University.

Cummins, Tom
  1984   Kinshape: The Design of the Hawaiian Feather Cloak. *Art History* 7(1): 1–20.

David, Nicholas, Kodzo Gavua, A. Scott MacEachern, and Judy Sterner
  1991   Ethnicity and Material Culture in North Cameroon. *Canadian Journal of Archaeology* 15: 171–177.

Davis, Dave D.
  1985   Hereditary Emblems: Material Culture in the Context of Social Change. *Journal of Anthropological Archaeology* 4(3): 149–176.

Deagan, Kathleen
  1983   *Spanish St. Augustine: The Archaeology of a Colonial Creole Community.* New York: Academic Press.

Dean, Jeffrey S.
  1969   Chronological Analysis of Tsegi Phase Sites in Northeastern Arizona. *Papers of the Laboratory of Tree-Ring Research* 3. Tucson: University of Arizona.
  1996   Kayenta Anasazi Settlement Transformations in Northeastern Arizona, A.D. 1150-1350. In *The Prehistoric Pueblo World, A.D. 1150–1350,* edited by Michael A. Adler, pp. 29–47. Tucson: University of Arizona Press.
  2000   [Editor] *Salado.* Albuquerque: University of New Mexico Press.

Dean, Jeffrey S., and John C. Ravesloot
  1993   The Chronology of Cultural Interaction in the Gran Chichimeca. In *Culture and Contact, Charles C. Di Peso's Gran Chichimeca,"* edited by Anne I. Woosley and John C. Ravesloot, pp. 88-103. Albuquerque: University of New Mexico Press.

Dean, Jeffrey S., William H. Doelle, and Janet D. Orcutt
  1994   Adaptive Stress, Environment, and Demography. In *Themes in Southwest Prehistory*, edited by George J. Gumerman, pp. 53–86. Santa Fe: School of American Research Press.

Deaver, William L., Robert B. Neily, Su Benaron, Richard Ciolek-Torrello, Jeffrey A. Homburg, Robert P. Jones, Lee W. Lindsay, Jr., and Steven D. Shelley
  1994   The Lower Verde Archaeological Project, Vol. 2: Site Descriptions for Habitation and Non-agricultural Sites (1994 draft). *Technical Series.* Tucson: Statistical Research.

DeBoer, Warren R.
  1990   Interaction, Imitation, and Communication as Expressed in Style: The Ucayali Experience. In *The Uses of Style in Archaeology*, edited by Margaret W. Conkey and Christine A. Hastorf, pp. 82-104. Cambridge: Cambridge University Press.

DeCorse, Christopher R.
  1989   Material Aspects of Limba, Yalunka and Kuranko Ethnicity: Archaeological Research in Northeastern Sierra Leone. In *Archaeological Approaches to Cultural Identity*, edited by S. J. Shennan, pp. 125–140. London: Unwin Hyman.
  1992   Culture Contact, Continuity, and Change on the Gold Coast, A.D. 1400–1900. *African Archaeological Review* 10: 163–196.

DeFrance, Susan D.
  1996   Iberian Foodways in the Moquegua and Torata Valleys of Southern France. *Historical Archaeology* 30(3): 20–48.

Dering, J. Phil
  1994   Plant Remains from Six Roosevelt and Gila Phase Sites. In "Archaeology of the Salado in the Livingston Area of Tonto Basin: Roosevelt Platform Mound Study, Report on the Livingston Management Group, Pinto Creek Complex," by David F. Jacobs. *Roosevelt Monograph Series* 3, *Anthropological Field Studies* 32: 867–882. Tempe: Office of Cultural Resource Management, Arizona State University.
  1997   Plant Remains from the Schoolhouse Point Mesa Sites. In "The Archaeology of Schoolhouse Point

Mesa: Roosevelt Platform Mound Study," by Owen Lindauer, pp. 491–506. *Roosevelt Monograph Series* 8. *Anthropological Field Studies* 37. Tempe: Office of Cultural Resource Management, Arizona State University.

De Vos, George A.
1975   Ethnic Pluralism: Conflict and Accommodation. In *Ethnic Identity: Cultural Continuities and Change*, edited by George De Vos and Lola Romanucci-Ross, pp. 5–41. Chicago: University of Chicago Press.

De Vos, George A., and Lola Romanucci-Ross, Editors
1975   *Ethnic Identity: Cultural Continuities and Change.* Chicago: University of Chicago Press.

Diehl, Michael, Jennifer A. Waters, and J. Homer Thiel
1998   Acculturation and the Composition of the Diet of Tucson's Overseas Chinese Gardeners at the Turn of the Century. *Historical Archaeology* 32(4): 19–33.

Di Peso, Charles C.
1958   The Reeve Ruin of Southeastern Arizona: A Study of Prehistoric Western Pueblo Migration into the Middle San Pedro Valley. *Amerind Foundation* 8. Dragoon, Arizona: Amerind Foundation.
1976   Gila Polychrome in the Casas Grandes Region. In "The 1976 Salado Conference," edited by David E. Doyel and Emil W. Haury. *The Kiva* 42(1): 57–63.

Doelle, William H.
1995   Tonto Basin Demography in a Regional Perspective. In "The Roosevelt Community Development Study: New Perspectives on Tonto Basin Prehistory," edited by Mark D. Elson, Miriam T. Stark, and David A. Gregory. *Anthropological Papers* 15: 201–226. Tucson: Center for Desert Archaeology.

Doelle, William H., David A. Gregory, and Henry D. Wallace
1995   Classic Period Platform Mound Systems in Southern Arizona. In "The Roosevelt Community Development Study: New Perspectives on Tonto Basin Prehistory," edited by Mark D. Elson, Miriam T. Stark, and David A. Gregory. *Anthropological Papers* 15: 385–440. Tucson: Center for Desert Archaeology.

Dolukhanov, P. M.
1989   Cultural and Ethnic Processes in Prehistory as Seen Through the Evidence of Archaeology and Related Disciplines. In *Archaeological Approaches to Cultural Identity*, edited by S. J. Shennan, pp. 267–277. London: Unwin Hyman.

Dothan, Trude
1982   *The Philistines and Their Material Culture.* New Haven: Yale University Press.

Downum, Christian E., John E. Douglas, and Douglas B. Craig
1993   The Cerro Prieto Site. In "Between Desert and River: Hohokam Settlement and Land Use in the Los Robles Community," by Christian E. Downum. *Anthropological Papers of the University of Arizona* 57: 53–95. Tucson: University of Arizona Press.

Doyel, David E.
1974   Excavations in the Escalante Ruin Group, Southern Arizona. *Arizona State Museum Archaeological Series* 37. Tucson: University of Arizona.
1976   Salado Cultural Development in the Tonto Basin and Globe-Miami Areas, Central Arizona. In "The 1976 Salado Conference," edited by David E. Doyel and Emil W. Haury. *The Kiva* 42(1): 5–16.
1978   The Miami Wash Project: Hohokam and Salado in the Globe-Miami Area, Central Arizona. *Contribution to Highway Salvage Archaeology in Arizona* 52. Tucson: Arizona State Museum, University of Arizona.
1991   Hohokam Cultural Evolution in the Phoenix Basin. In *Exploring the Hohokam: Prehistoric Desert Peoples of the American Southwest*, edited by George J. Gumerman, pp. 231–278. Albuquerque: University of New Mexico Press.
1992   On Models and Methods: Comments on the History of Archaeological Research in the Southern Southwest. In "Proceedings of the Second Salado Conference, Globe, AZ 1992," edited by Richard C. Lange and Stephen Germick, pp. 345–351. *Arizona Archaeological Society Occasional Paper.* Phoenix: Arizona Archaeological Society.

Doyel, David E., and Emil W. Haury, Editors
1976   The 1976 Salado Conference. *The Kiva* 42(1): 1–134.

Dozier, Edward P.
1966   *Hano: a Tewa Indian Community in Arizona.* New York: Holt, Rinehart, and Winston.

Duff, Andrew I.
1998   The Process of Migration in the Late Prehistoric Southwest. In "Migration and Reorganization: The Pueblo IV Period in the American Southwest," edited by Katherine A. Spielmann. *Anthropological Research Papers* 51: 31–52. Tempe: Arizona State University.

Dunnell, Robert C.
1978   Style and Function: A Fundamental Dichotomy. *American Antiquity* 43(2): 192–202.

Earle, Timothy
1990   Style and Iconography as Legitimation in Complex Chiefdoms. In *The Uses of Style in Archaeology*, edited by Margaret W. Conkey and Christine A. Hastorf, pp. 73–81. Cambridge: Cambridge University Press.

Elson, Mark D.

1994   The Pyramid Point Site, AZ V:5:1/25 (ASM/ TNF). In "The Roosevelt Community Development Study, Vol. 2: Meddler Point, Pyramid Point, and Griffin Wash Sites," by Mark D. Elson, Deborah L. Swartz, Douglas B. Craig, and Jeffery J. Clark. *Anthropological Papers* 13(2): 199–295. Tucson: Center for Desert Archaeology.

1995   Assessment of Chronometric Methods and Dates. In "The Roosevelt Community Development Study: New Perspectives on Tonto Basin Prehistory," edited by Mark D. Elson, Miriam T. Stark, and David A. Gregory. *Anthropological Papers* 15: 39–60. Tucson: Center for Desert Archaeology.

1996   *An Ethnographic Perspective on Prehistoric Platform Mounds of the Tonto Basin, Central Arizona*. Doctoral dissertation, University of Arizona, Tucson. Ann Arbor: University Microfilms.

1998   Expanding the View of Hohokam Platform Mounds: An Ethnographic Perspective. *Anthropological Papers of the University of Arizona* 63. Tucson: University of Arizona Press.

Elson, Mark D., and Douglas B. Craig

1992   The Rye Creek Project: Archaeology in the Upper Tonto Basin. 3 vols. *Anthropological Papers* 11. Tucson: Center for Desert Archaeology.

Elson, Mark D., and Michael Lindeman

1994   The Eagle Ridge Site, AZ V:5:104/1045 (ASM/ TNF). In "The Roosevelt Community Development Study, Vol. 1: Introduction and Small Sites," by Mark D. Elson and Deborah L. Swartz. *Anthropological Papers* 13(1): 23–116. Tucson: Center for Desert Archaeology.

Elson, Mark D., and Brenda G. Randolph

1994   The Porcupine Site, AZ V:5:106/217 (ASM/ TNF). In "The Roosevelt Community Development Study, Vol. 1: Introduction and Small Sites," by Mark D. Elson and Deborah L. Swartz. *Anthropological Papers* 13(1): 141–179. Tucson: Center for Desert Archaeology.

Elson, Mark D., David A. Gregory, and Miriam T. Stark

1995   New Perspectives on Tonto Basin Prehistory. In "The Roosevelt Community Development Study: New Perspectives on Tonto Basin Prehistory," edited by Mark D. Elson, Miriam T. Stark, and David A. Gregory. *Anthropological Papers* 15: 441–479. Tucson: Center for Desert Archaeology.

Elson, Mark D., Miriam T. Stark, and David A. Gregory, Editors

1995   The Roosevelt Community Development Study: New Perspectives on Tonto Basin Prehistory. *Anthropological Papers* 15. Tucson: Center for Desert Archaeology.

Elson, Mark D., Suzanne K. Fish, Steven R. James, and Charles H. Miksicek

1995   Prehistoric Subsistence in the Roosevelt Community Development Study Area. In "The Roosevelt Community Development Study, Vol. 3: Paleobotanical and Osteological Analyses," edited by Mark D. Elson and Jeffery J. Clark. *Anthropological Papers* 14(3): 217–260. Tucson: Center for Desert Archaeology.

Elson, Mark D., Deborah L. Swartz, Douglas B. Craig, and Jeffery J. Clark

1994   The Roosevelt Community Development Study, Vol. 2: Meddler Point, Pyramid Point, and Griffin Wash Sites. *Anthropological Papers* 13(2). Tucson: Center for Desert Archaeology.

Emberling, Geoff

1997   Ethnicity in Complex Societies: Archaeological Perspectives. *Journal of Archaeological Research* 5(4): 295–343.

Esse, Douglas L.

1992   Collared Pithos at Megiddo: Ceramic Distribution and Ethnicity. *Journal of Near Eastern Studies* 51(2): 81–103.

Evans, Jr., Williams S.

1980   Food and Fantasy: Material Culture of the Chinese in California and the West, Circa 1850–1900. In *Archaeological Perspectives on Ethnicity in America, Afro-American and Asian American Culture History*, edited by Robert L. Schuyler, pp. 89–96. Farmingdale, New York: Baywood.

Ezzo, Joseph A.

1991   *Dietary Change at Grasshopper Pueblo, Arizona: The Evidence from Bone Chemistry Analysis*. Doctoral dissertation, University of Wisconsin, Madison. Ann Arbor: University Microfilms.

Ferguson, Leland G.

1992   *Uncommon Ground: Archaeology and Early African America, 1650–1800*. Washington: Smithsonian Institution Press.

Ferguson, T. J.

1996   Historic Zuni Architecture and Society: An Archaeological Application of Space Syntax. *Anthropological Papers of the University of Arizona* 60. Tucson: University of Arizona Press.

Fewkes, Jesse Walter

1912   Casa Grande, Arizona. In *28th Annual Report of the Bureau of American Ethnology to the Secretary of the Smithsonian Institution, 1906–07*, pp. 25–179. Washington: Smithsonian Institution.

Fish, Suzanne K., and Paul R. Fish

1993   An Assessment of Abandonment Processes in the Hohokam Classic Period of the Tucson Basin. In *Abandonment of Settlements and Regions: Ethno-*

archaeological and Archaeological Approaches, edited by Catherine M. Cameron and Steve A. Tomka, pp. 99–109. Cambridge: Cambridge University Press.

Fitting, James E.
1972 Preliminary Notes on Cliff Valley Settlement Patterns. *The Artifact* 10(4): 15–30.

Flannery, Kent V.
1972 The Origins of the Village as a Settlement Type in Mesoamerica and the Near East: A Comparative Study. In *Man, Settlement, and Urbanism*, edited by Peter J. Ucko, Ruth Tringham, and G. W. Dimbleby, pp. 23–53. London: Duckworth.

Friedman, Jonathan, and M. J. Rowlands
1977 Notes toward an Epigenetic Model of the Evolution of "Civilization." In *The Evolution of Social Systems*, edited by Jonathan Friedman and M. J. Rowlands, pp. 201–276. London: Duckworth.

Fritz, John M.
1987 Chaco Canyon and Vijayanagara: Proposing Spatial Meaning in Two Societies. In *Mirror and Metaphor: Material and Social Constructions of Reality*, edited by Daniel W. Ingersoll, Jr., and Gordon R. Bronitsky, pp. 313–349. Landham, Maryland: Unversity of America Press.

Futrell, Mary E.
1998 Social Boundaries and Interaction: Ceramic Zones in the Northern Rio Grande Pueblo IV Period. In "Migration and Reorganization: The Pueblo IV Period in the American Southwest," edited by Katherine A. Spielmann. *Anthropological Research Papers* 51: 285-292. Tempe: Arizona State University.

Geary, Patrick J.
1983 Ethnic Identity as a Situational Construct in the Early Middle Ages. *Mitteilungen der Anthropologischen Gesellschaft in Wein* 113: 15–26.

Gellner, Ernest
1983 *Nations and Nationalism*. Oxford: Basil Blackwell.

Germick, Stephen, and Joseph S. Crary
1992 From Shadow to Substance: An Alternative Perspective on the Roosevelt Phase. In "Proceedings of the Second Salado Conference, Globe, AZ, 1992," edited by Richard C. Lange and Stephen Germick, pp. 286–303. *Arizona Archaeological Society Occasional Paper*. Phoenix: Arizona Archaeological Society.

Gladwin, Winifred, and Harold S. Gladwin
1929 The Red-on-Buff Culture of the Gila Basin. *Medallion Papers* 3. Globe, Arizona: Gila Pueblo.
1930a The Western Range of the Red-on-Buff Culture. *Medallion Papers* 5. Globe, Arizona: Gila Pueblo.
1930b Some Southwestern Pottery Types, Series I. *Medallion Papers* 8. Globe, Arizona: Gila Pueblo.

1934 A Method for the Designation of Cultures and Their Variations. *Medallion Papers* 15. Globe, Arizona: Gila Pueblo.
1935 The Eastern Range of the Red–on–Buff Culture. *Medallion Papers* 16. Globe, Arizona: Gila Pueblo.

Gmelch, George
1980 Return Migration. *Annual Review of Anthropology* 9: 135–159.

Goody, Jack, Editor
1971 *The Developmental Cycle in Domestic Groups*. Cambridge: Cambridge University Press.

Graebner, Fritz
1911 *Methode der Ethnologie*. Heidelberg: C. Winter.

Graves, Michael W.
1982 Breaking Down Ceramic Variation: Testing Models of White Mountain Redware Design Style Development. *Journal of Anthropological Archaeology* 1(4): 305–354.
1994 Community Boundaries in Late Prehistoric Puebloan Society: Kalinga Ethnoarchaeology as a Model for the Southwestern Production and Exchange of Pottery. In *The Ancient Southwestern Community: Models and Methods for the Study of Prehistoric Social Organization*, edited by Wirt H. Wills and Robert D. Leonard, pp. 149–169. Albuquerque: University of New Mexico Press.

Graves, William M., and Suzanne L. Eckert
1998 Decorated Ceramic Distributions and Ideological Developments in the Northern and Central Rio Grande Valley, New Mexico. In "Migration and Reorganization: The Pueblo IV Period in the American Southwest," edited by Katherine A. Spielmann. *Anthropological Research Papers* 51: 263-283. Tempe: Arizona State University.

Green, Roger C.
1987 The Initial Identification of a People as Polynesian as a Race, Language and Culture. In *Ethnicity and Culture*, edited by R. Auger, M. Glass, S. MacEachern, and P. McCartney, pp. 175–180. Calgary: University of Calgary Press.

Greene, Kevin
1987 Gothic Material Culture. In *Archaeology as Long-Term History*, edited by Ian Hodder, pp. 117–131. Cambridge: Cambridge University Press.

Gregory, David A.
1987 The Morphology of Platform Mounds and the Structure of Classic Period Hohokam Sites. In *The Hohokam Village: Site Structure and Organization*, edited by David E. Doyel, pp. 183–210. Glenwood Springs, Colorado: American Association for the Advancement of Science, Southwestern and Rocky Mountain Division.

Gregory, David A. (*continued*)
1995a A Cultural Resources Overview of the Rye Creek Geographic Study Area, Payson and Tonto Basin Ranger Districts, Tonto National Forest, Gila County, Arizona. *Technical Report* 95-10. Tucson: Center for Desert Archaeology.
1995b Prehistoric Settlement Patterns in the Eastern Tonto Basin. In "The Roosevelt Community Development Study: New Perspectives on Tonto Basin Prehistory," edited by Mark D. Elson, Miriam T. Stark, and David A. Gregory. *Anthropological Papers* 15: 127–184. Tucson: Center for Desert Archaeology.

Gumerman, George J., and Carol S. Weed
1976 The Question of Salado in the Agua Fria and New River Drainages of Central Arizona. In "The 1976 Salado Conference," edited by David E. Doyel and Emil W. Haury. *The Kiva* 42(1): 105–112.

Haas, Jonathan
1971 The Ushklish Ruin: A Preliminary Report on Excavations of a Colonial Period Hohokam Site in the Lower Tonto Basin, Central Arizona. MS on file, Arizona State Museum, University of Arizona, Tucson.

Hammack, Laurens C.
1969 Highway Salvage Excavations in the Upper Tonto Basin, Arizona. *The Kiva* 34(2–3): 132–175.

Hammel, E. A.
1980 Household Structure in Fourteenth Century Macedonia. *Journal of Family History* 5: 242–273.
1984 On the *** of Studying Household Form and Function. In *Households: Comparative and Historical Studies of the Domestic Group*, edited by Robert McC. Netting, Richard R. Wilk, and Eric J. Arnould, pp. 29–43. Berkeley: University of California Press.

Handler, Jerome S.
1996 A Prone Burial from a Plantation Slave Cemetery in Barbados, West Indies: Possible Evidence for an African-type Witch or Other Negatively Viewed Person. *Historical Archaeology* 30(3): 76–86.

Haury, Emil W.
1930 A Report on Excavations at the Rye Creek Ruin. MS on file, Tonto National Forest, Arizona.
1932 Roosevelt:9:6: A Hohokam Site of the Colonial Period. *Medallion Papers* 11. Globe, Arizona: Gila Pueblo.
1934 The Canyon Creek Ruin and The Cliff Dwellings of the Sierra Ancha. *Medallion Papers* 14. Globe, Arizona: Gila Pueblo.
1936 The Mogollon Culture of Southwestern New Mexico. *Medallion Papers* 20. Globe, Arizona: Gila Pueblo.

1945 The Excavation of Los Muertos and Neighboring Ruins in the Salt River Valley, Southern Arizona. *Papers of the Peabody Museum of American Archaeology and Ethnology* 24(1). Cambridge: Harvard University.
1958 Evidence at Point of Pines for a Prehistoric Migration from Northern Arizona. In "Migrations in New World Culture History," edited by Raymond H. Thompson. *University of Arizona Bulletin* 29(2), *Social Science Bulletin* 27: 1–8. Tucson: University of Arizona.
1985 *Mogollon Culture in the Forestdale Valley, East-Central Arizona*. Tucson: University of Arizona Press.

Hegmon, Michelle
1989 Social Integration and Architecture. In "The Architecture of Social Integration in Prehistoric Pueblos," edited by William D. Lipe and Michelle Hegmon. *Crow Canyon Archaeological Center Occasional Paper* 1: 5–14. Cortez: Crow Canyon Archaeological Center.
1992 Archaeological Research on Style. *Annual Review of Anthropology* 21: 517–536.

Heidke, James M.
1995 Overview of the Ceramic Collection. In "The Roosevelt Community Development Study, Vol. 2: Ceramic Chronology, Technology, and Economics," edited by James M. Heidke and Miriam T. Stark. *Anthropological Papers* 14(2): 7–18. Tucson: Center for Desert Archaeology.

Heidke, James M., and Miriam T. Stark
1995 Ceramic Chronology, Technology, and Economics in the Roosevelt Community Development Study Area. In "The Roosevelt Community Development Study, Vol. 2: Ceramic Chronology, Technology, and Economics," edited by James M. Heidke and Miriam T. Stark. *Anthropological Papers* 14(2): 395–408. Tucson: Center for Desert Archaeology.

Henige, David P.
1974 *The Chronology of Oral Tradition; Quest for a Chimera*. Oxford: Clarendon Press.

Herr, Sarah, and Jeffery J. Clark
1997 Patterns in the Pathways: Early Historic Migrations in the Rio Grande Pueblos. *Kiva* 62(4): 365–389.

Hill, Carol W.
1989 Who is What? A Preliminary Enquiry into Cultural and Physical Identity. In *Archaeological Approaches to Cultural Identity*, edited by S. J. Shennan, pp. 233–241. London: Unwin Hyman.

Hillier, Bill, and Julienne Hanson
1984 *The Social Logic of Space*. Cambridge: Cambridge University Press.

Hodder, Ian
1979   Economic and Social Stress and Material Culture Patterning. *American Antiquity* 44(3): 446–454.
1982   *Symbols in Action: Ethnoarchaeological Studies of Material Culture.* Cambridge: Cambridge University Press.

Hohmann, John W.
1985   Hohokam and Salado Hamlets in the Tonto Basin: Site Descriptions. *Report* 64. Tempe: Office of Cultural Resource Management, Arizona State University.

Hohmann, John W., and Linda B. Kelley
1988   Erich F. Schmidt's Investigations of Salado Sites in Central Arizona: The Mrs. W. B. Thompson Archaeological Expedition of the American Museum of Natural History. *Museum of Northern Arizona Bulletin* 56. Flagstaff: Museum of Northern Arizona.

Holmlund, James P., Jeffery J. Clark, and Douglas B. Craig
1994   The Roosevelt Community Development Study, Vol. 2 Supplement: Meddler Point Map Packet. *Anthropological Papers* 13(2). Tucson: Center for Desert Archaeology.

Hough, Walter
1907   Antiquities of the Upper Gila and Salt River Valleys in Arizona and New Mexico. *Bureau of American Ethnology Bulletin* 35. Washington: Smithsonian Institution.

Huber, Edgar K., and William D. Lipe
1992   Excavations at the Green Lizard Site. In "The Sand Canyon Archaeological Project: A Progress Report," edited by William D. Lipe. *Crow Canyon Archaeological Center Occasional Paper* 2: 69–77. Cortez: Crow Canyon Archaeological Center.

Huckell, Bruce B.
1973   The Hardt Creek Site. *The Kiva* 39(2): 171–197.
1978   The Oxbow Hill–Payson Project. *Contribution to Highway Salvage Archaeology in Arizona* 48. Tucson: Arizona State Museum, University of Arizona.

Isajiw, Wsevolod W.
1984   Symbols and Ukrainian Canadian Identity: Their Meaning and Significance. In *Visible Symbols*, edited by M. R. Lupul, pp. 119–128. Edmonton: Canadian Institute of Ukrainian Studies.

Jacobs, David F.
1994   Archaeology of the Salado in the Livingston Area of Tonto Basin: Roosevelt Platform Mound Study, Report on the Livingston Management Group, Pinto Creek Complex. *Roosevelt Monograph Series* 3, *Anthropological Field Studies* 32. Tempe: Office of Cultural Resource Management, Arizona State University.

1997   A Salado Platform Mound on Tonto Creek: Roosevelt Platform Mound Study. *Roosevelt Monograph Series 7, Anthropological Field Studies 36.* Tempe: Office of Cultural Resource Management, Arizona State University.

Jeter, Marvin D.
1978   The Reno–Park Creek Project: Archaeological Investigations in Tonto Basin, Arizona. *Contribution to Highway Salvage Archaeology in Arizona* 49. Tucson: Arizona State Museum, University of Arizona.

Johnson, Alfred E.
1965   The Development of Western Pueblo Culture. MS, Doctoral dissertation, Unversity of Arizona, Tucson.

Johnson, Alfred E., and William W. Wasley
1966   Archaeological Excavations Near Bylas, Arizona. *The Kiva* 31(4): 205–253.

Jordan, Terry G., and Matti Kaups
1989   *The American Backwoods Frontier: An Ethnic and Ecological Interpretation.* Baltimore: Johns Hopkins University Press.

Judge, W. James
1991   Chaco: Current Views of Prehistory and the Regional System. In *Chaco & Hohokam: Prehistoric Regional Systems in the American Southwest*, edited by Patricia L. Crown and W. James Judge, pp. 11–30. Santa Fe: School of American Research Press.

Kamp, Kathryn A., and Norman Yoffee
1980   Ethnicity in Ancient Western Asia during the Early Second Millennium B.C.: Archaeological Assessments and Ethnoarchaeological Prospectives. *Bulletin of the American Schools of Oriental Research* 237: 85–103.

Kent, Susan
1990   Segmentation, Architecture, and Space. In *Domestic Architecture and the Use of Space: An Interdisciplinary Cross-Cultural Study*, edited by Susan Kent, pp. 127–152. Cambridge: Cambridge University Press.

Kidder, Alfred V.
1924   An Introduction to the Study of Southwestern Archaeology, with a Preliminary Account of the Excavations at Pecos. *Papers of the Phillips Academy, Southwestern Expedition* 1. New Haven: Yale University Press for Phillips Academy, Andover.

Kimmel, Richard H.
1993   Notes on the Cultural Origins and Functions of Sub-Floor Pits. *Historical Archaeology* 27(3): 102–113.

Kintigh, Keith W.
1994   Chaco, Communal Architecture, and Cibolan Aggregation. In *The Ancient Southwestern Community: Models and Methods for the Study of Pre-*

Kintigh, Keith (*continued*)
   historic Social Organization, edited by Wirt H. Wills and Robert D. Leonard, pp. 131–140. Albuquerque: University of New Mexico Press.

Klingelhofer, Eric
   1987   Aspects of Early Afro–American Material Culture: Artifacts from the Slave Quarters at Garrison Plantation, Maryland. *Historical Archaeology* 21(2): 112–119.

Kluckhohn, Clyde
   1936   Some Reflections on the Method and Theory of the Kulturkreislehre. *American Anthropologist* 38(2): 157–196.

Kobylínski, Zbigniew
   1989   An Ethnic Change or a Socio–Economic One? The 5th and 6th Centuries A.D. in the Polish Lands. In *Archaeological Approaches to Cultural Identity*, edited by S. J. Shennan, pp. 303–312. London: Unwin Hyman.

Kossinna, G.
   1911   *Die Herkunft der Germanen. Zur Methode der Siedlungarchäologie.* Mannus–Bibliothek 6. Würzburg: Kabitzsch.

Kramer, Carol
   1977   Pots and People. In *Mountains and Lowlands: Essays in the Archaeology of Greater Mesopotamia*, edited by L. D. Levine and T. C. Young, Jr., pp. 91–112. Malibu: Undena.

Kus, Susan, and V. Raharijaona
   1990   Domestic Space and the Tenacity of Tradition among Some Betsileo of Madagascar. In *Domestic Architecture and the Use of Space: An Interdisciplinary Cross-Cultural Study*, edited by Susan Kent, pp. 21–33. Cambridge: Cambridge University Press.

Lange, Charles H., and Carroll L. Riley, Editors
   1970   *The Southwestern Journals of Adolph F. Bandelier, 1883–1884.* Albuquerque: University of New Mexico Press.

Lange, Richard C., and Stephen Germick, Editors
   1992   Proceedings of the Second Salado Conference, Globe, AZ 1992. *Arizona Archaeological Society Occasional Paper.* Phoenix: Arizona Archaeological Society.

Langenwalter II, Paul E.
   1980   The Archaeology of 19th Century Chinese Subsistence at the Lower China Store, Madera County, California. In *Archaeological Perspectives on Ethnicity in America, Afro-American and Asian American Culture History*, edited by Robert L. Schuyler, pp. 102–112. Farmingdale, New York: Baywood.

Larick, Roy
   1987   Men of Iron and Social Boundaries in Northern Kenya. In *Ethnicity and Culture*, edited by Régi-

nald Auger, Margaret F. Glass, Scott MacEachern, and Peter H. McCartney, pp. 67–76. Calgary: University of Calgary Press.

Larsen, Mogens T.
   1976   *The Old Assyrian City-State and Its Colonies.* Copenhagen: Akademisk Forlag.

Larsson, Lars
   1989   Ethnicity and Traditions in Mesolithic Mortuary Practices of Southern Scandinavia. In *Archaeological Approaches to Cultural Identity*, edited by S. J. Shennan, pp. 210–218. London: Unwin Hyman.

Lawrence, Denise L., and Setha M. Low
   1990   The Built Environment and Spatial Form. *Annual Review of Anthropology* 19: 453–505.

LeBlanc, Steven A.
   1998   Settlement Consequences of Warfare during the Late Pueblo III and Pueblo IV Periods. In "Migration and Reorganization: The Pueblo IV Period in the American Southwest," edited by Katherine A. Spielmann. *Anthropological Research Papers* 51: 115-135. Tempe: Arizona State University.

LeBlanc, Steven A., and Ben A. Nelson
   1976   The Salado in Southwestern New Mexico. In "The 1976 Salado Conference," edited by David E. Doyel and Emil W. Haury. *The Kiva* 42(1): 71–79.

Lechtman, Heather
   1977   Style in Technology—Some Early Thoughts. In *Material Culture: Styles, Organization, and Dynamics of Technology*, edited by Heather Lechtman and R. S. Merrill, pp. 3–20. St. Paul: West Publishing.

Lefferts, H. L., Jr.
   1977   Frontier Demography: An Introduction. In *The Frontier: Comparative Studies*, Vol. 1, edited by D. H. Miller and J. O. Steffan, pp. 33–55. Norman: University of Oklahoma Press.

Lekson, Stephen H.
   1978   Settlement Patterns in the Redrock Valley of the Gila River, New Mexico. MS, Master's thesis, Department of Anthropology, Eastern New Mexico University, Portales.

   1986   *Great Pueblo Architecture of Chaco Canyon, New Mexico.* Albuquerque: University of New Mexico Press. Originally published in 1984 as *Publications in Archeology* 18B, Chaco Canyon Studies, National Park Service, U.S. Department of the Interior, Albuquerque.

   1992   Salado of the East. In "Proceedings of the Second Salado Conference, Globe, AZ, 1992," edited by Richard C. Lange and Stephen Germick, pp. 17–21. *Arizona Archaeological Society Occasional Paper.* Phoenix: Arizona Archaeological Society.

1996 Southwestern New Mexico and Southeastern Arizona, A.D. 900 to 1300. In *The Prehistoric Pueblo World, A.D. 1150–1350*, edited by Michael A. Adler, pp. 170–176. Tucson: University of Arizona Press.

Lekson, Stephen H., Mark D. Elson,
and Douglas B. Craig
1992 Previous Research and Culture History. In "Research Design for the Roosevelt Community Development Study," by William H. Doelle, Henry D. Wallace, Mark D. Elson and Douglas B. Craig. *Anthropological Papers* 12: 19–33. Tucson: Center for Desert Archaeology.

Lemonnier, Pierre
1986 The Study of Material Culture Today: Toward an Anthropology of Technical Systems. *Journal of Anthropological Archaeology* 5(2): 147–186.

Leroi-Gourhan, André
1964 Geste et la Parole I, Technique et Langage. Paris: Albin Michel.

Lindauer, Owen
1991 Site AR-003-12-04-22 (TNF), The Mayfield Canyon Site. In "The Archaeology of Star Valley, Arizona: Variations in Small Communities," edited by Owen Lindauer, Ronna J. Bradley, and Charles L. Redman. *Anthropological Field Studies* 24: 146–153. Tempe: Arizona State University.
1994a Site V:5:128/1011, Saguaro Muerto. In "Archaeology of the Salado in the Livingston Area of Tonto Basin: Roosevelt Platform Mound Study, Report on the Livingston Management Group, Pinto Creek Complex," by David F. Jacobs. *Roosevelt Monograph Series* 3, Part 1, *Anthropological Field Studies* 32: 399–462. Tempe: Office of Cultural Resource Management, Arizona State University.
1994b Systematics of Decorated Wares. In "Archaeology of the Salado in the Livingston Area of Tonto Basin: Roosevelt Platform Mound Study, Report on the Livingston Management Group, Pinto Creek Complex," by David F. Jacobs. *Roosevelt Monograph Series* 3, Part 2, *Anthropological Field Studies* 32: 605–633. Tempe: Office of Cultural Resource Management, Arizona State University.
1995 Where the Rivers Converge: Roosevelt Platform Mound Study, Report on the Rock Island Complex. *Roosevelt Monograph Series* 4, *Anthropological Field Studies* 33. Tempe: Office of Cultural Resource Management, Arizona State University.
1996 The Place of the Storehouses: Report on the Schoolhouse Point Mound, Pinto Creek Complex, Roosevelt Platform Mound Study. *Roosevelt Monograph Series* 6, *Anthropological Field Studies* 35. Tempe: Office of Cultural Resource Management, Arizona State University.
1997 The Archaeology of Schoolhouse Point Mesa: Roosevelt Platform Mound Study. *Roosevelt Monograph Series* 8, *Anthropological Field Studies* 37. Tempe: Office of Cultural Resource Management, Arizona State University.

Lindauer, Owen, Ronna J. Bradley,
and Charles L. Redman, Editors
1991 The Archaeology of Star Valley, Arizona: Variation in Small Communities. *Anthropological Field Studies* 24. Tempe: Office of Cultural Resource Management, Arizona State University.

Lindeman, Michael W., and Jeffery J. Clark
2000 Granary Row (U:3:299/199). In "Tonto Creek Archaeological Project: Archaeological Investigations along Tonto Creek, Vol. 2: Site Descriptions for the Punkin Center Section," edited by Jeffery J. Clark and James M. Vint. *Anthropological Papers* 22: 445–505. Tucson: Center for Desert Archaeology.

Lindsay, Jr., Alexander Johnston
1987 Anasazi Population Movements to Southeastern Arizona. *American Archeology* 6(3): 190–198.

Lindsay, Jr., Alexander Johnston,
and Calvin H. Jennings
1968 Salado Redware Conference, Ninth Ceramic Seminar. *Museum of Northern Arizona Ceramic Series* 4. Flagstaff: Museum of Northern Arizona.

Lister, Florence C., and Robert H. Lister
1974 Maiolica in Colonial Spanish America. *Historical Archaeology* 8: 17–52.

Longacre, William A.
1970 Archaeology as Anthropology: A Case Study. *Anthropological Papers of the University of Arizona* 17. Tucson: University of Arizona Press.

Lowell, Julie C.
1991 Prehistoric Households at Turkey Creek Pueblo, Arizona. *Anthropological Papers of the University of Arizona* 54. Tucson: University of Arizona Press.

Lucius, William A.
1983 Modeling Anasazi Origins: The Frontier Approach. In *Proceedings of the Anasazi Symposium 1981*, edited by Jack E. Smith, pp. 53–56. Mesa Verde National Park, Colorado: Mesa Verde Museum Association.

Lyons, Patricia
1987 Language and Style in the Peruvian Montaña. In *Ethnicity and Culture*, edited by Réginald Auger, Margaret F. Glass, Scott MacEachern, and Peter H. McCartney, pp. 101–114. Calgary: University of Calgary Press.

Mabry, Jonathan B.
1996   The Ethnology of Local Irrigation. In *Canals and Communities*, edited by Jonathan B. Mabry, pp. 3-30. Tucson: University of Arizona Press.

Macnider, Barbara S., and Richard W. Effland, Jr.
1989   Cultural Resources Overview: The Tonto National Forest. Tonto National Forest Cultural Resources Inventory Report 88-12-312A. *Cultural Resources Report* 51. Phoenix: Archaeological Consulting Services.

Maquet, J.
1970   Rwanda Castes. In *Arabic and Islamic Studies in Honor of Hamilton A. R. Gibb*, edited by G. Makdisi, pp. 358-376. Leiden: E. J. Brill.

Markell, Ann, Martin Hall, and Carmel Schire
1995   The Historical Archaeology of Vergelegen. *Historical Archaeology* 29(1): 10-34.

Marshall, Michael P., and Henry J. Walt
1984   *Rio Abajo: Prehistory and History of a Rio Grande Province*. Santa Fe: New Mexico Historic Preservation Program.

Martin, Paul Schultz
1973   The Discovery of America. *Science* 179(4077): 969-974.

Martin, Paul Sidney, William A. Longacre, and James N. Hill
1967   Chapters in the Prehistory of Eastern Arizona, III. *Fieldiana: Anthropology* 57. Chicago: Field Museum of Natural History.

Martin, Paul S., John B. Rinaldo, Elaine A. Bluhm, and Hugh C. Cutler
1956   Higgins Flat Pueblo, Western New Mexico. *Fieldiana: Anthropology* 45. Chicago: Chicago Natural History Museum.

Martin, Paul Sidney, John B. Rinaldo, William A. Longacre, Leslie G. Freeman, Jr., James A. Brown, Richard H. Hevly, and M. E. Cooley
1964   Chapters in the Prehistory of Eastern Arizona, II. *Fieldiana: Anthropology* 55. Chicago: Field Museum of Natural History.

McGimsey III, Charles R.
1980   Mariana Mesa: Seven Prehistoric Settlements in West-Central New Mexico. *Papers of the Peabody Museum of Archaeology and Ethnology* 72. Cambridge: Harvard University.

McGuire, Randall H.
1982   The Study of Ethnicity in Historical Archaeology. *Journal of Anthropological Archaeology* 1(2): 159-178.

McGuire, Randall H., and Ann V. Howard
1987   The Structure and Organization of Hohokam Shell Exchange. *The Kiva* 52(2): 113-146.

McGuire, Randall H., and Michael B. Schiffer
1983   A Theory of Architectural Design. *Journal of Anthropological Archaeology* 2(3): 277-303.

McIntosh, Susan K., and R. J. McIntosh
1984   The Early City in West Africa: Towards an Understanding. *The African Archaeological Review* 2: 73-98.

McLaughlin, Castle
1987   Style as a Social Boundary Marker: A Plains Indian Example. In *Ethnicity and Culture*, edited by Réginald Auger, Margaret F. Glass, Scott MacEachern, and Peter H. McCartney, pp. 55-66. Calgary: University of Calgary Press.

Miksa, Elizabeth, and James M. Heidke
1995   Drawing a Line in the Sands: Models of Ceramic Temper Provenance. In "The Roosevelt Community Development Study, Vol. 2: Ceramic Chronology, Technology, and Economics," edited by James M. Heidke and Miriam T. Stark. *Anthropological Papers* 14(2): 133-204. Tucson: Center for Desert Archaeology.

Mills, Barbara J.
1998   Migration and Pueblo IV Community Reorganization in the Silver Creek Area, East-Central Arizona. In "Migration and Reorganization: The Pueblo IV Period in the American Southwest," edited by Katherine A. Spielmann. *Anthropological Research Papers* 51: 65-80. Tempe: Arizona State University.

Mills, Jack P., and Vera M. Mills
1969   The Kuykendall Site. *El Paso Archaeological Society Special Report* 6. El Paso: El Paso Archaeological Society.
1972   The Dinwiddie Site: A Prehistoric Salado Ruin on Duck Creek, Western New Mexico. *The Artifact* 10(2): 1-50.
1975   *The Meredith Ranch Site, VIV Ruin, a Prehistoric Salado Pueblo in the Tonto Basin, Central Arizona*. Privately printed by Jack and Vera Mills, Elfrida, Arizona.

Montgomery, Barbara K.
1992   *Understanding the Formation of the Archaeological Record: Ceramic Variability at Chodistaas Pueblo, Arizona*. Doctoral dissertation, University of Arizona, Tucson. Ann Arbor: University Microfilms.

Nelson, Ben A.
2000   Salado at the End of the Twentieth Century. In *Salado*, edited by Jeffrey S. Dean, pp. 321-326. Albuquerque: University of New Mexico Press.

Nelson, Ben A., and Steven A. LeBlanc
1986   *Short-Term Sedentism in the American Southwest: The Mimbres Valley Salado*. Albuquerque: Maxwell Museum of Anthropology and University of New Mexico Press.

Nelson, Rueben H.
1993   Casa de Piedras Site Report: Archaeological Investigations on the Agua Fria River Valley of

Arizona. *Arizona Archaeological Society Occasional Paper* 3. Phoenix: Arizona Archaeological Society.

Nesbitt, Paul H.
1938   Starkweather Ruin: A Mogollon–Pueblo Site in the Upper Gila Area of New Mexico, and Affiliative Aspects of the Mogollon Culture. *Publications in Anthropology Bulletin* 6. Beloit: The Logan Museum, Beloit College.

Netting, Robert McC.
1977   *Cultural Ecology*. Menlo Park: Cummings.
1993   *Smallholders, Householders: Farm Families and the Ecology of Intensive, Sustainable Agriculture*. Stanford: Stanford University Press.

Newcomb, Joanne
1997   Prehistoric Population Movements in the Silver Creek Drainage, Arizona. MS, Master's thesis, Department of Anthropology, University of Arizona, Tucson.

Newton, Dorothy
1974   The Timbara Hammock as a Cultural Indicator of Social Boundaries. In *The Human Mirror*, edited by Miles Richardson, pp. 231–251. Baton Rouge: Lousiana State University Press.

Ninsheng, Wang
1989   Ancient Ethnic Groups as Represented on Bronzes from Yunnan, China. In *Archaeological Approaches to Cultural Identity*, edited by S. J. Shennan, pp. 195–209. London: Unwin Hyman.

Oliver, Theodore J., and David F. Jacobs
1997   Salado Residential Settlements on Tonto Creek: Roosevelt Platform Mound Study. *Roosevelt Monograph Series 9, Anthropological Field Studies* 38. Tempe: Office of Cultural Resource Management, Arizona State University.

Olson, Alan P.
1959   An Evaluation of the Phase Concept in Southwestern Archaeology: As Applied to the Eleventh and Twelfth Century Occupations at Point of Pines, East-Central Arizona. MS, Doctoral dissertation, University of Arizona, Tucson.

O'Shea, John M.
1984   *Mortuary Variability: An Archaeological Investigation*. Orlando: Academic Press.

Otto, John Solomon
1980   Race and Class on Antebellum Plantations. In *Archaeological Perspectives on Ethnicity in America, Afro-American and Asian American Culture History*, edited by Robert L. Schuyler, pp. 3–13. Farmingdale, New York: Baywood.
1984   *Cannon's Point Plantation, 1794–1860: Living Conditions and Status Patterns in the Old South*. Orlando: Academic Press.

Pálóczi-Horváth, Andras
1989   Steppe Traditions and Cultural Assimilation of a Nomadic People: The Cumanians in Hungary in the 13th–14th Century. In *Archaeological Approaches to Cultural Identity*, edited by S. J. Shennan, pp. 291–302. London: Unwin Hyman.

Plog, Stephen
1980   *Stylistic Variation in Prehistoric Ceramics: Design Analysis in the American Southwest*. Cambridge: Cambridge University Press.
1990   Sociopolitical Implications of Stylistic Variation in the American Southwest. In *The Uses of Style in Archaeology*, edited by Margaret W. Conkey and Christine A. Hastorf, pp. 61–72. Cambridge: Cambridge University Press.

Pollock, Susan
1983   Style and Information: An Analysis of Susiana Ceramics. *Journal of Anthropological Archaeology* 2: 354–390.

Potter, James M.
1998   The Structure of Open Space in Late Prehistoric Settlements in the Southwest. In "Migration and Reorganization: The Pueblo IV Period in the American Southwest," edited by Katherine A. Spielmann. *Anthropological Research Papers* 51: 137–163. Tempe: Arizona State University.

Preucel, Robert W.
1990   *Seasonal Circulation and Dual Residence in the Pueblo Southwest: A Prehistoric Example from the Pajarito Plateau, New Mexico*. New York and London: Garland Publishing.

Prudden, T. Mitchell
1903   The Prehistoric Ruins of the San Juan Watershed of Utah, Arizona, Colorado, and New Mexico. *American Anthropologist* n.s. 5(2): 224–288.

Rapoport, Amos
1969   *House Form and Culture*. Englewood Cliffs, New Jersey: Prentice-Hall.
1990   Systems of Activities and Their Settings. In *Domestic Architecture and the Use of Space*, edited by Susan Kent, pp. 9–20. Cambridge: Cambridge University Press.

Rathje, William L.
1971   The Origin and Development of Lowland Classic Maya Civilization. *American Antiquity* 36(3): 275–285.

Redman, Charles L.
1993   *People of the Tonto Rim: Archaeological Discovery in Prehistoric Arizona*. Washington: Smithsonian Institution Press.

Reed, Erik K.
1942   Implications of the Mogollon Concept. *American Antiquity* 8(1): 27–32.

Regan, Marcia H., and Christy G. Turner II
1997   Physical Anthropology and Human Taphonomy of the Schoolhouse Point Mesa Sites. In "The Archaeology of Schoolhouse Point Mesa: Roose-

Regan, Marcia H., and Christy G. Turner II
(*continued*)

    velt Platform Mound Study," edited by Owen Lindauer. *Roosevelt Monograph Series* 8, *Anthropological Field Studies* 37: 631-667. Tempe: Office of Cultural Resource Management, Arizona State University.

Reid, J. Jefferson

1982   [Editor] Cholla Project Archaeology. *Arizona State Museum Archaeological Series* 161. Tucson: University of Arizona.

1989   A Grasshopper Perspective on the Mogollon of the Arizona Mountains. In *Dynamics of Southwestern Prehistory*, edited by Linda S. Cordell and George J. Gumerman, pp. 65–97. Washington: Smithsonian Institution Press.

1997   Return to Migration, Population Movement, and Ethnic Identity in the American Southwest. In *Vanishing River: Landscapes and Lives of the Lower Verde River*, edited by Stephanie M. Whittlesey, Richard Ciolek-Torrello, and Jeffrey H. Altschul, pp. 629-638. Tucson: SRI Press.

Reid, J. Jefferson, John R. Welch,
Barbara K. Montgomery, and
María Nieves Zedeño

1996   A Demographic Overview of the Late Pueblo III Period in the Mountains of East–Central Arizona. In *The Prehistoric Pueblo World, A.D. 1150–1350*, edited by Michael A. Adler, pp 73–85. Tucson: University of Arizona Press.

Renfrew, Colin

1975   Trade as Action at a Distance: Questions of Integration and Communication. In *Ancient Civilization and Trade*, edited by Jeremy A. Sabloff and C. C. Lamberg–Karlovsky, pp. 3–59. Albuquerque: University of New Mexico Press.

1987   *Archaeology and Language: The Puzzle of Indo-European Origins*. Cambridge: Cambridge University Press.

Renfrew, Colin, and John F. Cherry, Editors

1986   *Peer Polity Interaction and Socio–Political Change*. Cambridge: Cambridge University Press.

Rice, Glen E.

1985   [Editor] Studies in the Hohokam and Salado of the Tonto Basin. *OCRM Report* 63. Tempe: Office of Cultural Resource Management, Arizona State University.

1990a   Variability in the Development of Classic Period Elites. In "A Design for Salado Research," edited by Glen E. Rice. *Roosevelt Monograph Series* 1, *Anthropological Field Studies* 22: 31-40. Tempe: Office of Cultural Resource Management, Arizona State University.

1990b   Toward a Study of the Salado of the Tonto Basin. In "A Design for Salado Research," edited by

Glen E. Rice. *Roosevelt Monograph Series* 1, *Anthropological Field Studies* 22: 1–19. Tempe: Office of Cultural Resource Management, Arizona State University.

1998   Migration, Emulation, and Tradition in Tonto Basin Prehistory. In "A Synthesis of Tonto Basin Prehistory: The Roosevelt Archaeology Studies, 1989-1998," edited by Glen E. Rice. *Roosevelt Monograph Series* 12, *Anthropological Field Studies* 41: 231-241. Tempe: Office of Cultural Resource Management, Arizona State University.

2000   Hohokam and Salado Segmentary Organization: The Evidence from the Roosevelt Platform Mound Study. In *Salado*, edited by Jeffrey S. Dean, pp.143-166. Albuquerque: University of New Mexico Press.

Rice, Glen E., and Theodore J. Oliver

1998   Settlement Patterns and Subsistence. In "A Synthesis of Tonto Basin Prehistory: The Roosevelt Archaeology Studies, 1989-1998," edited by Glen E. Rice. *Roosevelt Monograph Series* 12, *Anthropological Field Studies* 41: 85-104. Tempe: Office of Cultural Resource Management, Arizona State University.

Rice, Glen E., Charles L. Redman,
David F. Jacobs, and Owen Lindauer

1998   Architecture, Settlement Types, and Settlement Complexes. In "A Synthesis of Tonto Basin Prehistory: The Roosevelt Archaeology Studies, 1989-1998," edited by Glen E. Rice. *Roosevelt Monograph Series* 12, *Anthropological Field Studies* 41: 55-83. Tempe: Office of Cultural Resource Management, Arizona State University.

Rice, Prudence

1981   Evolution of Specialized Pottery Production: A Trial Model. *Current Anthropology* 22(3): 219-240.

Riggs, Charles

1998   The Social Process of Migration and Its Influence on Community Organization: An Example from East-Central Arizona. Paper presented at the 63rd Annual Meeting of the Society for American Archaeology, Seattle.

Roberts, Jr., Frank H. H.

1929   Shabik'eshchee Village: A Late Basketmaker Site in the Chaco Canyon, New Mexico. *Bureau of American Ethnology Bulletin* 92. Washington.

Rouse, Irving

1958   The Inference of Migrations from Anthropological Evidence. In "Migrations in New World Culture History," edited by Raymond H. Thompson. *University of Arizona Bulletin* 29(2), *Social Science Bulletin* 27: 63–67. Tucson: University of Arizona.

Ruble, Ellen
1996 Macaws in the Southwest. MS, Master's thesis, Department of Anthropology, Northern Arizona University, Flagstaff.

Russell, Aaron E.
1997 Material Culture and African-American Spirituality at the Hermitage. *Historical Archaeology* 31(2): 63–80.

Sackett, James R.
1973 Style, Function, and Artifact Variability in Palaeolithic Assemblages. In *The Explanation of Culture Change*, edited by Colin Renfrew, pp. 317–325. London: Duckworth.
1977 The Meaning of Style in Archaeology: A General Model. *American Antiquity* 42(3): 369–380.
1982 Approaches to Style in Lithic Archaeology. *Journal of Anthropological Archaeology* 1(1): 59–112.
1985 Style and Ethnicity in the Kalahari: A Reply to Wiessner. *American Antiquity* 50(1): 154–159.
1986 Isochrestism and Style: A Clarification. *Journal of Anthropological Archaeology* 5(3): 266–277.
1990 Style and Ethnicity in Archaeology: The Case for Isochrestism. In *The Uses of Style in Archaeology,* edited by Margaret W. Conkey and Christine A. Hastorf, pp. 32–43. Cambridge: Cambridge University Press.

Sanders, William
1956 The Central Mexican Symbiotic System: A Study in Prehistoric Settlement Patterns. In *Prehistoric Settlement Patterns in the New World*, edited by Gordon Willey, pp. 115-127. New York: Wenner-Gren Foundation.

Santley, Robert S., Clare Yarborough, and Barbara A. Hall
1987 Enclaves, Ethnicity, and the Archaeological Record at Matacapan. In *Ethnicity and Culture*, edited by Réginald Auger, Margaret F. Glass, Scott MacEachern, and Peter H. McCartney, pp. 85–100. Calgary: University of Calgary Press.

Schmidt, Erich F.
1928 Time-relations of Prehistoric Pottery Types in Southern Arizona. *Anthropological Papers of the American Museum of Natural History* 30(5): 245–302.

Schroeder, Albert H.
1953 The Problem of Hohokam, Sinagua, and Salado Relations in Southern Arizona. *Plateau* 26(2): 75–83.

Shafer, Harry J.
1988 *Archaeology at the NAN Ranch Ruin: The 1987 Season.* College Station, Texas: Department of Anthropology, Texas A & M University.

Shennan, Stephen J.
1989 Introduction: Archaeological Approaches to Cultural Identity. In *Archaeological Approaches to Cultural Identity*, edited by S. J. Shennan, pp. 1–32. London: Unwin Hyman.

Sherratt, Andrew
1990 The Genesis of Megaliths: Monumentality, Ethnicity and Social Complexity in Neolithic North-West Europe. *World Archaeology* 22(2): 147–167.

Simon, Arleyn W.
1994a Analysis of Plain Ware Ceramic Assemblages. In "Archaeology of the Salado in the Livingston Area of Tonto Basin: Roosevelt Platform Mound Study, Report on the Livingston Management Group, Pinto Creek Complex," by David F. Jacobs. *Roosevelt Monograph Series* 3, Part 2, *Anthropological Field Studies* 32: 635–646. Tempe: Office of Cultural Resource Management, Arizona State University.
1994b Compositional Analysis of the Livingston Ceramic Assemblage. In "Archaeology of the Salado in the Livingston Area of Tonto Basin: Roosevelt Platform Mound Study, Report on the Livingston Management Group, Pinto Creek Complex," by David F. Jacobs. *Roosevelt Monograph Series* 3, Part 2, *Anthropological Field Studies* 32: 647–662. Tempe: Office of Cultural Resource Management, Arizona State University.
1997 Plain, Red, and Other Ceramic Wares from the Schoolhouse Point Mesa Sites. In "The Archaeology of Schoolhouse Point Mesa, Roosevelt Platform Mound Study," by Owen Lindauer, pp. 301–376. *Roosevelt Monograph Series* 8, *Anthropological Field Studies* 37. Tempe: Office of Cultural Resource Management, Arizona State University.

Simon, Arleyn W., Jean-Christophe Komorowski, and James H. Burton
1998 Ceramic Production and Exchange in Tonto Basin: The Mineralogical Evidence. In "Salado Ceramics and Social Organization: Prehistoric Interactions in Tonto Basin: The Roosevelt Archaeology Studies, 1989-1998," edited by Arleyn W. Simon. *Roosevelt Monograph Series* 11, *Anthropological Field Studies* 40: 93-127. Tempe: Office of Cultural Resource Management, Arizona State University.

Sires, Jr., Earl W.
1984 Hohokam Architecture and Site Structure. In "Hohokam Archaeology along the Salt-Gila Aqueduct, Central Arizona Project, Vol. 9: Synthesis and Conclusions," edited by Lynn S. Teague and Patricia L. Crown. *Arizona State Museum Archaeological Series* 150(9): 115–140. Tucson: Arizona State Museum, University of Arizona.
1987 Hohokam Architectural Variability and Site Structure during the Sedentary-Classic Transition.

Sires, Jr., Earl W. (*continued*)
    In *The Hohokam Village: Site Structure and Organization*, edited by David E. Doyel, pp. 171–182. Glenwood Springs, Colorado: American Association for the Advancement of Science.

Slaughter, Mark C., and Heidi Roberts, Editors
1996   *Excavation of the Gibbon Springs Site: A Classic Period Village in the Northeastern Tucson Basin*. Report No. 94-87. Tucson: SWCA.

Smith, M. G.
1986   *The Ethnic Origins of Nations*. Oxford: Basil Blackwell.

Spielmann, Katherine A., Editor
1998   The Pueblo IV Period in the American Southwest. *Anthropological Research Papers* 51: 65-80. Tempe: Arizona State University.

Stanislawski, Michael B.
1973   Ethnoarchaeology and Settlement Archaeology. *Ethnohistory* 20(4): 375–392.

Stark, Miriam T.
1995a   The Early Ceramic Horizon and Tonto Basin Prehistory. In "The Roosevelt Community Development Study, Vol. 2: Ceramic Chronology, Technology, and Economics," edited by James M. Heidke and Miriam T. Stark. *Anthropological Papers* 14(2): 249–272. Tucson: Center for Desert Archaeology.
1995b   Cultural Identity in the Archaeological Record: The Utility of Utilitarian Ceramics. In "The Roosevelt Community Development Study, Vol. 2: Ceramic Chronology, Technology, and Economics," edited by James M. Heidke and Miriam T. Stark. *Anthropological Papers* 14(2): 331–362. Tucson: Center for Desert Archaeology.
1995c   The Utilitarian Ceramic Collection: Plainware, Redware, and Corrugated Ceramics. In "The Roosevelt Community Development Study, Vol. 2: Ceramic Chronology, Technology, and Economics," edited by James M. Heidke and Miriam T. Stark. *Anthropological Papers* 14(2): 205–248. Tucson: Center for Desert Archaeology.
1995d   Commodities and Interaction in the Prehistoric Tonto Basin. In "The Roosevelt Community Development Study: New Perspectives on Tonto Basin Prehistory," edited by Mark D. Elson, Miriam T. Stark, and David A. Gregory. *Anthropological Papers* 15: 307–342. Tucson: Center for Desert Archaeology.

Stark, Miriam T., and Mark D. Elson
1995   Introduction. In "The Roosevelt Community Development Study: New Perspectives on Tonto Basin Prehistory," edited by Mark D. Elson, Miriam T. Stark, and David A. Gregory. *Anthropological Papers* 15: 1–37. Tucson: Center for Desert Archaeology.

Stark, Miriam T., and James M. Heidke
1992   The Plainware and Redware Ceramic Assemblages. In "The Rye Creek Project: Archaeology in the Upper Tonto Basin, Vol. 2: Artifact and Specific Analyses," by Mark D. Elson and Douglas B. Craig. *Anthropological Papers* 11: 89–214. Tucson: Center for Desert Archaeology.
1995   Early Classic Period Variability in Utilitarian Ceramic Production and Distribution. In "The Roosevelt Community Development Study, Vol. 2: Ceramic Chronology, Technology, and Economics," edited by James M. Heidke and Miriam T. Stark. *Anthropological Papers* 14(2): 363–393. Tucson: Center for Desert Archaeology.

Stark, Miriam T., Jeffery J. Clark, and Mark D. Elson
1995   Social Boundaries and Cultural Identity in the Tonto Basin. In "The Roosevelt Community Development Study: New Perspectives on Tonto Basin Prehistory," edited by Mark D. Elson, Miriam T. Stark, and David A. Gregory. *Anthropological Papers* 15: 343–368. Tucson: Center for Desert Archaeology.

Stark, Miriam T., Mark D. Elson, and Jeffery J. Clark
1998   Social Boundaries and Technical Choices in Tonto Basin Prehistory. In *The Archaeology of Social Boundaries*, edited by Miriam T. Stark, pp. 208–231. Washington and London: Smithsonian Institution Press.

Stark, Miriam T., James M. Vint,
and James M. Heidke
1995   Compositional Variability in Utilitarian Ceramics at a Colonial Period Site. In "The Roosevelt Community Development Study, Vol. 2: Ceramic Chronology, Technology, and Economics," edited by James M. Heidke and Miriam T. Stark. *Anthropological Papers* 14(2): 273–295. Tucson: Center for Desert Archaeology.

Steen, Charlie R.
1962   Excavations at the Upper Ruin, Tonto National Monument. In "Archaeological Studies at Tonto National Monument," edited by Louis R. Caywood. *Southwestern Monuments Association Technical Series* 2: 1–30. Globe, Arizona.

Sterner, Judy
1989   Who is Signalling Whom? Ceramic Style, Ethnicity and Taphonomy Among the Sirak Bulahay. *Antiquity* 63(240): 451–459.

Steward, Julian H.
1955   *Theory of Culture Change: The Methodology of Multilinear Evolution*. Urbana: University of Illinois Press.

Stine, Linda Francis, Melanie A. Cabak,
and Mark D. Groover
1996   Blue Beads as African-American Cultural Symbols. *Historical Archaeology* 30(3): 49–75.

Stone, Glenn Davis
1996 *Settlement Ecology: The Social and Spatial Organization of Kofyar Agriculture.* Tucson: University of Arizona Press.

Swartz, Deborah L.
1992 The Deer Creek Site, AZ O:15:52 (ASM). In "The Rye Creek Project: Archaeology in the Upper Tonto Basin, Vol. 1: Introduction and Site Descriptions," by Mark D. Elson and Douglas B. Craig. *Anthropological Papers* 11(1): 93–164. Tucson: Center for Desert Archaeology.

Swartz, Deborah L., and Mark D. Elson
1994 Tested Sites. In "The Roosevelt Community Development Study, Vol. 1: Introduction and Small Sites," by Mark D. Elson and Deborah L. Swartz. *Anthropological Papers* 13(1): 181–294. Tucson: Center for Desert Archaeology.

Swartz, Deborah L., and Brenda G. Randolph
1994a The Hedge Apple Site, AZ V:5:189/1605 (ASM/TNF). In "The Roosevelt Community Development Study, Vol. 1: Introduction and Small Sites," by Mark D. Elson and Deborah L. Swartz. *Anthropological Papers* 13(1): 117–140. Tucson: Center for Desert Archaeology.
1994b The Griffin Wash Site, AZ V:5:90/96 (ASM/TNF). In "The Roosevelt Community Development Study, Vol. 2: Meddler Point, Pyramid Point, and Griffin Wash Sites," by Mark D. Elson, Deborah L. Swartz, Douglas B. Craig, and Jeffery J. Clark. *Anthropological Papers* 13(2): 297–416. Tucson: Center for Desert Archaeology.

Swartz, Deborah L., Penny D. Minturn,
and Dana Hartman
1995 The Mortuary Assemblage. In "The Roosevelt Community Development Study, Vol. 3: Paleobotanical and Osteological Analyses," edited by Mark D. Elson and Jeffery J. Clark. *Anthropological Papers* 14(3): 169–216. Tucson: Center for Desert Archaeology.

Tainter, Joseph A.
1978 Mortuary Practices and the Study of Prehistoric Social Systems. In *Advances in Archaeological Method and Theory*, Vol. 1, edited by Michael B. Schiffer, pp. 105–141. New York: Academic Press.

Tainter, Joseph A., and Fred T. Plog
1994 Strong and Weak Patterning in Southwestern Prehistory: The Formation of Puebloan Archaeology. In *Themes in Southwestern Prehistory*, edited by George J. Gumerman, pp. 165–181. Santa Fe: School of American Research Press.

Teague, Lynn S.
1998 *Textiles in Southwestern Prehistory.* Albuquerque: University of New Mexico Press.

Towner, Ronald H., and Jeffrey S. Dean
1992 LA 2298: The Oldest Pueblito Revisited. *Kiva* 57(4): 315–329.

Triadan, Daniela
1997 Ceramic Commodities and Common Containers: Production and Distribution of White Mountain Red Ware in the Grasshopper Region, Arizona. *Anthropological Papers of the University of Arizona* 61. Tucson: University of Arizona Press.
1998 Socio-Demographic Implications of Pueblo IV Ceramic Production and Circulation: Sourcing White Mountain Red Ware from the Grasshopper Region, Arizona. In "Migration and Reorganization: The Pueblo IV Period in the American Southwest," edited by Katherine A. Spielmann. *Anthropological Research Papers* 51: 233-252. Tempe: Arizona State University.

Turner II, Christy G.
1998 The Salado Dentition: Univariate Comparisons within the Greater Southwest. In "A Synthesis of Tonto Basin Prehistory: The Roosevelt Archaeology Studies, 1989-1998," edited by Glen E. Rice. *Roosevelt Monograph Series* 12, *Anthropological Field Studies* 41: 153-179. Tempe: Office of Cultural Resource Management, Arizona State University.

Turner II, Christy G., Marica H. Regan, and Joel D. Irish
1994 Physical Anthropology of the Roosevelt Lake Livingston Study Area. In "Archaeology of the Salado in the Livingston Area of Tonto Basin: Roosevelt Platform Mound Study, Report on the Livingston Management Group, Pinto Creek Complex" by David Jacobs. *Roosevelt Monograph Series* 3, Part 2, *Anthroplogical Field Studies* 32: 819-832. Tempe: Office of Cultural Resource Management, Arizona State University.

Underhill, Ruth
1944 *Pueblo Crafts.* Washington: United States Department of Interior, Branch of Education.

Upham, Steadman, Kent G. Lightfoot, and Gary M. Feinman
1981 Explaining Socially Determined Ceramic Distributions in the Prehistoric Plateau Southwest. *American Antiquity* 46(4): 822–833.

Vargas, Victoria D.
1995 Copper Bell Trade Patterns in the Prehispanic U.S. Southwest and Northwest Mexico. *Arizona State Museum Archaeological Series* 187. Tucson: University of Arizona.

Varien, Mark D., William D. Lipe, Michael A. Adler,
Ian M. Thompson, and Bruce A. Bradley
1996 Southwestern Colorado and Southeastern Utah Settlement Patterns: A.D. 1100 to 1300. In *The Prehistoric Pueblo World, A.D. 1150–1350*, edited by Michael A. Adler, pp. 86–113. Tucson: University of Arizona Press.

Veit, Uhlrich
1989   Ethnic Concepts in German Prehistory: A Case Study on the Relationship between Cultural Identity and Archaeological Objectivity. In *Archaeological Approaches to Cultural Identity*, edited by S. J. Shennan, pp. 35–56. London: Unwin Hyman.

Wallace, Henry D.
1995   Decorated Buffware and Brownware Ceramics. In "The Roosevelt Community Development Study, Vol. 2: Ceramic Chronology, Technology, and Economics," edited by James M. Heidke and Miriam T. Stark. *Anthropological Papers* 14(2): 19–84. Tucson: Center for Desert Archaeology.

Wallace, Henry D., and James P. Holmlund
1984   The Classic Period in the Tucson Basin. *The Kiva* 49(3–4): 167–194.

Wallace, Henry D., James M. Heidke, and William H. Doelle
1995   Hohokam Origins. *Kiva* 60(4): 575–618.

Wallerstein, Emmanuel
1973   The Two Modes of Ethnic Consciousness: Soviet Central Asia in Transition? In *The Nationality Question in Soviet Central Asia*, edited by E. Allworth, pp. 168–169. New York: Praeger.

Washburn, Dorothy K.
1989   The Property of Symmetry and the Concept of Ethnic Style. In *Archaeological Approaches to Cultural Identity*, edited by S. J. Shennan, pp. 157–173. London: Unwin Hyman.

Wasley, William W.
1966   Classic Period Hohokam. MS on file, Arizona State Museum, Tucson.

Wasley, William W., and David E. Doyel
1980   Classic Period Hohokam. *The Kiva* 45(4): 337–352.

Waters, Michael R.
1998   Geoarchaeological Investigations in the Tonto Basin. In "Environment and Subsistence in the Classic Period Tonto Basin: The Roosevelt Archaeological Studies, 1989-1998," edited by Katherine A. Spielmann. *Roosevelt Monograph series* 10, *Anthropological Field Studies* 39. Tempe: Office of Cultural Resource Management, Arizona State University.

Weaver, Jr., Donald E.
1976   Salado Influences in the Lower Salt River Valley. *The Kiva* 42(1): 17–26.

Wegars, Priscilla
1991   Who's Been Workin' on the Railroad? An Examination of the Construction, Distribution, and Ethnic Origins of Domed Rock Ovens on Railroad–Related Sites. *Historical Archaeology* 25(1): 37–65.

Weigand, Phil C., and Garman Harbottle
1993   The Role of Turquoises in the Ancient Mesoamerican Trade Structure. In *The American Southwest and Mesoamerica: Systems of Prehistoric Exchange*, edited by Jonathon E. Ericson and Timothy G. Baugh, pp. 159–177. New York: Plenum Press.

Wheat, Joe Ben
1954   Crooked Ridge Village (Arizona W:10:15). *University of Arizona Bulletin* 25(3), *Social Science Bulletin* 24. Tucson: University of Arizona.
1955   Mogollon Culture Prior to A.D. 1000. *Memoirs of the Society for American Archaeology* 10.

Whiteley, Peter M.
1988   *Bacavi: Journey to Reed Springs*. Flagstaff: Northland Press.

Whittlesey, Stephanie M.
1978   *Status and Death at Grasshopper Pueblo: Experiments toward an Archaeological Theory of Correlates*. Doctoral dissertation, University of Arizona. Ann Arbor: University Microfilms.

Whittlesey, Stephanie M., and Richard Ciolek-Torrello
1992   A Revolt against Rampant Elites: Toward an Alternative Paradigm. In "Proceedings of the Second Salado Conference, Globe, AZ, 1992," edited by Richard C. Lange and Stephen Germick, pp. 312–324. *Occasional Paper of the Arizona Archaeological Society*. Phoenix.

Whittlesey, Stephanie M., and J. Jefferson Reid
1982   Cholla Project Perspectives on Salado. In "Cholla Project Archaeology, Vol. 1: Introduction and Special Studies," edited by J. Jefferson Reid. *Arizona State Museum Archaeological Series* 161(1): 63–80. Tucson: University of Arizona.

Whittlesey, Stephanie M., Richard S. Ciolek-Torrello, and J. Jefferson Reid
2000   Salado: The View from the Mountains. In *Salado*, edited by Jeffrey S. Dean, pp. 241-261. Albuquerque: University of New Mexico Press.

Wiessner, Polly
1983   Style and Social Information in Kalahari San Projectile Points. *American Antiquity* 48(2): 253–276.
1984   Reconsidering the Behavioral Basis for Style: A Case Study among the Kalahari San. *Journal of Anthropological Archaeology* 3(3): 190–234.
1985   Style or Isochrestic Variation? A Reply to Sackett. *American Antiquity* 50(1): 160–166.
1990   Is There a Unity to Style? In *The Uses of Style in Archaeology*, edited by Margaret W. Conkey and Christine A. Hastorf, pp. 105–112. Cambridge: Cambridge University Press.

Wilcox, David R.
1979   The Hohokam Regional System. In "An Archaeological Test of Sites in the Gila Butte-Santan

Region, South–Central Arizona," by Glen E. Rice, David R. Wilcox, Kevin Rafferty, and James Schoenwetter. *Anthropological Research Papers* 18: 77–116. Tempe: Arizona State University.

1991   The Mesoamerican Ballgame in the American Southwest. In *The Mesoamerican Ballgame*, edited by Vernon L. Scarborough and David R. Wilcox, pp 101–128. Tucson: University of Arizona Press.

Wilcox, David R., and Jonathan Haas

1994   The Scream of the Butterfly: Competition and Conflict in the Prehistoric Southwest. In *Themes in Southwest Prehistory*, edited by George J. Gumerman, pp. 211–238. Santa Fe: School of American Research Press.

Wilcox, David R., and Charles Sternberg

1983   Hohokam Ballcourts and Their Interpretation. *Arizona State Museum Archaeological Series* 160. Tucson: University of Arizona.

Wilcox, David R., Thomas R. McGuire,
and Charles Sternberg

1981   Snaketown Revisited. *Arizona State Museum Archaeological Series* 155. Tucson: University of Arizona.

Wilk, Richard R.

1991   *Household Ecology: Economic Change and Domestic Life Among the Kekchi Maya in Belize.* Tucson: University of Arizona Press.

Wilk, Richard R., and Robert McC. Netting

1984   Households: Changing Forms and Functions. In *Households: Comparative and Historic Studies of the Domestic Group*, edited by Robert McC. Netting, Richard R. Wilk, and Eric J. Arnould, pp. 1–28. Berkeley: University of California Press.

Wilkie, Laurie

1996   Glassknapping at a Louisiana Plantation: Afro-American Tools. *Historical Archaeology* 30(4): 37–49.

Williams, Brackette F.

1992   Of Straightening Combs, Sodium Hydroxide, and Potassium Hydroxide in Archaeological and Cultural–Anthropological Analyses of Ethnogenesis. *American Antiquity* 57(4): 608–612.

Wilson, C. Dean

1988   An Evaluation of Individual Migration as an Explanation for the Presence of Smudged Ceramics in the Dolores Project Area. In *Dolores Archaeological Program: Additive and Reductive Technologies*, edited by Eric Blinman, Carl J. Phagan, and Richard Wilshusen, pp. 425–434. Denver: Bureau of Reclamation Engineering and Research Center, Department of the Interior.

Wobst, H. Martin

1977   Stylistic Behavior and Information Exchange. In

"For the Director: Research Essays in Honor of James B. Griffin," edited by Charles E. Cleland. *Museum of Anthropology Anthropological Paper* 61: 317–342. Ann Arbor: University of Michigan.

Wolf, Eric R.

1984   Culture: Panacea or Problem? *American Antiquity* 49(2): 393–400.

Wood, J. Scott

1985   The Northeastern Periphery. In "Proceedings of the 1983 Hohokam Symposium," edited by Alfred E. Dittert, Jr., and Donald E. Dove. *Arizona Archaeological Society Occasional Paper* 2: 239–262. Phoenix: Arizona Archaeological Society.

1987   Checklist of Pottery Types for the Tonto National Forest: An Introduction to the Archaeological Ceramics of Central Arizona. *The Arizona Archaeologist* 21. Phoenix: Arizona Archaeological Society.

1989   Vale of Tiers, Too: Late Classic Period Salado Settlement Patterns and Organizational Models for Tonto Basin. Preliminary Report. *Cultural Resources Inventory Report* 89–12–280. Phoenix: Tonto National Forest.

1995   Review of Draft RCDS "New Perspectives in Tonto Basin Prehistory." Tonto National Forest File Code 2360. MS on file, Tonto National Forest, Phoenix.

2000   Vale of Tiers Palimpsest: Salado Settlement and Internal Relationships in the Tonto Basin Area. In *Salado*, edited by Jeffrey S. Dean, pp. 107-141. Albuquerque: University of New Mexico Press.

Wood, J. Scott, and John W. Hohmann

1985   Foundation's Edge: The Northeastern Periphery and the Development of the Hohokam Classic Period. Paper presented at the 50th Annual Meeting of the Society for American Archaeology, Denver.

Wood, J. Scott, and Martin E. McAllister

1980   Foundation and Empire: The Colonization of the Northeastern Hohokam Periphery. In "Current Issues in Hohokam Prehistory," edited by David E. Doyel and Fred T. Plog. *Anthropological Research Papers* 23: 180–200. Tempe: Arizona State University.

1982   The Salado Tradition. An Alternative View. In "Cholla Project Archaeology, Vol. 1: Introduction and Special Studies," edited by J. Jefferson Reid. *Arizona State Museum Archaeological Series* 161(1): 81–94. Tucson: University of Arizona.

Wood, J. Scott, Michael A. Sullivan, Steve Germick,
and Linda B. Kelley

1989   Tonto National Forest Cultural Resources Assessment and Management Plan. *Cultural Resources*

Wood, J. Scott, Michael A. Sullivan, Steve Germick,
and Linda B. Kelley (*continued*)
      Inventory Report 89–235. Phoenix: Tonto Na-
      tional Forest.
Woodson, M. Kyle
   1995   The Goat Hill Site: A Western Anasazi Pueblo in
the Safford Valley of Southeastern Arizona. MS,
Master's Thesis, Department of Anthropology,
University of Texas, Austin.
   1999   Migrations in Late Anasazi Prehistory: The Evidence from the Goat Hill Site. *Kiva* 65(1): 63–
84.

Index

Abstract

T his monograph takes a fresh look at migration in light of the recent resurgence of interest in this topic within archaeology. A reliable approach for determining the scale and impact of migration is developed based on current conceptions of style in anthropology. Emphasis is placed on conservative material culture attributes that tend to be exclusively associated with the groups that produce them, and artifacts that are exchange goods or attributes that are likely to be emulated are avoided. Using this approach, migrant enclaves can be discerned from indigenous settlements in the culturally mixed communities that often form in the wake of large migration processes. This strategy is tested using ethnoarchaeological case studies from a variety of cultural and temporal contexts. Once the settlements of indigenous and various migrant groups have been pinpointed, other archaeological data can be used to reconstruct social and economic relations between groups. Regardless of whether these relations are cooperative or competitive, interaction between socially distant groups who suddenly find themselves neighbors can lead to the development of inequality and complexity.

The developed approach is used to evaluate pueblo migration into a community occupied during the early Classic period (A.D. 1200–1325) in the Tonto Basin of east-central Arizona. This community had been developing along internal lines with substantial Hohokam influence prior to this interval. Puebloan enclaves are differentiated from indigenous settlements based on differences in the organization of domestic space and technological styles reflected in house construction and utilitarian ceramic manufacture. Puebloan migration is determined to be limited in scale, at least initially, and this movement resulted in the co-residence of migrants and local groups within a single community.

Once the co-residence settlement pattern is reconstructed, relations between the two groups are examined and the short-term and long-term impacts of migration are assessed. Although initial relations were cooperative between migrants and locals, they were by no means equal. The migrants were at a distinct disadvantage with respect to land ownership and familiarity with the local subsistence strategy focused on canal irrigation. Several of these groups may have turned to alternative ways of obtaining food by producing pots and other commodities for exchange with local groups. The first platform mounds were constructed at local settlements in the basin shortly after the initial influx of migrants. One of the functions of these impressive constructions may have been to integrate a community that was becoming increasingly diverse as the result of continued migration. In addition, platform mounds may have been territorial markers that symbolized the first-comer status of local groups and legitimized the asymmetrical economic

Resumen

Esta monografía examina nuevamente la inmigración, en respuesta a una reciente resurgencia de este tópico en la arqueología. En base a conceptos de estilo en la antropología contemporánea, se desarrolla un enfoque confiable para determinar la escala e impacto de la migración. Se enfatizan los atributos de la cultura material más conservadores, los que tienden a estar asociados exclusivamente con los grupos que los producen, pero se evitan los artefactos y atributos obtenidos por intercambio o emulados, respectivamente. A través de este enfoque se disciernen énclaves de inmigrantes entre los asentamientos indígenas en comunidades culturalmente diversas que frequentemente se forman al principio de los procesos de inmigración. Esta estrategia se pone a prueba usando casos de estudio etnoarqueológicos en varios contextos culturales y temporales. Una vez que los asentamientos de grupos indígenas e inmigrantes han sido reconocidos, otros datos arqueológicos se pueden usar para reconstruir las relaciones sociales y económicas entre estos grupos. La interacción entre grupos socialmente distantes que repentinamente se vuelven vecinos puede llevar al desarrollo de desigualdad y complejidad, sin importar el que estas relaciones sean de cooperación o competencia.

Este enfoque se utiliza para evaluar la inmigración de gente Pueblo a una comunidad localizada en la Cuenca Tonto de Arizona centro-este, durante el período Clásico temprano (1200–1325 d.C.). Anteriormente a este período, la comunidad se desarrolló con substancial influencia Hohokam. Enclaves Pueblo se pueden diferenciar de los asentamientos indígenas en base a diferencias en la organización del espacio doméstico y los estilos tecnológicos reflejados en la construcción de casas y en la manufactura de cerámica utilitaria. Se determina que la inmigración Pueblo fue limitada en escala, al menos inicialmente, y que este movimiento resultó en la co-residencia de grupos indígenas e inmigrantes en la misma comunidad.

Una vez reconstruido el patrón de co-residencia, se examinan las relaciones entre los dos grupos en términos de impactos a corto y largo plazo. Las relaciones iniciales fueron de cooperación, pero no de igualdad. Los inmigrantes afrontaron desventajas en la propiedad de la tierra y debieron familiarizarse con el medioambiente local y la producción agrícola centrada en los canales de irrigación. Algunos de estos grupos adoptaron modos de subsistencia alternos, incluyendo la producción de cerámica y otros productos para intercambiar con los grupos locales. Los primeros montículos de plataforma fueron construidos en asentamientos locales en la cuenca poco después del arribo de los inmigrantes. Una de las funciones de estas impresionantes construcciones pudo haber sido la de integrar la comunidad en vista de la diversidad cultural creciente producida por la inmigración. Además, los montículos de plataforma podrían

arrangement between locals and migrants that favored the former. The leap toward complexity, evidenced by increased socioeconomic inequality and the development of new integrative institutions, was short-lived and the community collapsed after a generation or two.

The early Classic period is associated with the appearance of the Salado horizon in the Tonto Basin and elsewhere in the Southwest. The role of migration in generating this wide-spread horizon has been the topic of considerable debate in Southwest archaeology. This study shows that migration and co-residence occurred throughout the various basins and valleys within the Salado horizon, although each local sequence relates a unique story. The results have methodological and theoretical implications well beyond Salado and the Southwest, extending to any prehistoric study where the scale and impact of migration is contested.

haber servido como marcadores territoriales que simbolizaron los derechos de los fundadores y legitimizaron la economía asimétrica que favoreció a estos grupos locales. El salto hacia la complejidad, evidente en la creciente desigualdad socioeconómica y en el desarrollo de nuevas instituciones integradoras, duró poco tiempo y la comunidad se dispersó después de una o dos generaciones.

El período Clásico temprano está asociado con el surgimiento del horizonte Salado en la Cuenca Tonto y en el resto del suroeste norteamericano. El rol de la inmigración en el desarrollo de este horizonte ha sido un tópico de considerable debate en la arqueología regional. Este estudio demuestra que la inmigración y co-residencia se expandieron a través de varias cuencas y valles asociados con material Salado, aunque cada secuencia local relata su propia historia. Los resultados tienen implicaciones metodológicas y teóricas más allá de este horizonte y del suroeste norteamericano, y pueden extenderse a cualquier estudio prehistórico de la escala e impacto de la inmigración en comunidades indígenas.

ANTHROPOLOGICAL PAPERS OF THE UNIVERSITY OF ARIZONA

Anthropological Papers listed as O.P., D are available as Docutech reproductions (high quality xerox) printed on demand. They are tape or spiral bound and nonreturnable.